Ultimate Guide Instant Vort Fryer and Bread Machine

A Complete Guide With 400 + Tasty and Delicious Recipes for Cooking with your Instant Vortex and Bread Machine Cookbook

Michelle Crocker   Megan Buckley

TABLE OF CONTENT

Bread Machine Cookbook

Pro-Bakery Products Made at Home | Ultimate Bread Maker Guide for Beginners, With 200 Recipes to Impress With Homemade Bread Like Gluten-Free, Sourdough, Ketogenic & More

By

Michelle Crocker

Introduction

Homemade bread is nutritious and tasty, but to make it from scratch requires a huge amount of work. It requires a lot of effort, time, and patience to combine the ingredients, knead the dough, wait for it to rise, knead it again, and then bake it, but it does not have to be always this way. The bread maker can do all the hard work, and you have only to taste and appreciate the wonderful taste of homemade bread. If one is not yet persuaded and wonders if it is wise to invest in such an appliance, all the recipes in this book can reassure you of its merit. The bread-making process is slow and labor-intensive, and as many people do not have the patience to go through the entire process in this time, bread machines have become a requirement.

Although a person can still buy bread from markets, it would always be a better choice to bake bread at home, as bread can be optimized as per the tastes and health needs of the individual/family. A home machine for baking bread is a bread machine that transforms all the ingredients into tasty bread. The wonderful thing about an automated bread maker is that all these steps are completed for you. Basically, a bread-making appliance is a portable electric oven that contains a single wide bread tin. The tin is still a little unique; it has a bottom axle that attaches to the electric motor below it. Within the tin, a small metal paddle spins on the axle. A waterproof seal holds the axle, so the bread mixture cannot

leak. Bread has always been eaten along with all sorts of food, rendering it mandatory for all occasions, whether it be lunch, brunch, or dinner. Using a bread maker is better than purchasing the bread at a store.

Tore-bought bread is full of synthetic chemicals, but you only need natural ingredients at home with a bread machine. You may even incorporate specific ingredients, including grains or seeds, to make it much better; apart from flour, you will need yeast and water. Homemade bread is even tastier given the fact that you must always use fresh ingredients, and you can personalize ingredients according to the particular preference. Even if that's not enough, after traditional bread-making, many dishes have to be washed too. One has to put in the ingredients with a bread machine, and after the bread is baked, clean the tin.

Current bread machines bring a lot of special controls that allow several bread specialties to be prepared. For individuals who are intolerant or sensitive to such foods, such as gluten, a bread machine may be especially useful. This book will provide you with all sorts of recipes. These devices can also be used for recipes other than bread, such as jelly, fruit jam, scrambled eggs, tomato sauce, and casseroles, and even some desserts, with a couple of ingredients variations. All you have to do is use fresh ingredients and walk away.

Chapter 1: Easy Baking with Bread Machine

Since the beginning of baking, freshly made bread is the best thing ever. The only trouble is, time and commitment are required. Many individuals have never baked bread in their lives and will never think of doing so, but much of that has begun to shift with the new advent of automated bread-making machines. Today millions convert their homes into bakeries, and every day one can enjoy their own freshly made bread at a fraction of the price they might spend in a shop. There are different explanations for why an individual should suggest using a bread maker instead of any other choices that he has access to.

Bread machines in cafes, households, workplaces, etc., have often been more comfortable people's choice. The majority of available bread makers on the market are automatic.

Bread machines reduce effort and time by helping their customers. An ingredient may be added to it by a baker, homemaker, or any other user. It completes its work automatically, without any control on the part of its consumer. Bread machines allow consumers to do other required things, such as preparing the main course, dinner, etc., while reducing the workload.

It is necessary to remember, though, that not all bread machines are automated. Many Pricey bread makers only give automatic functions. To finish the bread-making method, you just need all the necessary ingredients. Bread makers are often simple to use and manage, much like ovens for bread makers. Assume an individual doesn't know how to bake or doesn't even want to bake; bread machines are the ideal substitute for those people. In addition, it is often likely that individuals wish to bake a certain form of bread at home, like French bread, but does not know how to use an oven for baking one. A bread maker allows us to produce such bread in these situations, while alternate cycles or settings also come with it.

The dough must go through 5 phases if you make bread the conventional way, primarily as mixing, kneading, rising, punching down, proving, and baking, but it's all in one move with the bread maker. All ingredients you have to add to the system, adjust the cycles, and let it do its thing. Each time, you'll get accurate outcomes.

1.1 Main Ingredients for Baking

Baking powder, produced from starch and tartar cream, is a fermenting agent that allows the batter to grow. It has an acidic ingredient incorporated into it, so one does not need to integrate something else for raising the flour. A bitter-tasting food can result from too much baking powder, whereas too little results in a hard cake with very little volume.

Baking soda is a simple sodium bicarbonate which has to be mixed with yogurt, honey, or cocoa, as an acidic ingredient. It's a fermenting product much like baking soda. Using baking soda too much will make the cake rough in texture. Baking soda and baking powder can lose their strength more easily than you would know. If the packages are not fresh, inspect them before using them. Place a couple of teaspoons of white vinegar in a tiny bowl to test the baking soda and incorporate a teaspoon of baking soda. It can vigorously foam out, and it will take some moments for the frothing to subside. The more bubbles, the stronger the baking soda would be. You should substitute the baking soda for fresh baking soda if there is no action, or it just ends up with a couple of tiny bubbles. To check the baking powder, add a spoon full of baking powder into a cup.

Fill the bowl with hot water to cover the baking powder; if it continues to burst furiously, it's safe to include it in the recipes. When weighing, do not add a wet spoon into the baking powder bag for better results.

The water can trigger the baking powder left unused in the can, and each time, it will not be as pleasant to use. If you can see lumps in the baking soda, it's typically a warning that humidity has made its way in the baking soda.

Butter, as a stable fat, butter is ideally used for baking than any other fat material. In fact, butter adds taste, with a melting point only below body temp. Hence certain cookies and bakery items appear to "melt in the

mouth."

Cornstarch has many uses based on the kind of recipe it's being incorporated in. Cornstarch is commonly either a binder or thickener, although it may be an anti-caking agent as well.

It's perfect to use to thicken custards sauces or in gluten-free cooking.

Eggs have many uses, but most significantly, they add volume to foods and are a binding agent, ensuring they hold together the final product.

For glazing, flavor, thickening, and binding, you can use the entire egg or just use the egg yolks and egg whites for different reasons. Egg whites, providing moisture and strength. Egg yolks contribute to shape and flavor.

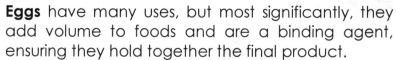

Flour has a very crucial part in making bread. Its major quality is that it binds all the products together.

It transforms into gluten as flour protein is mixed with heat and moisture.

Different flour varieties have different protein amounts and are ideal for various bakery products.

Milk provides softness, moisture, taste, and lightens color to baked goods.

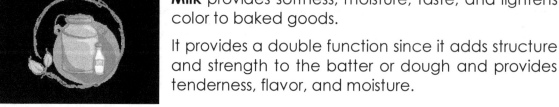

It provides a double function since it adds structure and strength to the batter or dough and provides tenderness, flavor, and moisture.

Sugar, in every particular recipe, sugar is executing a variety of functions. It provides texture, moisture, and holds the form.

Although operating in combination with eggs, fat, and liquid materials, it is also just another rising agent. Sugar gives "crunch" to certain cookies and cakes.

1.2 Bread Machine Cycles

Like in any other bread making, the bread machine also goes through cycles to make you the flavorful bread.

1.2.1 Kneading Cycle

The first cycle is kneading, and perhaps the most significant step in baking bread that includes yeast. Kneading combines all the ingredients absolutely well and is probably the bread machine's noisiest period. It will also take anywhere between 15 to 45minutes for this cycle. The time it takes depends on the bread machine, and the sort of bread one is making. In most machines at the bottom of the baking tin, kneading propellers completely combine everything.

1.2.2 Rest Cycle

The rest cycle makes the dough rest until it begins kneading again. Autolyzing is the scientific baking word for this. Essentially, it helps the moisture surrounding the dough to soak in the starch and gluten completely. It can take this process from only a couple of minutes to over 35 minutes.

1.2.3 Rise Cycle

It would require this cycle if the flour has gluten in it, so it will rise and make the bread airy and soft. It is a fermentation. Depending on the bread machine, this cycle can normally take about 40 to 50 minutes. It can take considerably longer occasionally, particularly if you're making French bread.

1.2.4 Punch Cycle

The next cycle is Punch Cycle after the dough has finished the rising cycle. In this cycle, the bread machine continues to knead the dough yet again. The distinction is that it is performed even more lightly at this point, and the goal is to remove the small air pockets produced in the growing period by the fermentation of the yeast. Usually, the Punch cycle, often referred to as the shape-forming cycle, is a short cycle that takes only seconds to complete, and it is still necessary.

1.2.5 Baking Cycle

This is the most important cycle. This is the cycle in which the bread maker bakes the bread. Depending on the bread maker and the kind of bread you are making, this cycle will take anywhere from half an hour to more than 90 minutes.

Other important baking modes of the bread machine are

- Basic Bread
- Sweet Bread
- Whole-Wheat Cycle
- Gluten-Free Bread
- Rapid Bake
- Cake & Jam—yes, you can make Jellies and Jam and sauces.

1.3 How easy are Bread Machines to use?

Bread machines are very easy and simple to use. Add in ingredients specifically in an order, following the bread machine's manufacturer suggested order. In most machines, add liquids first, then in dry ingredients, or as your machine specifies. All ingredients should be at room temperature or specified otherwise.

- Choose the type of bread you want to make (whole wheat, sweet, basic, multigrain, pizza, or French).
- Choose the baking mode (bake rapid, bake, sandwich, or dough). Choosing different modes changes the sequence of kneading, mixing, rising, and baking. In dough mode, for example, the bread maker will stop without actually baking the bread. You can open up the lid, take out the dough, and roll it out however you like. After that, you have to bake in the oven rather than a bread machine.
- Choose the bread loaf size if your machine has this feature. (1 lb., 1.5 lb. or 2 lb.).
- Choose the crust type to your liking.
- Click the Timer button if your machine has one. The bread maker will show you the time it will take to bake the bread.
- Now click the Start button, and your wait begins.
- When the loaf is baked (from three to four hours), you slowly open the lid, take the heated tin out of the bread machine, wait for ten or more minutes to take out the loaf, let it cool off. In the cleaning

process, you only have to wipe out the tin (which is non-stick), requiring only 30 seconds.

1.4 Choosing the Right Bread Machine

Think of yourself what the criteria will be before selecting the right kind of bread machine for yourself.

Timer: You can manually determine when to set the timer for a baking cycle. Then you have to come at the right time, to take the bread out of the maker. Otherwise, the bread would be preheated and cooked, or choose a one where the machine will calculate the time.

Size: Get the bread machine that carries a recipe comprising 3 cups of flour if one has a big family. Some can hold flour cups of up to 4 to 5-1/2.

Blades: Blades in horizontal pans do not often knead the dough too well, leaving the pan's corners with flour. A big negative is incomplete blending. However, the upright settings do a better job of mixing. Many new machines are made vertically, but some horizontal pans also offer two blades, so choose carefully.

How expensive does a bread machine be?

Some automated control machines are a bit pricey since they do not need your supervision, but some machines require your full-time attention, so keep that fact in mind.

1.5 Mistakes to Avoid While Using the Bread Maker

Here are some tips that will help you to avoid making mistakes while using a bread machine

- You must unplug the appliance before taking bread out.

- Failing to measure the ingredients precisely

- You must add ingredients accepted by the bread machine in the order suggested.

- Please consider the Kitchen's temperature.

- Not opening the lid: it's a good idea to open the lid and look at the dough, particularly in the kneading process, for about after ten minutes. Look at the dough's surface if it's too sticky and requires more flour if your finger is covered in the dough.

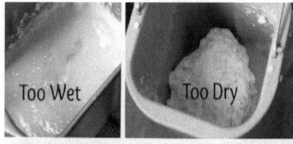

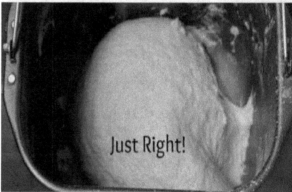

If the dough looks too dry, so it needs more water. Adding products is better than taking them out, so incorporate a vigilant quantity at once. To re-adjust the texture, add a teaspoon of water or flour at a time.

- As the bread bakes, you leave paddles in the machine: You can hear the bread maker begin beating down the dough before the bread reaches the final rise process. Now open the lid, shift the flour to the side of the tin, and gently bring the paddles out.

- Enabling the loaf to rise without reshaping the dough in the final period.

- Taking the bread out before it cools, try waiting for ten to fifteen minutes before taking out the bread.

1.6 Benefits of Using Bread Machine

- It is easier to bake bread in a bread machine.
- The process is cleaner and simpler than traditional bread baking.
- Every time the bread machine produces the same consistency & exceptional taste.
- The benefit of jam and jelly making.
- You're not going to do the kneading.
- Make your fresh bread, at home, for the sandwiches.
- You can add many ingredients to make the bread to your taste.
- It is convenient for busy people.
- Saves long-term resources and money.

Chapter 2: Basic Breads

2.1 Everyday White Bread

(Prep time: 20 minutes | Total time: 2 hours 30 minutes)

Ingredients

- 3 and 3/4 cups of flour
- Lukewarm water: 1 cup
- Butter: 3 tbsp.
- Lukewarm milk: 1/3 cup
- Bread machine Yeast: 2 tsp
- Sugar: 3 tbsp.
- Salt: 1 tsp

Instructions

- In the bread machine, add all the ingredients according to your machine's order.
- Select 2 pounds' loaf, and basic setting, medium crust. Click on start.
- After it's baked, let it cool down before slicing.

2.2 Honey Whole-Wheat Bread

(Prep time: 5 minutes | Total time: 3 hours 30 minutes)

Ingredients

- Olive oil: ⅓ cup
- 4 and a half cups of whole wheat flour
- 1 and a half cups of warm water
- Honey: ⅓ cup

- Yeast: 1 tablespoon
- Kosher salt: 2 tsp
- Gluten: 1 tsp (optional)

Instructions

- In the machine, add water, then oil, and then honey. Add half flour, salt, gluten, and the rest of the flour.
- Make a well in the center add yeast.
- Select whole wheat and light crust. Press start.
- Serve fresh bread.

2.3 Molasses Wheat Bread

(Prep time: 10 minutes | Total time: 4 hours 10 minutes)

Ingredients

- Whole wheat flour: 1 and 3⁄4 cups
- Water: 3⁄4 cup
- Melted butter: 3 tablespoons
- Milk: 1⁄3 cup
- Sugar: 2 tablespoons
- Molasses: 3 tablespoons
- Fast-rising yeast: 2 and 1⁄4 teaspoons
- Bread flour: 2 cups
- Salt: 1 teaspoon

Instructions

- Add all the ingredients to the machine according to your suggested machine's order. Make sure the ingredients are at room temperature
- Use light crust, basic setting.
- Serve fresh.

2.4 100 Percent Whole-Wheat Bread

(Prep time: 10 minutes | Total time: 4 hours 10 minutes)

Ingredients

- 3 and 1/3 cups of whole wheat flour
- Powdered milk: 2 tablespoons
- 1 and a half cups of water
- Honey: 2 tablespoons
- Molasses: 2 tablespoons
- Margarine: 2 tablespoons
- Salt: 1 and a half teaspoons
- Yeast: 1 and a half teaspoons

Instructions

- Add liquid ingredients before dry ingredients or as per your machine's order.
- Mix the powdered milk and water. Heat in microwave for 30 seconds, then adds in the bread machine followed by rest of the ingredients.
- Select 2 lb. loaf and whole wheat bread press start.
- Serve fresh.

2.5 Crusty French Bread

(Prep time: 10 minutes | Total time: 3 hours 35 minutes)

Instructions

- Instant yeast: 1 teaspoon
- 1 and a half teaspoons of sugar
- Lukewarm water: 1 cup
- 1 and a half teaspoons salt
- 1 and a half teaspoons of butter
- Bread flour: 3 cups

Glaze:

- 1 teaspoon water
- One egg white

Instructions

- Add all the ingredients to the bread machine as per your machine's suggested order.
- Select the dough cycle. Adjust the consistency of dough after 5 to 10 minutes by adding one tbsp. of water at a time for very dry dough or one tbsp. of flour if it's too sticky.
- It should pull away after sticking to the sides.
- After the machine is done, take out the dough on a clean, floured surface. Shape into cylinder shape loaves. Shape into French bread.
- Place the loaves in oiled baking pans. Cover with a towel and let it rise in a warm place.
- Let the oven preheat to 425 F. make the glaze by mixing water with egg.
- Coat the loaf's surface with a glaze.
- Make cuts onto the dough surface.
- Bake in the oven for 20 minutes.
- Lower the oven's temperature to 350 F, bake for 5 to 10 minutes more or until golden brown.
- Check the bread's internal temperature. It should be 195 F.
- Cool slightly and Serve fresh

2.6 Pumpernickel Bread

(Prep time: 10 minutes | Total time: 3 hours 45 minutes)

Ingredients

- 1 and a half tablespoons of vegetable oil
- 1 and ⅛ cups of warm water
- Cocoa: 3 tablespoons

- Caraway seed: 1 tablespoon
- Molasses: ⅓ cup
- 1 and a half cups of bread flour
- Whole wheat flour: 1 cup
- 1 and a half teaspoons of salt
- Bread machine yeast: 2 and a half teaspoons
- Rye flour: 1 cup
- Wheat gluten: 1 and a half tablespoons

Instructions

- Add all ingredients in the bread machine in the suggested order by the manufacturer.
- Select the basic cycle and press start.
- Serve fresh bread.

2.7 Lovely Oatmeal Bread

(Prep time: 10 minutes | Total time: 3 hours 15 minutes)

Ingredients

- 3 Tablespoons of sliced Unsalted Butter
- Lukewarm milk: one cup
- 1 and a half Teaspoons of Bread Machine Yeast
- Old Fashioned Oatmeal: 3/4 Cup
- 2 and 1/4 Cups of Bread Flour
- 1 and a half Teaspoons of Salt
- Brown Sugar (packed): 1/4 Cup for sweet and 1 tbsp. for non-sweet

Instructions

- Add all ingredients in the bread machine in the suggested order by the manufacturer.
- Select 1.5 lb. loaf. Light crust and basic setting. Press start.
- Before the baking cycle begins, add some oatmeal to the top.
- Serve fresh bread.

2.8 Oat Bran Molasses Bread

(Prep time: 10 minutes | Total time: 3 hours 20 minutes)

Ingredients

- Whole wheat flour: 3 cups
- Warm water: 1 cup
- Molasses: 1/4 cup
- Melted margarine: 2 tablespoons
- Yeast: 2 and a 1/4 tsp
- Half teaspoon of salt
- Oat bran: 1 cup

Instructions

- Add all ingredients in the bread machine in the suggested order by the manufacturer.
- Click one lb. loaf, whole wheat, and press start.

2.9 Whole-Wheat Buttermilk Bread

(Prep time: 10 minutes | Total time: 3 hours 10 minutes)

Ingredients

- Bread flour: 2 cups
- Whole wheat flour: 2 cups
- 2 tablespoons olive oil (or other oil)
- 1 3⁄4 teaspoons salt
- 6 tablespoons water

- 1 cup buttermilk
- Sugar: 3 tablespoons
- 1 and a half teaspoons of caraway seeds
- 1 and a half teaspoons of celery seeds
- Bread machine yeast: 2 teaspoons
- Half teaspoon of mustard seeds
- 1 and a half teaspoons of sesame seeds

Instructions

- Place all ingredients in the pan of the bread machine, in the suggested order by the manufacturer.
- Add the yeast on top after making a well.
- Select basic cycle, light crust. Press start
- Serve fresh

2.10 Soft Egg Bread

(Prep time: 10 minutes | Total time: 2 hours 10 minutes)

Ingredients

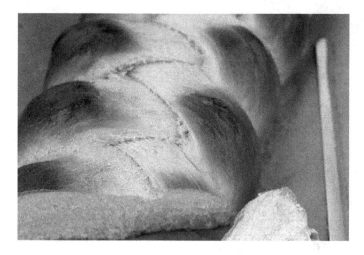

- Bread machine flour: 3 cups
- Milk: 2⁄3 cup
- Softened butter: 2 tablespoons
- Sugar: 2 tablespoons
- Bread machine yeast: 2 teaspoons
- 2 whole eggs
- Salt: 1 teaspoon

Instructions

- Add all ingredients to the bread machine in the suggested order by the manufacturer.
- Add all ingredients to the bread machine in the suggested order by the manufacturer.
- Select white bread, light crust. Press start.
- Serve fresh.

2.11 Healthy Bran Bread

(Prep time: 5 minutes | Total time: 3 hours 45 minutes)

Ingredients

- One egg beaten mixed with enough water to make one cup
- 1 and a half teaspoons of Kosher salt
- 1 Tablespoon of honey
- 1 Tablespoon of olive oil
- Half teaspoon of bread machine yeast
- 5 and a half Tablespoons of unprocessed wheat bran
- 3 cups of bread flour

Instructions

- Add all ingredients to the bread machine in the suggested order by the manufacturer.
- Adjust the consistency of the dough by adding water or more flour.
- Select the basic cycle—press start.
- Serve fresh

2.12 Dark Rye Bread

(Prep time: 5 minutes | Total time: 3 hours 10 minutes)

Ingredients

- 2 and a half cups of bread flour
- Warm water: 1 and 1/4 cups
- Yeast: 2 and 1/4 teaspoons
- 1 cup of rye flour
- Molasses: 1/3 cup
- Half teaspoon of salt
- Caraway seed: 1 tablespoon
- Vegetable oil: 1/8 cup
- Cocoa powder: 1/8 cup

Instructions

- Add ingredients in the bread machine in the suggested order by the manufacturer.
- Select white bread—press start.
- Serve fresh

2.13 Golden Raisin Bread

(Prep time: 10 minutes | Total time: 3 hours 10 minutes)

Ingredients

- 1 Cup of quick Oatmeal
- Warm Milk: 1 and 1/3 Cups
- 2 Teaspoons of Bread Machine Yeast
- 3 Cups of Bread Flour
- Half cup of Brown Sugar
- Molasses: 2 Teaspoons
- Sliced Butter: 4 Tablespoons

- Golden Raisins: 1 Cup
- Salt: 2 Teaspoons

Instructions

- Add all ingredients except raisins to the bread machine in the suggested order by the manufacturer.
- Select basic, light crust and 2 lb. loaf.
- Press start.
- After the machine completes its first cycle of kneading, add raisins.
- Serve fresh.

2.14 Golden Corn Bread

(Prep time: 10 minutes | Total time: 3 hours 10 minutes)

Ingredients

- 1 cup of cornmeal
- 2 eggs, lightly beaten
- Melted butter: 1/4 cup
- 1 and a 1/4 cup of bread flour
- 1 cup of milk
- Baking powder: 4 teaspoons
- Vanilla: 1 teaspoon
- Sugar: 1/4 cup
- Salt: 1 teaspoon

Instructions

- Add all ingredients to the bread machine in the suggested order by the manufacturer.
- Select light crust and cake setting if available, or quick setting.
- Press start.
- Serve fresh.

2.15 English Muffin Bread

(Prep time: 15 minutes | Total time: 3 hours 40 minutes)

Ingredients

- Lukewarm milk: 1 cup
- Vinegar: 1 teaspoon
- Butter: 2 tablespoons
- 1/3 to 1/4 cup of water
- 1 and a half teaspoons of salt
- Instant yeast: 2 and 1/4 teaspoons
- 3 and a half cups of all-purpose flour
- 1 and a half teaspoons of sugar
- Half teaspoon of baking powder

Instructions

- In the tin of bread machine, add all ingredients. Use less water in a humid environment and more water in a dry or colder environment.
- Select basic and light crust. Press start. Adjust dough consistency by adding more flour if too sticky and add water if too dry.
- Serve fresh.

2.16 Traditional Italian Bread

(Prep time: 10 minutes | Total time: 3 hours 10 minutes)

Ingredients

- Sugar: 1 tablespoon
- Cold water: 3/4 cup
- Salt: 1 teaspoon
- 2 cups of bread flour
- Active dry yeast: 1 teaspoon

- Olive oil: 1 tablespoon

Instructions

- Add all ingredients in the pan of the bread machine in the suggested order by the manufacturer.
- Select Italian cycle or basic cycle. Light crust. Press start.
- Serve fresh.

2.17 Cocoa Bread

(Prep time: 10 minutes | Total time: 3 hours 5 minutes)

Ingredients

- 1 whole egg
- 1 cup of milk
- One yolk only
- Salt: 1 teaspoon
- Canola oil: 3 tablespoons
- Vanilla extract: 1 teaspoon
- Wheat gluten: 1 tablespoon
- 3 cups of bread flour
- Half cup of brown sugar
- 2 and a half teaspoons of bread machine yeast
- Cocoa powder: 1/3 cup

Instructions

- Add all the ingredients in the bread machine in the suggested order by the manufacturer.
- Select white bread, medium crust. Press start.
- Serve fresh.

Chapter 3: Spice & Herb Breads

3.1 Fragrant Herb Bread

(Prep time: 10 minutes | Total time: 3 hours 5 minutes)

Ingredients

- Olive oil: 2 tablespoons
- Warm water: 1 cup
- 1 egg, lightly beaten
- Dried rosemary leaves: 2 teaspoons
- White sugar: 2 tablespoons
- 1 teaspoon of salt
- Dried oregano: 1 teaspoon
- Bread machine yeast: 2 teaspoons
- Dried basil: 1 teaspoon
- All-purpose flour: 3 cups + 2 tablespoons

Instructions

- Add all ingredients in the pan of the bread machine, as per the suggested order.
- Select large loaf, light crust. Press start.
- Serve fresh

3.2 Rosemary Bread

(Prep time: 10 minutes | Total time: 3 hours 15 minutes)

Ingredients

- Onion Powder: 1 Tablespoon
- Butter: 4 Tablespoons
- Bread Flour: 3 Cups

- 1 and 1/3 Cups of warm Milk
- One Minute Oatmeal: 1 Cup
- Salt: 1 Teaspoon
- 1 and a half Teaspoons of Bread Machine Yeast
- White Granulated Sugar: 6 Teaspoons
- Dried Rosemary: 1 Tablespoon

Instructions

- Add all ingredients to the bread machine in the suggested order by the manufacturer.
- Select 2 lb. loaf, basic and light crust.
- Press start.
- Before the baking cycle begins, sprinkle some rosemary on top and let it bake.
- Serve fresh.

3.3 Spicy Cajun Bread

(Prep time: 10 minutes | Total time: 2 hours 20 minutes)

Ingredients

- Bread flour: 2 cups
- 1/4 cup of diced green bell pepper
- Half cup of water
- 1/4 cup of chopped onion
- 2 teaspoons of soft butter
- 2 teaspoons finely chopped garlic
- Active dry yeast: 1 teaspoon
- Sugar: 1 tablespoon
- Cajun seasoning: 1 teaspoon
- Half teaspoon of salt

Instructions

- Place all ingredients into the bread machine in the suggested order by the manufacturer.
- Select white bread, dark or medium crust, and not the delay cycle.
- Press start.
- Serve fresh

3.4 Aromatic Lavender Bread

(Prep time: 10 minutes | Total time: 2 hours 55 minutes)

Ingredients

- Water: 1/3 cup
- Buttermilk: 3/4 cup
- Fresh lavender flowers, finely chopped: 1 teaspoon
- Bread flour: 3 cups
- Olive oil: 3 tablespoons
- Fresh lavender leaves, finely chopped: 2 tablespoons
- Gluten: 1 tablespoon
- One lemon: zest
- 2 and a half tsp. of bread machine yeast
- 1 and a half teaspoons of salt

Instructions

- Add all ingredients to the bread machine in the suggested order by the manufacturer.
- Select dark crust, basic cycle, and press start.
- Serve fresh.

3.5 Cracked Black Pepper Bread

(Prep time: 10 minutes | Total time: 2 hours 45 minutes)

Ingredients

- Minced chives: 3 tablespoons
- Olive oil: 3 tablespoons
- Sugar: 3 tablespoons
- 1 and a half cups water
- Cracked black pepper: 1 teaspoon
- Salt: 2 teaspoons
- Garlic cloves: 2 minced
- Dried basil: 1 teaspoon
- Garlic powder: 1 teaspoon
- Active dry yeast: 2 and a half teaspoons
- Grated parmesan cheese: 1/4 cup
- Bread flour: 4 cups

Instructions

- Add all ingredients in the bread machine in the suggested order by the manufacturer.
- Select basic, light crust. Do not use the time delay—press start.
- Serve fresh.

3.6 Herb & Garlic Cream Cheese Bread

(Prep time: 10 minutes | Total time: 2 hours 15 minutes)

Ingredients

- Bread flour: 3 cups
- Active dry yeast: 2 teaspoons
- Warm water: 1 cup
- 1 and a half teaspoons of salt

- Dry herbs: 1 teaspoon
- Butter: 1 tablespoon
- Sugar: 1 tablespoon
- Garlic powder: 2 teaspoons
- Powdered milk: 1 tablespoon

Instructions

- Add all ingredients to the bread machine in the suggested order by the manufacturer.
- Select knead or mix cycle. After ten minutes, check dough consistency, adjust if too dry or too wet by adding one tbsp. of water or flour one at a time.
- Select basic setting, light crust. Press start.

3.7 Honey-Spice Egg Bread

(Prep time: 10 minutes | Total time: 3 hours 25 minutes)

Ingredients

- 2 Fresh eggs
- Warm water: 1 Cup
- 1 and a half Tablespoons of unsalted butter
- Honey: 2 Tablespoons
- Salt: 1 teaspoon
- Powdered milk: 3 Tablespoons
- Bread flour: 3 Cups
- Active dry yeast: 2 teaspoons
- Cinnamon: 1 teaspoon
- Cardamom: 1 teaspoon
- Ginger: 1 teaspoon
- Nutmeg: 1 teaspoon

Instructions

- Place all ingredients into the bread machine in the suggested order by the manufacturer.
- Select white bread, light crust. Press start.
- Serve warm with honey or butter.

3.8 Cinnamon Swirl Bread

(Prep time: 10 minutes | Total time: 3 hours 25 minutes)

Ingredients

- 1 and a half tbsp. of butter
- Warm milk: ¾ cup
- 1 whole egg
- 1 tbsp. of brown sugar
- Half teaspoon of salt
- Instant Yeast: 1 ¾ tsp
- 2 and a half cups of bread flour

For Cinnamon Swirl

- Half tbsp. of cinnamon
- 3 tbsp. of white sugar
- Raisins: 1 ¼ cups

Instructions

- Warm the milk to 110 F. Mix with butter and stir, so it melts.
- Add to the bread machines. Add the rest of the ingredients as per the suggested order.
- Select basic. Choose crust to your liking. Select knead. Meanwhile, combine the swirl ingredients.
- After the second knead cycle's beeping, add the swirl ingredients.
- After the third kneading cycle's beeping, remove paddles and place the dough back in the machine.
- Serve fresh.

3.9 Simple Garlic Bread

(Prep time: 10 minutes | Total time: 3 hours 15 minutes)

Ingredients

- 1 tablespoon of butter
- Warm water: 1 cup (110 F)
- Powdered milk: 1 tablespoon
- White sugar: 1 tablespoon
- 1 and a half teaspoons of salt
- Active dry yeast: 2 teaspoons
- Minced garlic: 3 teaspoons

- 1 and a half tablespoons of dried parsley
- Bread flour: 3 cups

Instructions

- Add all ingredients to the bread machine in the suggested order by the manufacturer.
- Select the basic cycle, and press start.
- Serve fresh.

3.10 Herbed Pesto Bread

(Prep time: 10 minutes | Total time: 2 hours 5 minutes)

Ingredients

- 3 cups bread flour
- 1 and a half teaspoons of sugar
- 1 cup of water
- 1 teaspoon salt
- Pesto sauce: 1/4 cup
- 2 and a 1/4 teaspoons of bread machine yeast
- Lemon juice: 1 teaspoon

Instructions

- Add all ingredients to the bread machine in the suggested order by the manufacturer.
- Select basic cycle and 1.5 lb.
- Press start and serve fresh.

3.11 Caraway Rye Bread

(Prep time: 10 minutes | Total time: 4 hours 10 minutes)

Ingredients

- Dry milk powder: 2 tablespoons
- 1 and a 1/4 cups of lukewarm water (100 F)
- Brown sugar: 2 tablespoons
- 1 teaspoon of salt
- Butter: 2 tablespoons
- 3/4 cup of rye flour
- Whole wheat flour: 3/4 cup

- Molasses: 2 tablespoons
- 1 and a ¾ teaspoons of active dry yeast
- 1 and a ¾ cups of bread flour
- 1 and a half tablespoons of caraway seeds

Instructions

- Add all ingredients to the bread machine in the suggested order by the manufacturer.
- Select grain, the crust of your liking. Press start.
- Serve fresh.

3.12 Anise Lemon Bread

(Prep time: 10 minutes | Total time: 3 hours 5 minutes)

Ingredients

- Water
- 1 lemon: juice and zest
- Olive oil: 1 tablespoon
- Half cup of milk (110 F).
- 2 tablespoons of honey
- Instant active dry yeast: 3 teaspoons
- Anise seeds: 1 tablespoon
- 1 teaspoon of salt
- 3 cups of bread flour

Instructions

- Add lemon juice to a cup and enough lukewarm water to make a half cup.
- Heat this mixture to 110 F.
- Add to the bread machine, then lemon zest and rest of the ingredients.
- Select basic and crust to your liking—press start.

- After 10 minutes, check the dough's consistency. Add more flour or water if required.
- Serve fresh.

3.13 Fragrant Cardamom Bread

(Prep time: 5 minutes | Total time: 1 hour 5 minutes)

Ingredients

- 1 whole egg
- Half cup of milk
- Honey: 1/4 cup
- Ground cardamom: 1 teaspoon
- Unsweetened applesauce: 1/4 cup
- Active dry yeast: 2 teaspoons
- 1 teaspoon of salt
- Bread flour: 2 and a 3/4 cups

Instructions

- Add all ingredients to the bread machine in the suggested order by the manufacturer.
- Select basic, light crust—press start.
- Serve warm with butter.

3.14 Chocolate Mint Bread

(Prep time: 10 minutes | Total time: 3 hours 5 minutes)

Ingredients

- Softened butter: 2 tablespoons
- Water: 1 and a 1/4 cups + 2 tbsp.
- 1 and a 1/4 teaspoons of salt
- 4 cups of bread flour
- 2 and a half teaspoons of bread machine dry yeast

- Sugar: 1/3 cup
- Mint chocolate chips: 2/3 cup

Instructions

- Carefully measure and place all ingredients in the bread pan as per the order suggested by the manufacturer.
- Select the sweet cycle. Light crust. Press start.
- Serve fresh.

3.15 Molasses Candied-Ginger Bread

(Prep time: 10 minutes | Total time: 3 hours 10 minutes)

Ingredients

- Molasses: 1/4 cup
- 3 and 1/3 cups of bread flour
- 1 whole egg
- Milk: 3/4 cup
- 3 tablespoons of butter
- Brown sugar: 1 tablespoon
- Ginger: 3/4 teaspoon
- Raisins: 1/3 cup
- Salt: 3/4 teaspoon
- Cinnamon: 3/4 teaspoon
- Active dry yeast: 2 and a 1/4 teaspoons

Instructions

- Add all ingredients to the bread machine in the suggested order by the manufacturer. Do not add raisins yet.
- Select white bread and light crust—press start.
- Add raisins on ingredient beeping.
- Serve warm.

Chapter 4: Grain, Seed & Nuts Breads

4.1 Whole-Wheat Seed Bread

(Prep time: 10 minutes | Total time: 3 hours 10 minutes)

Ingredients

- 1 and 1/3 cups of whole wheat bread flour
- 1 and 1/3 cups of water
- Honey: 3 tablespoons
- Salt: 1 teaspoon
- Softened Butter: 2 tablespoons
- Half cup of flaxseed
- 1 and a half cups of bread flour
- Half cup of sunflower seeds
- Active dry yeast: 1 teaspoon

Instructions

- Add all ingredients to the bread machine in the manufacturer's suggested order, except for sunflower seeds.
- Select basic cycle, and press start.
- Add sunflower seeds on the beeping of the kneading cycle.
- Serve fresh.

4.2 Multigrain Bread

(Prep time: 10 minutes | Total time: 2 hours 40 minutes)

Ingredients

- Multigrain Cereal: 3/4 Cup
- Softened Unsalted Butter: 3 tbsp.
- 2 and a 1/4 Cups of Bread Flour
- Warm Milk: 1 Cup
- 1 Teaspoon of Bread Machine Yeast
- Brown Sugar packed: 1/4 Cup
- 1 teaspoon of Salt

Instructions

- Add all ingredients to the bread machine in the suggested order by the manufacturer.
- Select basic cycle, Light crust, and press start.
- Serve fresh

4.3 Toasted Pecan Bread

(Prep time: 10 minutes | Total time: 3 hours 5 minutes)

Ingredients

- 2 and a half tablespoons of butter
- 1 and 1⁄4 cups of water
- Half cup of old-fashioned oatmeal
- bread flour: 3 cups
- Half cup chopped pecans
- bread machine yeast: 2 teaspoons
- Dry milk: 2 tablespoons
- Sugar: 3 tablespoons
- 1 and a 1⁄4 teaspoons of salt

Instructions

- Add all ingredients to the bread machine in the suggested order by the manufacturer.
- Select Grain and light crust. Press start.
- Serve fresh.

4.4 Market Seed Bread

(Prep time: 10 minutes | Total time: 3 hours 10 minutes)

Ingredients

- Olive oil: 2 tablespoons
- Tepid water: 1 cup
- Whole wheat bread flour: 1 cup
- 1/3 cup mixed seeds (pumpkin, sunflower, sesame, linseed, & poppy)
- 1 teaspoon of salt
- 1 and a half teaspoons of dried yeast
- Sugar: 1 tablespoon
- White bread flour: 2 cups

Instructions

- Add all ingredients to the bread machine in the suggested order by the manufacturer. Add seeds in the end.
- Select white bread cycle—press start. Check the dough's consistency if it needs more water or flour. Add one tbsp at a time.
- Serve fresh.

4.5 Cracked Wheat Bread

(Prep time: 10 minutes | Total time: 1 hour 10 minutes)

Ingredients

- 1 and a half teaspoons of salt
- 2 and 1/4 cups of bread flour

- 1 and a half tablespoons of butter
- One and a 1/3 cup of water
- Honey: 2 tablespoons
- 2 and a 1/4 teaspoons of active dry yeast
- 1 and 1/4 cups of whole wheat flour
- Half cup of cracked wheat

Instructions

- Put all ingredients in the pan of the bread machine, as per the suggested order.
- Select basic setting, the crust of your liking. Press start.
- Serve fresh and enjoy.

4.6 Double Coconut Bread

(Prep time: 10 minutes | Total time: 4 hours 10 minutes)

Ingredients

- 1 egg yolk only
- 1 cup of unsweetened coconut milk
- 1 and a half teaspoons of coconut extract
- White flour: 3 cups
- 3/4 teaspoon of salt
- 1 and a half tablespoons of vegetable oil
- 1/3 cup of coconut
- 1 and a half teaspoons of bread machine yeast
- 2 and a half tablespoons of sugar

Instructions

- Add all ingredients to the bread machine in the suggested order by the manufacturer.
- Select sweet cycle—press start.
- Serve fresh and enjoy

4.7 Honeyed Bulgur Bread

(Prep time: 10 minutes | Total time: 2 hours 10 minutes)

Ingredients

- 2 tbsp. of honey
- 1/4 cup of extra coarse bulgur wheat
- Boiling water: 1/4 cup
- 1 package of active dry yeast
- 1 teaspoon of salt
- Half cup of bread flour
- 1 tbsp. of vegetable oil
- 1 and 1/4 cups of all-purpose flour
- 3/4 cup of water
- 1 tablespoon of skim milk

Instructions

- Add all ingredients to the bread machine in the suggested order by the manufacturer.
- Select basic cycle and press start.
- Enjoy fresh.

4.8 Flaxseed Honey Bread

(Prep time: 10 minutes | Total time: 3 hours 40 minutes)

Ingredients

- Vegetable oil: ¼ cup
- 1 and a half cup of bread flour
- Honey: 3 tablespoons
- 1 and a half teaspoon of salt
- Ground ginger: 1 teaspoon
- 1 and a half cup of whole wheat flour

- 1 and a 1/3 cup of lukewarm water
- 1 and a half teaspoon of instant yeast
- Half cup of ground flax seed

Instructions

- Put all the ingredients in the pan of the bread machine as per the suggested order.
- Select the basic cycle and medium crust—press start.
- Check dough. It should not be too sticky or too dry. Add water or flour one tbsp. at a time.
- Enjoy fresh with butter.

4.9 Chia Sesame Bread

(Prep time: 10 minutes | Total time: 3 hours 10 minutes)

Ingredients

- Organic apple cider vinegar: 1 tablespoon
- 1/4 cup of olive oil
- 2 teaspoons of salt
- Almond meal flour: 2/3 cup
- 3 whole eggs, whisked
- 1 cup of ground sesame seeds
- Half cup of gluten-free tapioca flour
- 1 cup of ground chia seeds
- 1 cup of warm water
- Gluten-free coconut flour: 1/3 cup
- Psyllium husks ground: 3 tablespoons

Instructions

- In a bowl, add all dry ingredients and sift them together. Take out any large bits.

- Add all ingredients to the bread machine in the suggested order by the manufacturer.

- Select gluten-free, press start, and check dough's consistency. It should not be too wet or too dry. Add one tbsp. of water or flour if it's too dry or too wet.

- Serve fresh.

4.10 Quinoa Whole Wheat Bread

(Prep time: 10 minutes | Total time: 3 hours 10 minutes)

Ingredients

- Honey: 2 tbsp.

- 1 and ¼ cups of water

- Olive oil: 1 tbsp.

- Half tsp. of salt

- Whole wheat flour: 1 and ¾ cups

- Bread flour: 1 and 3/4 cups

- Toasted sesame oil: one dash

- Uncooked quinoa: 1/3 cup

- Active dry yeast: 1 3/4 teaspoons

Instructions

- Add all ingredients to the bread machine in the suggested order by the manufacturer.

- Select basic, light crust—press start.

- Serve fresh.

4.11 Peanut Butter Bread

(Prep time: 10 minutes | Total time: 3 hours 10 minutes)

Ingredients

- 1 and a half cups of bread flour
- Half cup of peanut butter
- Half teaspoon of salt
- 1 and a half cups of whole wheat flour
- 2 and a 1/4 teaspoons of active dry yeast
- Gluten flour: 3 tablespoons
- 1 and 1/4 cups of warm water
- Brown sugar: 1/4 cup

Instructions

- Add all ingredients to the bread machine in the suggested order by the manufacturer.
- Select whole wheat, light crust. Press start.
- Serve fresh.

4.12 Toasted Hazelnut Bread

(Prep time: 10 minutes | Total time: 2 hours 45 minutes)

Ingredients

- Hazelnut liqueur: 2 tablespoons
- 3 cups of flour
- Chopped hazelnuts: ¾ cups
- 1 whole egg
- Sugar: 3 tablespoons
- ¾ teaspoon of salt
- Active dry yeast: 1 teaspoon
- Butter: 3 tablespoons

- 1 cup of milk

For Glaze

- 1-2 teaspoons of milk
- Hazelnut liqueur: 1 tablespoon
- Half cup of powdered sugar

Instructions

- Add all ingredients to the bread machine in the suggested order by the manufacturer except for nuts.
- Select basic and light crust. Press start.
- Add nuts on the signal.
- Meanwhile, mix all the ingredients of glaze. Drizzle over warm bread and serve.

4.13 Oatmeal Seed Bread

(Prep time: 10 minutes | Total time: 3 hours 10 minutes)

Ingredients

- Softened Butter: 2 tablespoons
- 1 and 3⁄4 cups of water
- Olive oil: 1 tablespoon
- 2 cups of bread flour
- 1⁄4 cup of honey
- Quick-cooking oats: 2⁄3 cup
- Whole wheat flour: 2 cups
- Half cup of sunflower seeds
- Dry milk: 2 tablespoons
- 2 and a half teaspoons of bread machine yeast
- 1 and a 1⁄4 teaspoons of salt

Instructions

- Add all ingredients to the bread machine in the suggested order by the manufacturer, except for seeds.
- Select basic, light crust. Do not try the delay cycle.
- Press start.
- Serve fresh.

4.14 Nutty Wheat Bread

(Prep time: 10 minutes | Total time: 3 hours 10 minutes)

Ingredients

- 1 and a half tablespoons of unsalted butter, cut into half-inch pieces ·
- 1 and a ⅓ cups of buttermilk
- 1 and a half tablespoons of maple syrup
- 1 teaspoon of salt
- 1 and a ¼ cups of bread flour
- 2 and a ¼ teaspoons bread machine yeast
- ¾ cups of mixed seeds and nuts (pecans, sunflower seeds, pumpkin seeds, and walnuts)
- 2 and a ¼ cups of whole wheat flour

Instructions

- All ingredients should be at room temperature
- Add all ingredients to the bread machine in the suggested order by the manufacturer. Do not add seeds and nuts yet.
- Select whole wheat, light crust. Press start.
- Add in the seeds, nuts on the ingredients signal.
- Serve warm.

4.15 Sunflower Bread

(Prep time: 10 minutes | Total time: 2 hours 10 minutes)

Ingredients

- 2 and a half cups of white bread flour
- 1 and 1/4 cups of water
- Dry milk: 2 tablespoons
- Half cup of sunflower seeds
- Half teaspoon of salt
- Wheat bread flour: 3/4 cup
- Butter: 2 tablespoons
- Fast rise yeast: 2 teaspoons
- Honey: 3 tablespoons

Instructions

- Add all ingredients to the bread machine in the suggested order by the manufacturer.
- Select the cycle you like the best. Even use the delay cycle.
- Press start and enjoy fresh bread.

4.16 Raisin Seed Bread

(Prep time: 10 minutes | Total time: 3 hours 10 minutes)

Ingredients

- Cinnamon: 2 teaspoons
- Half teaspoon of salt
- Whole-wheat flour: 3 cups
- 1 cup of warm water
- Raisins: 1 cup
- Four tablespoons of honey
- One teaspoon of seeds

- Half cup of coconut oil
- Active dry yeast: 2 teaspoons

Instructions

- Add all ingredients to the bread machine in the suggested order by the manufacturer.
- Select whole-wheat crust to your liking—press start.

4.17 Quinoa Oatmeal Bread

(Prep time: 10 minutes | Total time: 3 hours 50 minutes)

Ingredients

- Half cup of whole wheat flour
- Buttermilk: 1 cup
- 1 and a half of bread flour
- Half cup of quick-cooking oats
- 1 and a half teaspoons of bread machine yeast
- 2/3 cup of water
- Honey: 1 tablespoon
- 1/3 cup of uncooked quinoa
- 4 tablespoons of melted unsalted butter
- Salt: 1 teaspoon
- Sugar: 1 tablespoon

Instructions

- Cook quinoa in 2/3 cup of water. Cool it.
- Add all ingredients with cooked quinoa to the bread machine in the suggested order by the manufacturer.

- Select whole grain and press start.
- Enjoy fresh.

Chapter 5: Cheese Breads

5.1 Cheesy Chipotle Bread

(Prep time: 10 minutes | Total time: 3 hours 10 minutes)

Ingredients

- 1 and a half teaspoons of salt
- Shredded Mexican Cheese: 1 cup
- Chipotle Chili powder: 1 teaspoon
- Sugar: 1/4 cup
- 1 and 1/4 cups of lukewarm water
- Bread machine yeast: 1 teaspoon
- Bread flour: 4 cups
- 3 tablespoons of dry milk

Instructions

- Add all the ingredients to the bread machine's pan in the suggested order by the manufacturer.
- Select white bread cycle, light crust. Press start.
- Do not use a delay cycle.
- Enjoy fresh.

5.2 Roasted Garlic Asiago Bread

(Prep time: 10 minutes | Total time: 3 hours 15 minutes)

Ingredients

- 1 cup of white bread flour

- Gluten flour: 1/4 cup
- 1 and a 3/4 cup of whole wheat flour
- Grated Asiago cheese: 3/4 cup
- Fresh rosemary minced: 2 teaspoons
- Dry milk: 2 tablespoons
- 3 roasted crushed garlic cloves
- Fresh basil minced: 1 tablespoon
- Fresh oregano minced: 2 teaspoons
- 4 teaspoons of active dry yeast
- 1 and 1/4 cups of water
- Honey: 1 teaspoon
- 1 teaspoon of salt
- Olive oil: 2 tablespoons

Instructions

- Add all the ingredients to the bread machine in the suggested order by the manufacturer.
- Select whole wheat cycle, crust to your liking.
- Serve fresh.

5.3 Cheddar Cheese Basil Bread

(Prep time: 10 minutes | Total time: 3 hours 10 minutes)

Ingredients

- Softened Unsalted Butter: 4 Tablespoons
- 1 and 1/8 Cups (2tbsp.) of lukewarm Milk
- 1 Cup of Shredded Cheese
- 3 Cups of Bread Flour
- Brown Sugar: 1 Tablespoon
- Basil: 1 Teaspoon
- 1 and a half Teaspoons of Bread Machine Yeast

- 1 and a half Teaspoons of Salt

Instructions

- Put all ingredients into the bread machine in the suggested order by the manufacturer.
- Select basic setting, light crust. Press start.
- Before the baking cycle, add some cheese on top of the bread loaf, if you like.
- Enjoy fresh.

5.4 Jalapeño Corn Bread

(Prep time: 10 minutes | Total time: 2 hours 50 minutes)

Ingredients

- Thawed frozen corn: 2/3 cup, drained
- Water: ¾ cup + 2 tablespoons
- jalapeño chili, chopped: 1 tablespoon
- Softened Butter: 2 tablespoons
- Sugar: 2 tablespoons
- Bread flour: 3 and a ¼ cups
- 2 and a half teaspoons of bread machine
- Cornmeal: 1/3 cup
- 1 and a half teaspoons of salt

Instructions

- Add all ingredients to the bread machine in the suggested order by the manufacturer.
- Select White cycle and Light crust—press start. Do not use a delay cycle.
- Enjoy fresh.

5.5 Olive Cheese Bread

(Prep time: 10 minutes | Total time: 4 hours 10 minutes)

Ingredients

- Half cup of small stuffed olives, drained
- Sharp cheddar cheese, shredded: 1 cup
- 3 and 1/4 cups of flour
- 1 and a 1/4 teaspoons of yeast
- 1 cup of water
- Sugar: 1 teaspoon
- Salt: 1 teaspoon

Instructions

- Place all ingredients in the pan of the bread machine, except for olives. Select basic. Press start.
- Add olives when ten minutes are left in the kneading cycle.
- Serve fresh.

5.6 Blue Cheese Onion Bread

(Prep time: 10 minutes | Total time: 3 hours 50 minutes)

Ingredients

- Powdered milk: 3 tablespoons
- Dried onion flakes: 2 tablespoons
- Sugar: 2 tablespoons
- 1 and 1/3 cups of water
- Salt, a pinch
- 4 cups of white flour
- 1 and a 1/4 teaspoons of bread machine yeast
- Shredded blue cheese: 1/4 cup

Instructions

- Add all ingredients to the bread machine in the suggested order by the manufacturer.
- Select sweet bread cycle and dark crust, if you like—press start.
- Serve fresh

5.7 Double Cheese Bread

(Prep time: 10 minutes | Total time: 3 hours 5 minutes)

Ingredients

- Bread flour: 3 cups
- 1 teaspoon of salt
- 1 teaspoon of coarse black pepper
- 1 and a half cups of shredded sharp cheddar (at room temperature)
- Sugar: 2 tablespoons
- 1 and a 1/4 cup of Luke warm water
- 1 and a 1/4 teaspoon of bread machine yeast
- 1 tablespoon of soft butter
- Dry milk powder: 1/4 cup
- Parmesan cheese, finely grated: 1/3 cup

Instructions

- Add all ingredients to the bread machine in the suggested order by the manufacturer.
- Select white bread, medium crust. Press start.
- When 15-20 minutes of the baking cycle is left, sprinkle shredded cheese on top of the loaf.
- Serve fresh.

5.8 Mozzarella & Salami Bread

(Prep time: 10 minutes | Total time: 3 hours 10 minutes)

Ingredients

- Shredded mozzarella cheese: 1/3 cup
- 1 and a half teaspoons of dried oregano
- Warm water: 1 cup + 2 tablespoons
- 2 tablespoons of sugar
- 1 and a half teaspoons of garlic salt
- 1 and a half teaspoons of active dry yeast
- Diced salami: 2/3 cup
- 3 and a 1/4 cup of bread flour

Instructions

- Add all ingredients to the bread machine in the suggested order by the manufacturer except for salami.
- Select basic cycle. Do not use the time delay.
- Add salami before final kneading.
- Enjoy fresh.

5.9 Simple Cottage Cheese Bread

(Prep time: 10 minutes | Total time: 3 hours 10 minutes)

Ingredients

- Bread flour: 3 cups
- 1/3 cup of water
- 2 Tbsp. of Butter
- 1% Cottage Cheese: 1 cup
- 1 whole Egg
- 1 Tablespoon of Sugar
- 2 teaspoons of yeast
- 1/4 tsp of Baking Soda
- 1 tsp of salt

Instructions

- Add all ingredients to the bread machine in the suggested order by the manufacturer.
- Select basic, light crust—press start.
- Enjoy warm.

5.10 Chile Cheese Bacon Bread

(Prep time: 10 minutes | Total time: 3 hours 20 minutes)

Ingredients

- Bread flour: 4 cups
- Vegetable oil: 2 tablespoons
- 1 and a 1/4 teaspoon of salt
- Mexican cheese: 2 cups
- 1 and 1/3 cups of water
- Dry milk: 3 tablespoons
- 3 tablespoons of bacon bits
- Sugar: 2 tablespoons+ 1 and a half tsp.
- Dry active yeast: 2 teaspoons

Instructions

- Add all ingredients to the bread machine in the manufacturer's suggested order, except for bacon and cheese.
- Select basic setting, crust to your liking.
- Add bacon and cheese at the nut & fruit signal.
- Serve fresh.

5.11 Italian Parmesan Bread

(Prep time: 10 minutes | Total time: 3 hours 5 minutes)

Ingredients

- 4 cups of flour
- parmesan cheese: 1/4 cup
- 1 and a half cups of water
- 1 and a half teaspoons of salt
- 2 and a half teaspoons of yeast
- Garlic powder: 1 teaspoon
- Italian/pizza seasoning: 1 teaspoon

Instructions

- Add all ingredients to the bread machine in the suggested order by the manufacturer.
- Select basic or delay cycle—press start.
- Serve fresh

5.12 Rich Cheddar Bread

(Prep time: 10 minutes | Total time: 3 hours 10 minutes)

Ingredients

- 2 and a half tablespoons of Parmesan cheese
- 1 cup of warm water
- Half teaspoon of salt
- 3 and a half teaspoons of sugar
- 1 and a 1/4 cup of freshly grated cheddar cheese
- Dry mustard: 1 teaspoon
- 2 and a half tablespoons of softened butter
- 2 and a half cups of bread flour
- 1 and a half teaspoons of paprika
- Active dry yeast: 2 teaspoons

- 2 and a half tablespoons of minced onions

Instructions

- Place all ingredients in the bread machine in the suggested order by the manufacturer.
- Select white setting, crust to your liking.
- Press start and assess dough's consistency if it needs water or more flour.
- Add one tbsp. of flour or water if required.
- Serve fresh.

5.13 Feta Oregano Bread

(Prep time: 10 minutes | Total time: 3 hours 10 minutes)

Ingredients

- 1 and a half tablespoons of olive oil
- 3 cups of bread flour
- Half cup of crumbled feta cheese
- 1 cup of water
- Active dry yeast: 2 teaspoons
- Dried leaf oregano: 1 tablespoon
- Salt: 1 teaspoon
- 3 tablespoons of sugar

Instructions

- Put all ingredients in the bread machine in the suggested order by the manufacturer.
- Select basic. Press start.
- Serve fresh.

5.14 Goat Cheese Bread

(Prep time: 10 minutes | Total time: 3 hours 10 minutes)

Ingredients

- 2 cups of bread flour
- Water: 3/4 cup less
- 1 and a half tsp of active dry yeast
- 1 tbsp. Of granulated sugar
- Half tsp of salt
- 3 Tbsp. of soft goat cheese
- 1 Tbsp. of nonfat dry milk
- 1 and a half tsp of cracked black pepper

Instructions

- All ingredients must be at room temperature
- Add all ingredients to the bread machine in the suggested order by the manufacturer.
- Select normal cycle—press start.
- Assess dough's consistency; it should not be too dry or too wet.
- Add one tbsp. of water or flour if required.
- Serve fresh

5.15 Mozzarella-Herb Bread

(Prep time: 10 minutes | Total time: 3 hours 10 minutes)

Ingredients

- Onion Powder: 1 Teaspoon
- Butter cut into slices: 6 Tablespoons
- lukewarm Milk: 1/3 Cup

- Bread Flour: 4 Cups
- 1 and a half teaspoons of Bread Machine Yeast
- 2 Tablespoons of Sugar
- Italian Herb Seasoning: 2 Tablespoons
- 1 and a half Teaspoons of Salt

Instructions

- Add all ingredients to the bread machine in the suggested order by the manufacturer.
- Select basic, light crust—press start.
- Before the baking cycle begins, sprinkle Italian seasoning on top.
- Enjoy fresh.

Chapter 6: Fruit Breads

6.1 Pineapple Coconut Bread

(Prep time: 10 minutes | Total time: 3 hours 10 minutes)

Ingredients

- Half cup of pineapple (crushed with juice)
- Milk: 1/4 cup
- Margarine: 1/4 cup
- Sugar: 1/3 cup
- coconut extract: 1 teaspoon
- 1 whole egg, beaten
- Half cup of mashed banana
- Flour: 3 cups
- Half teaspoon of salt
- 1 and a half teaspoons of bread machine yeast
- Half cup of instant potato flakes

Instructions

- Add all ingredients to the bread machine in the suggested order by the manufacturer.
- Select sweet bread and light crust—press start.
- Serve fresh.

6.2 Warm Spiced Pumpkin Bread

(Prep time: 10 minutes | Total time: 3 hours 10 minutes)

Ingredients

- Half cup white sugar
- Canned pumpkin: 1 cup, not pie filling
- 1/4 tsp. of salt
- Half cup of brown sugar
- 2 whole eggs
- 1 tsp. of vanilla
- 1 and a half cups of all-purpose flour
- 1 and a half tsp. of pumpkin pie spice
- Half cup of chopped walnuts
- Canola oil: 1/3 cup
- 2 tsp. of baking powder

Instructions

- Spray the bread machine pan with cooking oil.
- Add all ingredients to the bread machine in the suggested order by the manufacturer.
- Select Quick cycle, medium crust.
- After three minutes, clean the sides of the pan with a spatula.
- Start again, and serve fresh.

6.3 Black Olive Bread

(Prep time: 10 minutes | Total time: 2 hours 10 minutes)

Ingredients

- Warm water: 1 cup and half cup brine
- 1/3 -1/2 cup of brine (from olives)
- 3 cups of bread flour

- Olive oil: 2 tablespoons
- Active dry yeast: 2 teaspoons
- 1 and a half teaspoons of salt
- 1 and 2/3 cups of whole-wheat flour
- Sugar: 2 tablespoons
- Half to 2/3 cup of finely chopped olives
- 1 and a half teaspoons of dried basil

Instructions

- Mix water with brine.
- Add all ingredients, except for olives, to the bread machine in the manufacturer's suggested order.
- Select wheat or basic setting. Press start.
- Add the chopped olives to the ingredient signal.
- Serve fresh bread, and brush with olive oil.

6.4 Robust Date Bread

(Prep time: 10 minutes | Total time: 2 hours 10 minutes)

Ingredients

- Boiling water: 3/4 cup
- Unsalted butter: 3 tablespoons cut into half-inch pieces
- Granulated sugar: 2/3 cup
- Baking powder: 1 teaspoon
- 1 and a 1/3 cup of all-purpose flour
- Vanilla extract: 1 teaspoon
- Chopped dates: 3/4 cup
- Baking soda: 1 teaspoon
- Chopped walnuts: 1/3 cup
- Half teaspoon of salt

Instructions

- Add all ingredients to the bread machine in the suggested order by the manufacturer.
- Select basic and light crust.
- After 4 minutes, scrape the sides of the pan with a rubber spatula.
- Before baking starts, remove paddles.
- Enjoy fresh.

6.5 Apple Spice Bread

(Prep time: 10 minutes | Total time: 3 hours 35 minutes)

Ingredients

- Vegetable oil: 1/4 cup
- 1 cup of milk
- Half teaspoon of cinnamon
- 1 and a half teaspoons of salt
- 1 and a 1/3 cup of diced apples (peeled)
- 2 tablespoons of sugar
- 2 and a half teaspoons of yeast
- Bread flour: 3 cups

Instructions

- Add all ingredients to the bread machine, except for apples, in the manufacturer's suggested order.
- Select medium crust. Press start.
- Add apples at the ingredients signal.
- Serve fresh

6.6 Lemon-Lime Blueberry Bread

(Prep time: 10 minutes | Total time: 3 hours 10 minutes)

Ingredients

- 1/4 cup of lukewarm heavy cream

- 1 teaspoon of salt
- 1/3 cup of diced butter
- 3 whole eggs
- All-purpose flour: 1 and a half cup + 3 tbsp.
- 1 and a half cup of bread flour
- 1 and a half cup of blueberries
- Sugar: 3-4 tablespoons + 2 tablespoons
- 2 teaspoons of bread machine yeast
- 1/4 cup of lukewarm water
- Lime and lemon juice, 2 tablespoons of each

Instructions

- Add all ingredients to the bread machine, except blueberries, in the suggested order by the manufacturer.
- Select basic cycle, crust to your liking. Press start.
- Add blueberries to the ingredient signal.
- Serve fresh bread with sugar on top of the loaf.

6.7 Banana Whole-Wheat Bread

(Prep time: 10 minutes | Total time: 3 hours 10 minutes)

Ingredients

- 1 whole egg
- Softened butter: 1 tablespoon
- 1 and a half teaspoons of bread machine yeast
- 1/3 cup of ripe bananas, mashed
- 3 tablespoons of sugar
- 1/4 cup of warm (80 F) water
- Half teaspoon of salt
- 1 and 1/4 cups of bread flour

- Toasted chopped pecans: 1/3 cup
- 3/4 cup of whole wheat flour

Instructions

- Add all ingredients, except nuts, to the bread machine in the suggested

  order by the manufacturer. Add banana with water.
- Select white bread cycle. Light crust. Press start. Add nuts at the ingredient signal. Do not use the delay feature.
- Enjoy fresh.

6.8 Orange Cranberry Bread

(Prep time: 10 minutes | Total time: 3 hours 5 minutes)

Ingredients

- 1 cup of dried cranberries
- All-purpose flour: 3 cups
- Half cup of warm water
- Active dry yeast: 2 teaspoons
- Honey: 3 tablespoons
- ¾ cup of plain yogurt
- Melted butter: 1 tablespoon
- Orange oil: 1 teaspoon
- 1 and a half teaspoons of salt

Instructions

- Add all ingredients to the bread machine in the suggested order by the manufacturer.
- Select basic and light crust. Press start.
- Serve fresh bread

6.9 Plum Orange Bread

(Prep time: 10 minutes | Total time: 3 hours 10 minutes)

Ingredient

- 1 and a 1/4 cups of warm (100 F) water
- Packed brown sugar: 1/4 cup
- 1 and a half teaspoons of bread machine yeast.
- 3 and a 3/4 cup of bread flour
- Orange juice: 2 tbsp.
- Plums: 3/4 cups
- Vegetable oil: 2 tablespoons
- Salt: 1 teaspoon

Instructions

- Place all ingredients in the bread machine in the suggested order by the manufacturer.
- Select basic with medium crust.
- Press start. Enjoy fresh bread.

6.10 Peaches & Cream Bread

(Prep time: 15 minutes | Total time: 3 hours 10 minutes)

Ingredients

- 1 whole egg, beaten
- 1 and a half teaspoon of salt
- 1 and a half cups of chopped peaches
- 1 and a half tablespoons of vegetable oil

- Sugar: 3 tablespoons
- 1/2 teaspoon of cinnamon
- 3 and a half cups of bread flour
- 1 and a half teaspoons of active dry yeast
- Heavy cream: 1/4 cup
- 1/4 teaspoon of nutmeg
- Half cup of rolled oats

Instructions

- Add all ingredients to the bread machine in suggested order by the manufacturer
- Select basic setting. Press start.
- Enjoy fresh bread.

6.11 Fresh Blueberry Bread

(Prep time: 10 minutes | Total time: 3 hours 10 minutes)

Instructions

- 8 Tablespoons of melted Butter
- 2 Eggs, whisked
- Vanilla Extract: 1 Teaspoon –
- 3 ripe Bananas mashed
- Packed Light Brown Sugar: 1 Cup
- All-purpose flour: 2 Cups
- Half Teaspoon of Salt
- Baking Powder: 1 Teaspoon
- Baking Soda: 1 Teaspoon
- 1 Cup of Blueberries

Instructions

- All ingredients should be at room temperature.
- Add all ingredients, except blueberries, to the bread machine in the manufacturer's suggested order.
- Select Quick bread, light crust—press start.
- After the first kneading, add blueberries.
- Enjoy.

6.12 Blueberry Oatmeal Bread

(Prep time: 10 minutes | Total time: 3 hours 10 minutes)

Ingredients

- 2 cups of all-purpose flour
- 1 cup of quick-cooking Oatmeal
- 1 teaspoon of grated lemon
- Half teaspoon of salt
- Half teaspoon of Baking soda
- 1/3 cup of Vegetable oil
- 2 teaspoons of Baking Powder
- 2 teaspoons of Vanilla
- 3/4 cup of Sugar
- 1 cup of thawed Blueberries
- 1 and a 1/4 cup of Skim milk
- 2 Eggs, lightly whisked

Instructions

- Dust lightly the thawed blueberries with flour.
- With cooking oil, spray the bread pan.
- Add already mixed ingredients to the bread machine.
- Select quick or cake cycle—press start.
- Serve fresh bread.

6.13 Fragrant Orange Bread

(Prep time: 10 minutes | Total time: 3 hours 45 minutes)

Ingredients

- Half teaspoon of grated orange
- orange juice concentrate: 3 tablespoons
- 1 whole egg
- 3 cups of bread flour
- 1 and a ¼ teaspoons of salt
- Water: half cup+1 tablespoon
- Granulated sugar: ¼ cup
- Instant dry milk: 2 tablespoons
- 1 and a half tablespoons of softened butter
- Bread machine yeast: 2 teaspoons

For Orange Glaze

- Orange juice: 1 tablespoon
- ¾ cup of powdered sugar

Instructions

- Add all ingredients to the bread machine in the suggested order by the manufacturer.
- Select the white cycle. Do not use the delay feature. Select Light crust—press start.
- Meanwhile, mix the glaze ingredients.
- Drizzle the glaze over fresh bread.

6.14 Moist Oatmeal Apple Bread

(Prep time: 10 minutes | Total time: 3 hours 10 minutes)

Ingredients

- Unsweetened applesauce: 1/3 cup
- Water: 1/3 cup

- Unsweetened apple juice: 2/3 cup
- 3 tablespoons of honey
- Oat bran: 1/4 cup
- 2 tablespoons of vegetable oil
- Quick-cooking oats: 1/3 cup
- 1 and a half teaspoons of salt
- Bread flour: 3 cups
- 2 and a 1/4 teaspoons of bread machine yeast
- 1 and a half teaspoons of ground cinnamon

Instructions

- Add all ingredients to the bread machine in the suggested order by the manufacturer.
- Select basic cycle, light crust. Press start.
- Serve fresh bread.

6.15 Strawberry Shortcake Bread

(Prep time: 10 minutes | Total time: 3 hours 10 minutes)

Ingredients

- 2 and a half teaspoons of bread machine yeast
- Vanilla extract: 1 teaspoon
- Warm heavy whipping cream: 1/4 cup
- Bread machine flour: 3 cups
- 1/4 cup of warm water
- Sugar: 1 tablespoon
- Baking powder: 1/8 teaspoon
- 2 cups of fresh strawberries with 1/4 cup sugar

- Salt: 1 teaspoon

Instructions

•Add water, cream to the pan of the bread maker, mix with yeast and sugar. Let it rest for 15 minutes.

•Coat the sliced strawberries with ¼ cup of sugar.

- Add all ingredients, except for strawberries, to the bread machine in the manufacturer's suggested order.

- Add strawberries to the fruit hopper or add at the ingredients signal.

- Select basic, medium crust. Press start.

- Slice and serve fresh bread.

Chapter 7: Vegetable Breads

7.1 Yeasted Carrot Bread

(Prep time: 10 minutes | Total time: 4 hours 10 minutes)

Ingredients

- 2/3 cup of whole wheat flour
- 1 and a 1/3 cup of rolled oats
- 2 cups of bread flour
- 1 and a 1/3 tsp of salt
- 1 and a half Tbsp. of vegetable oil
- 1 cup of water
- Brown sugar: 2 Tbsp.
- 1/4 cup of dry milk powder
- 2 and a half tsp of active dry yeast
- 2/3 cup of grated carrot

Instructions

- Add all ingredients to the bread machine in the suggested order by the manufacturer.
- Select basic setting, light crust. Press start.
- Enjoy fresh bread.

7.2 Sauerkraut Rye Bread

(Prep time: 10 minutes | Total time: 3 hours 50 minutes)

Ingredients

- Bread flour: 2 cups
- 1 cup of rinsed & drained sauerkraut

- 1 and a half tablespoons of butter
- ¾ cup of warm water
- 1 and a half tablespoons of brown sugar
- 1 and a half teaspoons of active dry yeast
- 1 and a half tablespoons of molasses
- 1 and a half teaspoons of salt
- 1 teaspoon of caraway seed
- Rye flour: 1 cup

Instructions

- Add all ingredients to the bread machine in the suggested order by the manufacturer.
- Use Basic Cycle setting. Press start.
- Serve fresh bread.

7.3 Savory Onion Bread

(Prep time: 10 minutes | Total time: 3 hours 40 minutes)

Ingredients

For Caramelized Onions

- 2 sliced onions
- Butter: 1 tablespoon

For Bread

- Water: 1 cup
- Olive oil: 1 tablespoon
- Bread flour: 3 cups
- Sugar: 2 tablespoons
- 1 teaspoon of salt
- 1 and a ¼ teaspoons of bread machine

Instructions

- In a skillet, sauté onions over medium flame in butter until caramelized and brown. Turn off the heat.

- Add all ingredients to the bread machine in the manufacturer's suggested order, except for caramelized onion.

- Select Basic cycle, Press start. Do not use the delay feature. Add half a cup of onions at nut signal.

- Serve fresh bread.

7.4 Tomato Herb Bread

(Prep time: 10 minutes | Total time: 4 hours 10 minutes)

Ingredients

- 1 whole egg

- Olive oil: 2 tablespoons

- Dried minced onion: 2 teaspoons

- Warm milk: half cup + 2 tbsp. (70°-80° f)

- Half teaspoon of salt

- Minced fresh parsley: 2 tablespoons

- Sugar: 1 tablespoon

- 2 and a 1/4 teaspoons of active dry yeast

- Half teaspoon of garlic powder

- 1 can of (6 ounces) tomato paste

- Half teaspoon of dried tarragon

- Bread flour: 3 cups

Instructions

- Add all ingredients to the bread machine in the suggested order by the manufacturer.

- Use basic bread setting, crust to your liking.

- After five minutes, check the dough add flour if it's too wet and sticky.

- Add one tbsp. of flour if required. Serve fresh bread.

7.5 Mashed Potato Bread

(Prep time: 10 minutes | Total time: 3 hours 15 minutes)

Ingredients

- Dry milk powder: 1 tablespoon
- Sunflower oil: 2 tablespoons
- 3 and 1/4 cups of white bread flour
- 1 teaspoon of salt
- 0.8 cup of potato cooking water at room temperature
- 1 and a half cups of mashed potatoes
- 1 and a half teaspoons of dried yeast
- Sugar: 2 tablespoons

Instructions

- Add all ingredients to the bread machine in the suggested order by the manufacturer.
- Select basic setting, medium crust. Press start.
- Glaze the bread with milk with a brush at the start of cooking time.

7.6 Confetti Bread

(Prep time: 10 minutes | Total time: 3 hours 10 minutes)

Ingredients

- Instant skim-milk powder: 2 tsp
- Roughly chopped old cheddar cheese: 3/4 cup
- Salt: 3/4 tsp
- 1 tsp of sugar
- Water: 3/4 cup
- Half cup of shredded carrot
- White flour: 3 cups

- 1 and a 1/4 tsp of bread machine yeast
- Diced sweet mix bell pepper: 1/3 cup
- 2 tsp of dried Italian seasoning

Instructions

- Place all ingredients, except cheese, into the bread machine in the suggested order by the manufacturer.
- Select white bread cycle—press start. Add cheese at the ingredients signal.
- Serve fresh bread.

7.7 Pretty Borscht Bread

(Prep time: 10 minutes | Total time: 3 hours 10 minutes)

Ingredients

- 1 package of onion soup mix (dry)
- Tomato juice: 2/3 cup
- Ground ginger: 1/4 teaspoon
- 2 and a 1/4 teaspoons of active dry yeast
- All-purpose flour: 3 cups
- Grated carrot: 1/3 cup
- Wheat germ: 1 tablespoon
- Vegetable oil: 2 tablespoons
- Beet: 3/4 cup, cooked & chopped
- Half cup of sour cream
- Granulated sugar: 1/4 teaspoon

Instructions

- Add all ingredients to the bread machine in the suggested order by the manufacturer.
- Select the dough cycle. Take the dough out and let it rise for one and a half hours.
- Punch the dough, let it rise again for 60 minutes.

- Let the oven preheat to 350 F.
- Bake for 20-25 minutes.
- Serve fresh bread.

7.8 Yeasted Pumpkin Bread

(Prep time: 10 minutes | Total time: 3 hours 5 minutes)

Ingredients

- 1 cup of mashed pumpkin puree
- 1 and a 1/4 teaspoons of salt
- Sugar: 2 tablespoons
- Bread flour: 4 cups
- Milk: half cup + 2 tbsp.
- 2 and a 1/4 teaspoons active dry yeast
- Vegetable oil: 2 tablespoons

Instructions

- Place all ingredients in the pan of the bread machine, as per the manufacturer's suggested order.
- Select white bread and light crust—press start.
- Enjoy fresh bread.

7.9 Oatmeal Zucchini Bread

(Prep time: 10 minutes | Total time: 2 hours 10 minutes)

Ingredients

- 2 whole eggs
- 1/3 cup of packed brown sugar
- 3/4 cup of shredded zucchini
- 3 tablespoons of granulated sugar
- 1 and a half cups of all-purpose flour
- Vegetable oil: 1/3 cup

- 3⁄4 teaspoon of ground cinnamon
- Half teaspoon of baking powder
- 3⁄4 teaspoon of salt
- 1⁄4 teaspoon of ground allspice
- 1⁄3 cup of raisins
- Half teaspoon of baking soda
- 1⁄3 cup of oatmeal

Instructions

- Add all ingredients to the bread machine in the suggested order by the manufacturer.
- All ingredients should be at room temperature.
- Select Cake/Quick bread. Press Start.
- After 5 minutes, clean the pan's surface with a rubber spatula and let the cycle continue.
- Serve fresh bread.

7.10 Hot Red Pepper Bread

(Prep time: 10 minutes | Total time: 3 hours 10 minutes)

Ingredients

- Butter: 1 tablespoon
- Unsweetened yogurt: 2 tablespoons
- 2 cloves of garlic
- 3 cups of bread flour
- 3 tablespoons of parmesan cheese

- Roasted red pepper: 1/4 cup, chopped
- 1 and a half teaspoons of dried basil
- Water: 3/4 cup
- 2 tablespoons of sugar
- 2 teaspoons bread machine yeast
- 1 and a half teaspoons of salt

Instructions

- Add all ingredients to the bread machine in the suggested order by the manufacturer.
- Set basic setting, Light crust. Press start.
- Serve fresh bread.

7.11 French Onion Bread

(Prep time: 10 minutes | Total time: 3 hours 10 minutes)

Ingredients

- Unsalted Butter: 4 Tablespoons (softened)
- Half Onion diced and fried
- Onion Powder: 1 Tablespoon
- Bread Flour: 3 Cups
- 1 and a half Teaspoons of Bread Machine Yeast
- Lukewarm Milk: one cup
- White Sugar: 1 Tablespoon
- 1 and a half Teaspoons of Salt

Instructions

- Add all ingredients to the bread machine in the suggested order by the manufacturer.
- Select basic setting. Light crust. Press start.
- Enjoy fresh bread.

7.12 Golden Butternut Squash Raisin Bread

(Prep time: 10 minutes | Total time: 3 hours 10 minutes)

Ingredients

- Bread flour: 3 cups
- Nonfat milk powder: 3 tbsp.
- Active dry yeast: 4 tsp.
- Wheat germ: 3 tbsp.
- Gluten four: 3 tbsp.
- Salt: one and a half tsp.
- Butter: 3 tbsp.
- Butternut puree: 1 cup
- Water: 2/3 cup
- Raisins: half cup
- Sugar: 4 tbsp.
- Ground ginger: half tsp.
- Ground cinnamon: ¾ tsp

Instructions

- Add all ingredients to the bread machine in the suggested order by the

  manufacturer.
- Select basic and crust to your liking—press start.
- Serve fresh bread.

7.13 Sweet Potato Bread

(Prep time: 10 minutes | Total time: 3 hours 10 minutes)

Ingredients

- Half teaspoon of cinnamon
- Half cup of Luke warm water

- Flour: 4 cups
- Vanilla extract: 1 teaspoon
- 1/3 cup of packed brown sugar
- Butter: 2 tablespoons, softened
- 1 and a half teaspoons of salt
- Mashed sweet potatoes: 1 cup
- 2 tablespoons of powdered milk
- Yeast: 2 teaspoons

Instructions

- Add all ingredients to the bread machine in the suggested order by the manufacturer.
- Select white bread, light crust. Press start.
- Serve fresh bread.'

7.14 Potato Thyme Bread

(Prep time: 10 minutes | Total time: 3 hours 10 minutes)

Ingredients

- 1 and a half tsp of salt
- 2 tbsp. of butter softened
- 1 tbsp. of sugar
- 1.25 cups of lukewarm (110 F) water
- Bread machine yeast: 2 tsp
- Instant potato flakes: half cup
- Bread flour: 3 cups
- Dried thyme leaves: 2 tbsp.

Instructions

- Add all ingredients to the bread machine in the suggested order by the manufacturer.
- Select white cycle and dark crust if you like.

- Press start.
- Serve fresh bread.

7.15 Light Corn Bread

(Prep time: 10 minutes | Total time: 3 hours 10 minutes)

Ingredients

- 1 cup of milk
- 1/4 cup of sugar
- 2 whole eggs – lightly whisked
- 1 and a 1/4 cup of bread flour
- Baking powder: 4 teaspoons
- 1 cup of cornmeal
- 1/4 cup of melted butter
- Salt: 1 teaspoon
- Vanilla: 1 teaspoon

Instructions

- Add all ingredients to the bread machine in the suggested order by the manufacturer.
- Use cake cycle/quick cycle and a light crust. Press start.
- Serve fresh bread

Chapter 8: Sourdough Breads

8.1 Simple Sourdough Starter (No-Yeast Whole Wheat Sourdough Starter)

(Prep time: 10 minutes | Total time: 8 Days)

Ingredients

- Half a cup of cool water
- 1 cup of whole wheat or rye flour
- To feed the starter:
- Half cup of cool water (if the environment is warm) or lukewarm water (if the environment is cool)
- 1 cup of All-Purpose Flour Unbleached

Instructions

Day 1: In a one-quart glass container(preferably), mix the flour with cool water. Mix well, so there is no dry flour. Let it rest at (70 F) room temperature, loosely covered.

Day 2: It is possible there will be little bubbling or no activity in the first 24 hours. In any case, take out a half cup of flour and discard it. Add one cup of unbleached flour and a half cup of cool water to the mixture left. Mix well, let it rest at (70 F) room temperature, loosely covered.

Day 3: On the third day, there will be some activity like bubbling, fruity, fresh aroma, and expansion. Now you will start possibly two feedings each day. For every feeding, keep half of the mixture. Discard the rest. Add one cup of all-purpose flour and a half cup of water. Mix well with the mixture and let it sit at room temperature for 12 hours.

Day 4: Keep one cup of mixture and discard the rest. Again, add one cup of flour with a half cup of water.

Day 5: Repeat day 4. At the end of this day, it should be with a lot of bubbles and doubled with a tangy, acidic aroma. In any case, the starter has not doubled yet. Repeat the whole process after every 12 hours on the 6th and 7th day.

After the starter is ready, feed it for one last time. Discard half of it, mix the half with flour and water mix well. Let it rest at room temperature for 6-8 hours. It should be very bubbly and ready. Store in a jar for the long-term. Feed it again in the jar, let it rest for many hours at room temperature, then cover it. Cover lightly, even with a tight lid.

Keep in the fridge, feed it once a week with one cup flour and a half cup of water.

8.2 Basic Sourdough Bread

(Prep time: 10 minutes | Total time: 3 hours 22 minutes)

Ingredients

- 1 and a half teaspoons of salt
- Active dry yeast: 2 teaspoons
- 1 and a half teaspoons of sugar
- 4-6 tablespoons of lukewarm water
- 2 cups of ripe sourdough starter
- 2 and a half cups of All-Purpose Flour (Unbleached)
- 2 tablespoons of vegetable oil

Instructions

- Add all ingredients to the bread machine in the suggested order by the

  manufacturer.
- Select French bread or long-rise cycle. Press start.
- After ten minutes of kneading, check the dough and more flour or water if necessary, to make the dough smooth and soft.
- Serve fresh bread.

8.3 Whole-Wheat Sourdough Bread

(Prep time: 10 minutes | Total time: 3 hours 10 minutes)

Ingredients

- Vegetable oil: 1 tsp. + 1 tbsp.
- 2 tsp of sugar
- Water: half cup + 3 tbsp.
- Whole wheat sourdough starter: ¾ cup
- 1 and a half tsp of Active Dry Yeast
- 2 and a ¼ cups of whole wheat flour
- 1 tsp of salt

Instructions

- All the ingredients should be at room temperature, oil, and water at 80 F.
- Add all ingredients to the bread machine in the suggested order by the manufacturer.
- Select whole wheat and medium crust, not the delay feature. Check dough and add water and flour, if needed.
- Serve fresh bread.

8.4 Multigrain Sourdough Bread

(Prep time: 10 minutes | Total time: 3 hours 10 minutes)

Ingredients

- Sourdough Starter: 3/4 cup
- 7 Grain Cereal (Hot): 2/3 cup
- 1 and a half tbsp. of butter
- Sea Salt: 3/4 tsp
- Wheat Gluten: 1 Tbsp.
- 1-2 Tbsp. of Water or Flour to make the dough smooth
- 2 and a half Tbsp. of packed Brown Sugar

- All-Purpose Flour: 3 cups
- 1 and a half tsp. of Active Dry Yeast
- Water: 2/3 cup

Instructions

- Add all ingredients to the bread machine in the suggested order by the manufacturer.
- Select basic bread. Light crust. Press start.
- Serve fresh bread.

8.5 Faux Sourdough Bread

(Prep time: 10 minutes | Total time: 3 hours 10 minutes)

Ingredients

- 1 and a half teaspoon of salt
- Half cup of plain yogurt
- Lemon juice: 1 tablespoon
- Active dry yeast: 2 teaspoons
- Canola oil: 1 tablespoon
- 3 cups of bread flour
- 3/4 cup of water

Instructions

- Add all ingredients to the bread machine in the suggested order by the manufacturer.
- Select French or white bread cycle, light crust. Press start.
- Serve fresh bread.

8.6 Sourdough Milk Bread

(Prep time: 10 minutes | Total time: 3 hours 10 minutes)

Ingredients

- Sugar: 4 Tablespoons
- Bread flour: 4 cups

- 1 and a ¼ teaspoon of salt
- 1 and a half cups of sour milk or regular milk
- 1 and a ¾ teaspoons of active dry yeast
- 1 and a half Tablespoons of oil

Instructions

- If using sour milk, you can make it by adding one tbsp. of vinegar to one cup of room temperature milk. Let it rest for five minutes.
- Add all ingredients to the bread machine in the suggested order by the manufacturer.
- Select basic setting, medium crust. Press start.
- Check dough after 5-10 minutes of kneading, add one tbsp. of water or flour if the dough is too dry or too wet, respectively.

8.7 Lemon Sourdough Bread

(Prep time: 10 minutes | Total time: 3 hours 10 minutes)

Ingredients

- Lemon juice: 2 tsp
- 1/3 cup of plain yogurt
- Half cup of water
- Salt: 1 tsp
- Softened butter: 2 tsp
- 1 and a 3/4 tsp of regular active dry yeast
- 2 cups of bread flour
- Sugar: 2 tsp

Instructions

- Add all ingredients to the bread machine in the suggested order by the manufacturer.
- Do not use a delay cycle: select white bread or French bread—press start.
- Enjoy fresh bread.

8.8 San Francisco Sourdough Bread

(Prep time: 10 minutes | Total time: 3 hours 10 minutes)

Ingredients

- Lukewarm water: 3/4 cup
- 2 teaspoons of salt
- Baking soda: 1/4 teaspoon
- 1 cup of room temperature sourdough starter
- Bread flour: 3 cups

Glaze

- Cornstarch: 1 teaspoon
- Half cup of cold water

Instructions

- Place all ingredients in the pan of the bread machine.
- Select basic bread, light crust. Press start.
- Enjoy warm bread.

8.9 Sourdough Beer Bread

(Prep time: 10 minutes |
Total time: 3 hours 10
minutes)

Ingredients

- Vegetable oil: 2
  tablespoons
- 1 and 1/3 cups of
  sourdough starter
- Half cup of flat beer
- Bread flour: 3 cups
- 1 and a half
  teaspoons of salt
- 1/4 cup of water
- 1 and a half teaspoons of yeast
- Sugar: 1 tablespoon

Instructions

- Add all ingredients to the bread machine in the suggested order
  by the manufacturer.
- Select white bread, dark crust if you like—press start.
- Enjoy fresh bread.

8.10 Crusty Sourdough Bread

(Prep time: 10 minutes | Total time: 3 hours 40 minutes)

Ingredients

- Bread flour: 3 cups
- Half cup of water
- One cup of Sourdough Starter
- Sugar: 2 tablespoons
- Bread machine: 1 teaspoon

- 1 and a half teaspoons of salt

Instructions

- Add all ingredients to the bread machine in the suggested order by the manufacturer.
- Select white cycle, light crust. Press start.
- Enjoy fresh bread.

8.11 Sourdough Cheddar Bread

(Prep time: 10 minutes | Total time: 3 hours 10 minutes)

Ingredients

- Sourdough starter: 1 cup (at room temperature)
- 1 and a half teaspoons of salt
- 1 and a half teaspoons of yeast
- Half cup of warm water
- 1 and a half tablespoons of sugar
- Bread flour: 3 cups
- Grated sharp cheddar cheese: 3⁄4 cup

Instructions

- Add all ingredients to the bread machine in the suggested order by the manufacturer.
- Select French bread, light crust. Press start.
- Enjoy fresh bread.

8.12 Herb Sourdough

(Prep time: 10 minutes | Total time: 3 hours 10 minutes)

Ingredients

- 3 tablespoons of sugar
- 3⁄4 cup of water
- 1 and a half teaspoons of salt
- 3 or 3 and a half cups of bread flour

- dried parsley: 1 teaspoon
- 1 1/4 cups of sourdough starter
- 1 and a half teaspoons of dried Rosemary
- Soy margarine: 2 tablespoons

Instructions

- Add all ingredients to the bread machine in the suggested order by the manufacturer.
- Start with three cups of flour. Select basic cycle, light crust. Press start.
- Check dough after 5-10 minutes; if it needs more flour, then add one tbsp. of flour at a time.
- Serve fresh bread.

8.13 Cranberry Pecan Sourdough

(Prep time: 10 minutes | Total time: 3 hours 10 minutes)

Ingredients

- 1 dried package of (3 and a half ounce) sweetened cranberries
- Water: 2 tablespoons + 1 and a 1/4 cup
- Salt: 2 teaspoons
- Chopped pecans: 3/4 cup, toasted
- Bread flour: 4 cups
- Butter: 2 tablespoons
- 2 teaspoons of yeast
- Non-fat powdered milk: 2 tablespoons
- 1/4 cup of sugar

Instructions

- Place all ingredients in the bread machine as per the suggested order by the manufacturer.
- Select white bread setting, medium crust. Press start.

- Enjoy fresh bread.

8.14 Dark Chocolate Sourdough

(Prep time: 10 minutes | Total time: 3 hours 10 minutes)

Ingredients

- Lukewarm (110 F) Water: ¾ cup
- Half cup of cocoa powder
- Sourdough starter: 1 cup
- Sugar: 1 tablespoon
- dark chocolate: Half cup, finely diced

- 3 tablespoons of oil
- 2 teaspoons of salt
- Active dry yeast: 1 tablespoon
- 3 cups of bread flour

Instructions

- Add all ingredients to the bread machine in the suggested order by the manufacturer.
- Select basic cycle. Light crust. Press start.
- Check dough's consistency if it's too wet and sticky and requires more flour. Add one tbsp. of flour at a time.
- Serve fresh bread.

Chapter 9: Creative Combination Breads

9.1 Zucchini Pecan Bread

(Prep time: 10 minutes | Total time: 1 hour 40 minutes)

Ingredients

- 1/3 cup of Vegetable Oil
- Baking Powder: 2 tsp
- 3 whole Eggs, whisked
- Sugar: 3/4 cup
- 1 tsp of Baking Soda
- Half tsp of Allspice
- Half tsp of salt
- toasted pecan: Half cup chopped finely
- All-Purpose Flour: 2 cups
- 1 tsp of cinnamon
- Zucchini: 1 cup, shredded

Instructions

- Add oil and whisked eggs in the bread machine.
- Add flour, then add the rest of the ingredients, except for zucchini.
- Select the cake/quick cycle. Dark crust if you like.
- Press start.
- Add in the zucchini at the ingredient signal. Serve fresh.

9.2 Raisin Bran Bread

(Prep time: 10 minutes | Total time: 3 hours 10 minutes)

Ingredients

- 2 tablespoons of softened butter
- 2 and a 1/4 teaspoons of active dry yeast
- 1/4 cup of packed brown sugar
- 1 and a half cups of raisin bran
- Half teaspoon of salt
- Lukewarm water: 1 cup + 1 tbsp.
- 1/4 teaspoon of baking soda
- Half cup of raisins
- 2 and 1/4 cups of bread flour

Instructions

- Add all ingredients to the bread machine, except for raisins, in the manufacturer's suggested order.
- Select basic bread. Crust color to your liking.
- Check dough if it needs more water or flour add one tbsp. at a time.
- At the signal, add raisins.
- Serve fresh bread.

9.3 Lemon Poppy Seed Bread

(Prep time: 10 minutes | Total time: 3 hours 10 minutes)

Ingredients

- 3 cups of bread flour
- 1 and a half Tablespoons of dry milk
- ¾ cup of water
- 1 teaspoon of salt
- 1 and a half tablespoons of butter

- Honey: 2 Tablespoon
- Lemon extract: 2 teaspoons
- ¾ cup of lemon yogurt
- Half cup of toasted almonds, cut into slices
- Lemon peel: 1 tablespoon
- Yeast: 2 teaspoons
- Poppy seeds: 3 Tablespoons

Instructions

- Add all ingredients to the bread machine in the suggested order by the manufacturer.
- Select sweet bread cycle—press start.
- Enjoy fresh bread.

9.4 Mustard Rye Bread

(Prep time: 10 minutes | Total time: 3 hours 10 minutes)

Ingredients

- Ground mustard: 1⁄4 cup
- Butter: 1 tablespoon
- 1 and 1⁄4 cups of water
- Gluten flour: 2 tablespoons
- Bread flour: 2 cups
- 1 and a half cups of rye flour
- 3⁄4 teaspoon of salt
- 1 tbsp. of brown sugar
- 1 teaspoon of dry yeast
- 1 teaspoon of caraway seed

Instructions

- Add all ingredients to the bread machine in the suggested order by the manufacturer.

- Select whole wheat/ basic cycle.
- Serve fresh bread.

9.5 Ham & Cheese Bread

(Prep time: 10 minutes | Total time: 3 hours 10 minutes)

Ingredients

- Softened Butter: 2 tablespoons
- 1 and 1/3 cups of Luke warm water
- Non-fat dry milk powder: 1 tablespoon
- Active dry yeast: 1 tablespoon
- Mashed potato flakes: 3 tablespoons
- Cornmeal: 2 tablespoons
- 1 and a half teaspoons of salt
- Half cup of Swiss cheese, diced
- 4 cups of bread flour
- Half cup of cooked diced ham

Instructions

- Add all ingredients to the bread machine in the suggested order by the manufacturer.
- Select basic bread cycle. Light crust color. Press start.
- Enjoy fresh bread.

9.6 Sausage Herb Bread

(Prep time: 10 minutes | Total time: 3 hours 10 minutes)

Ingredients

- 3/4 teaspoon of Basil leaves
- 1 and a half tablespoon of Sugar
- 1 small Onion minced
- 2 and a 1/4 teaspoon of yeast

- 3/4 teaspoon of thyme leaves
- 3/4 teaspoon of rosemary leaves
- 3/8 cup of Wheat bran
- Half tablespoon of Salt
- 6 oz. of Italian sausage
- 3 cup of bread flour
- 3/4 teaspoon of Oregano leaves
- 1 and a half tablespoon of grated Parmesan
- 1 and 1/8 cup of warm water

Instructions

- Cook crumbled sausage for three minutes on medium flame. Add onion and cook for five minutes, until onion softens.
- Turn off the heat and let it cool. All the ingredients must be at room temperature.
- Add all ingredients to the bread machine in the suggested order by the manufacturer.
- Select white bread and press start. In humid, hot weather, use less water.
- Serve fresh bread.

9.7 Wild Rice Hazelnut Bread

(Prep time: 10 minutes | Total time: 3 hours 10 minutes)

Ingredients

- 1 and a 1/4 cup of water
- 3 cups of bread flour
- 1/4 cup of non-fat milk powder
- 2 tbsp. of liquid honey
- 1 and a 1/4 tsp of salt
- 1 tbsp. of olive oil
- Cooked wild rice: 3/4 cup

- Bread machine: 1 tsp
- Pine nuts: 1/4 cup
- Celery seeds: 3/4 tsp
- Hazelnuts: 2/3 cup
- Black pepper: 1/8 tsp

Instructions

- Add all ingredients to the bread machine, except cranberries, in the suggested order by the manufacturer.
- Select basic cycle light crust. Press start.
- Add cranberries at the ingredients signal.

9.8 Spinach Feta Bread

(Prep time: 10 minutes | Total time: 4 hours 10 minutes)

Ingredients

- 1 cup of water
- 1 cup of fresh spinach leaves, chopped
- 2 teaspoons of softened butter
- 1 teaspoon of sugar
- 3 cups of flour
- 1 teaspoon of salt
- 2 teaspoons of minced onion (instant)
- 1 and a 1/4 teaspoons of instant yeast
- Crumbled feta: 1 cup

Instructions

- Add all ingredients, except spinach, cheese, and yeast, to the bread machine in the manufacturer's suggested order.
- Add yeast to yeast hopper. In the kneading cycle (last), add cheese and spinach.
- Select basic cycle light crust.

- Enjoy.

9.9 Rum Raisin Bread

(Prep time: 10 minutes | Total time: 3 hours 35 minutes)

Ingredients

- 2 tablespoons of dark rum
- 3⁄4 cup of room temperature milk
- 1 teaspoon of salt
- Packed brown sugar: 2 tablespoons
- 1 whole egg
- 2 and 1⁄4 cups of bread flour
- 1 cup of raisins
- Half teaspoon of ground allspice
- 1 and a 3⁄4 teaspoons of bread machine yeast
- Softened Butter: 2 tablespoons

Instructions

- Place all ingredients into the pan of the bread machine, except raisins, according to the order suggested by the manufacturer.
- Use Sweet Cycle. At ingredient signal, add raisins.
- Serve fresh bread.

9.10 Bacon Corn Bread

(Prep time: 10 minutes | Total time: 2 hours 50 minutes)

Ingredients

- 2 tablespoons of oil
- 1 and 1/3 cups of water
- Dry active yeast: 2 teaspoons
- Sugar: 1 and a half tsp. + 2 tbsp.
- Bread flour: 4 cups

- 8 slices of bacon
- 1 and a 1/4 teaspoon of salt
- 3 tablespoons of skim dry milk
- Cheddar cheese: 2 cups

Instructions

- Add all ingredients, except bacon and cheese, to the bread machine in the manufacturer's suggested order.
- Add bacon, cheese at the ingredient signal.
- Select basic cycle. Press start.
- Enjoy.

9.11 Oatmeal Coffee Bread

(Prep time: 10 minutes | Total time: 3 hours 10 minutes)

Ingredients

- 1 + ¼ cup of Bread flour
- ½ cup + 2 tbsp. of Cake flour
- 1 and a half tbsp. of Coffee powder
- 2 tbsp. + 1 tsp of sugar
- ½ cup + 2 tbsp. of water/milk
- Half cup of oats
- 1 tbsp. + 1 tsp of Butter
- 3 tbsp. + 2 tsp of Milk powder
- 1 tsp of yeast

Instructions

- Add all ingredients, except butter, to the bread machine in the suggested order by the manufacturer.
- Select basic cycle, light crust. Add butter after the dough cycle.
- Serve fresh bread.

9.12 Cherry Pistachio Bread

(Prep time: 10 minutes | Total time: 3 hours 10 minutes)

Ingredients

- 1 whole egg
- Half cup of cherry preserves
- Half cup of water
- 1/4 cup of butter
- 1 teaspoon of salt
- 2 and a 1/4 teaspoons of active dry yeast
- Half teaspoon of almond extract
- Half cup of chopped pistachio
- 3 and a half cups of bread flour

Instructions

- Add all ingredients to the bread machine in the suggested order by the manufacturer.
- Select basic cycle. Press start. Check dough; it should be a smooth ball; add one tbsp. of water or flour if too dry or too sticky, respectively.
- Serve fresh bread.

9.13 Banana Coconut Bread

(Prep time: 10 minutes | Total time: 3 hours 10 minutes)

Ingredients

- 8 tablespoons of sugar
- 3 large ripe bananas
- 1 tsp. of baking powder
- 2 cups of plain flour
- 1 tsp. of salt
- Half cup of coconut flakes

- 2 whole eggs
- Half tsp. of vanilla
- Half tsp. of cinnamon

Instructions

- Mix the sugar with mashed bananas.
- Add all ingredients to the bread machine in the suggested order by the manufacturer.
- Select basic cycle. Press start.
- Enjoy fresh bread.

9.14 Easy Honey Beer Bread

(Prep time: 10 minutes | Total time: 1 hour 45 minutes)

Ingredients

- 2 tablespoons of olive oil
- 3⁄4 teaspoon of salt
- 3 and a half cups of bread flour
- 1 and a 3⁄4 teaspoons of fast-rising yeast
- 1 and 1⁄8 cups of flat beer
- 1⁄4 cup of honey

Instructions

- Add all ingredients to the bread machine in the suggested order by the manufacturer.
- Select basic cycle. Press start.
- Enjoy fresh bread.

9.15 Coffee Molasses Bread

(Prep time: 10 minutes | Total time: 2 hours 40 minutes)

Ingredients

- 3 tablespoons of honey
- Butter: 2 tablespoons

- 1 and a half teaspoons of salt
- 3 cups of bread flour
- 1 whole egg, whisked
- Instant coffer mixed in 1 cup of boiling water
- 1 tablespoon of dark molasses
- Half cup of oats
- 2 teaspoons of yeast

Instructions

- Mix oats with one cup of boiling water and set it aside. Let them come to

  110 F or lukewarm temperature.
- Add all ingredients to the bread machine in the suggested order by the manufacturer.
- Select basic cycle. Light crust. Press start.
- Serve fresh bread.

9.16 Pear Sweet Potato Bread

(Prep time: 10 minutes | Total time: 2 hours 25 minutes)

Ingredients

- Half teaspoon of almond extract

- 1 can of undrained (15 ounces) pear halves
- Mashed sweet potatoes: half cup
- 1 and a half teaspoons of salt
- 2 tablespoons of softened butter
- 3 and a half cups of bread flour
- 1 teaspoon of ground cinnamon
- 2 and a 1/4 teaspoons of active dry yeast
- 1/4 teaspoon of ground nutmeg

Instructions

- Puree the pear halves and juice in the blender. Add to the bread machine.
- Add the rest of the ingredients to the bread machine in the suggested order by the manufacturer.
- Select basic cycle. Press start.
- Enjoy fresh bread.

Chapter 10: Holiday Breads

10.1 Panettone Bread

(Prep time: 10 minutes | Total time: 3 hours 10 minutes)

Ingredients

- 1 and a half teaspoons of vanilla extract
- 3⁄4 cup of water
- 2 eggs, whisked
- 3 and 1⁄4 cups of flour
- 2 tablespoons of sugar
- 1⁄4 cup of softened butter
- 1 and a half teaspoons of salt
- Half cup mixed dried fruit, chopped
- 2 tablespoons of powdered milk
- 2 teaspoons of yeast

Instructions

- Add all ingredients, except dried fruits, to the bread machine in the manufacturer's suggested order.
- Select sweet bread cycle. Light crust. Press start.
- Enjoy fresh bread.

10.2 White Chocolate Cranberry Bread

(Prep time: 10 minutes | Total time: 3 hours 10 minutes)

Ingredients

- Softened butter: 4 teaspoons
- 1 cup of milk
- 3 tablespoons of water

- 1 and a half teaspoons vanilla
- 1 whole egg
- 4 cups of bread flour
- 6 tbsp. of chopped white baking bar
- Half cup of dried cranberries
- 2 tablespoons of sugar
- 1 and a ¼ teaspoons of bread machine yeast
- 1 teaspoon of salt

Instructions

- Add all ingredients, except cranberries, to the bread machine in the suggested order by the manufacturer.
- Select white bread cycle. Light crust. Press start.
- Add cranberries at the ingredient signal.
- Enjoy fresh bread.

10.3 Eggnog Bread

(Prep time: 10 minutes | Total time: 3 hours 10 minutes)

Ingredients

- 1 and a ¼ teaspoon of salt
- 4 cups of bread flour
- Half cup of dried cranberries or raisins
- Oil: 1 Tablespoon
- Half cup of milk
- 2 Tablespoons of sugar
- 1 cup of eggnog
- 1 and a ¾ teaspoons of active dry yeast
- 1 teaspoon of cinnamon

Instructions

- Add all ingredients to the bread machine in the suggested order by the manufacturer.
- Select basic cycle. Medium crust. Press start.
- Enjoy fresh bread.

10.4 Whole-Wheat Challah

(Prep time: 10 minutes | Total time: 3 hours 10 minutes)

Ingredients

- 2 whole eggs
- 1 cup of warm water
- 1/4 or half cup of honey
- Half tsp. of salt
- 1/4 tsp. of canola oil
- 2 and a half tsp. of instant yeast
- 4 cups of whole wheat flour
- 1 cup of white flour

Instructions

- Add all ingredients to the bread machine in the suggested order by the

  manufacturer.
- Select dough cycle. Press start.
- Take the dough out on a floured clean surface. Separate the dough into three long pieces.
- Bread the dough together. Brush with egg wash and seeds—Bake at 350 F for 30 minutes.
- Should sound hollow at tapping.
- Enjoy.

10.5 Portuguese Sweet Bread

(Prep time: 10 minutes | Total time: 3 hours 10 minutes)

Ingredients

- 1 whole egg, whisked
- 1/3 cup of sugar
- 3/4 teaspoon of salt
- 2 and a half teaspoons of yeast
- 1 cup of milk
- Margarine: 2 tablespoons
- 3 cups of bread flour

Instructions

- Add all ingredients to the bread machine in the suggested order by the manufacturer.
- Select sweet bread cycle—press start.
- Serve fresh bread.

10.6 Pecan Maple Bread

(Prep time: 10 minutes | Total time: 3 hours 10 minutes)

Ingredients

- 1 and ¼ cup of wholemeal flour
- 3 tablespoons maple syrup
- 3/4 teaspoon of yeast
- 1 and ¼ cup white flour
- Half cup of pecan pieces
- 1 teaspoon of salt
- 1 cup and 3 tbsp. of water
- 1 tbsp. of butter

Instructions

- Add all ingredients, except for pecans, to the bread machine in the manufacturer's suggested order.
- Select basic cycle. Light crust. Press start.
- Enjoy fresh bread.

10.7 Nana's Gingerbread

(Prep time: 10 minutes | Total time: 3 hours 10 minutes)

Ingredients

- 3 tbsp. of melted Butter
- 3/4 cup of Rye flour
- 1 and a 1/4 cup of milk
- 1/4 tsp. of grated Nutmeg
- 1 and a half tsp. of Salt
- 3/4 tsp. of ground Cinnamon
- 2 and 2/3 cup of bread flour
- 1/4 tsp. of ground Cloves
- 2 tsp. of ground Ginger
- 2 and a 1/4 tsp. of Active dry yeast
- 6 tbsp. of Brown sugar

Instructions

- Add milk to a pot, simmer it and mix with brown sugar and butter.
- Add the rest of the ingredients to the bread machine in the suggested order by the manufacturer.
- Select basic cycle. Press start.
- Serve fresh bread.

10.8 Bread Machine Brioche

(Prep time: 10 minutes | Total time: 3 hours 10 minutes)

Ingredients

- 2 tablespoons of bread flour
- 1 and a 3⁄4 teaspoons of active dry yeast
- 3 tablespoons of sugar
- 1 and 3⁄4 cups of bread flour
- 2 eggs + 1 yolk
- 1⁄4 cup of water
- 8 tablespoons of unsalted butter
- 3⁄4 teaspoon of salt
- 2 tablespoons of water

Instructions

- Place all ingredients in the pan of the bread machine, except butter, in the manufacturer's suggested order.
- Select basic cycle. Light crust. Press start.
- Dice butter into small pieces.
- After the end of the kneading cycle or after ten minutes, add butter one tbsp. of worth at a time.
- Serve fresh bread.

10.9 Traditional Paska

(Prep time: 10 minutes | Total time: 3 hours 10 minutes)

Ingredients

- Half cup of warm water
- 1⁄4 lemon: zest
- Fresh lemon juice: 1 teaspoon

- 1/4 orange: zest
- Half cup of warm milk
- 1 teaspoon of fresh orange juice
- 2 whole eggs+ 1 yolk
- Vanilla extract: 1/4 teaspoon
- 1 teaspoon of anise seed
- 1/3 cup of granulated sugar
- 3 and a half cups of flour
- 1 teaspoon of salt
- 1 and a half teaspoons of active dry yeast
- Half cup of butter at room temp

Instructions

- Add all ingredients, except anise seeds, to the bread machine in the manufacturer's suggested order.
- Select sweet bread cycle. Dark crust. Press start.
- Add seeds at the ingredient signal.
- Enjoy fresh bread.

10.10 Raisin & Nut Paska

(Prep time: 10 minutes | Total time: 4 hours 5 minutes)

Ingredients

- 1 package of yeast
- Sugar: 3 tablespoons
- 1/4 cup of water
- 4 tablespoons of cooled melted butter
- 1 and a half teaspoons of salt
- 3/4 cup of milk
- 2 whole eggs
- 1/3 cup of golden raisin

- Bread flour: 3 cups
- 1/4 cup of honey
- 3/4 cup of mixed nuts
- 1/3 cup of regular raisins

Instructions

- Add all ingredients to the bread machine in the suggested order by the manufacturer.
- Select basic cycle. Press start.
- Enjoy fresh bread.

10.11 Honey Cake

(Prep time: 10 minutes | Total time: 3 hours 10 minutes)

Ingredients

- 1-2 tablespoons of Milk
- 2 tbsp. + 1 tsp of Honey
- 1 and a ¼ cup of Pancake mix
- 2 whole eggs, whisked
- ¼ cup + 3 tbsp. of Unsalted butter at room temperature

Instructions

- Dice the butter into 1 cm pieces.
- Add all ingredients to the bread machine in the suggested order by the manufacturer.
- Select cake cycle. Press start.
- At the ingredient signal, with a rubber spatula, scrape the pan. Let the cycle continue
- Serve fresh bread.

10.12 Christmas Fruit Bread

(Prep time: 10 minutes | Total time: 3 hours 10 minutes)

Ingredients

- One and a half tbsp. of sugar
- 1 whole egg
- Bread machine yeast: 1 tsp
- Half tsp of ground cardamom
- Salt: 1 tsp
- Water: 1 cup + 2 tablespoons
- Mixed candied fruit: 1/3 cups
- 1/4 cup of softened butter
- Bread flour: 3 cups
- Raisins: 1/3 cups

Instructions

- Add all ingredients, except the candied fruits and raisins, to the bread machine in the manufacturer's suggested order.
- Select basic cycle. Medium crust. Press start.
- Add candied fruits and raisins at the ingredient signal.
- Enjoy fresh bread.

10.13 Stollen Bread

(Prep time: 10 minutes | Total time: 3 hours 10 minutes)

Ingredients

- 2 whole eggs
- 1/4 cup of non-fat milk powder
- 2 teaspoons of bread machine yeast
- 1 cup of water
- 3 and 3/4 cups of bread flour
- 2 Tablespoons of sugar
- 2 teaspoons of lemon zest
- 2 Tablespoons of butter
- 1 and a half tsp. of salt
- 3/4 teaspoon of ground nutmeg
- 1/4 cup of slivered almonds, cut into slices
- Half-cup of mixed candied fruit
- Half cup of raisins

Instructions

- Add all ingredients, except for raisins, some almonds slice, and candied fruits, to the bread machine in the manufacturer's suggested order.
- Select basic cycle. Light crust. Press start.
- Add raisins and candied fruit at the signal ingredient.
- Before the baking cycle begins, add the leftover almond slices to the loaf.
- Enjoy fresh bread.

10.14 Julekake

(Prep time: 10 minutes | Total time: 3 hours 10 minutes)

Ingredients

- Bread machine yeast: 1 teaspoon
- Half teaspoon of ground cardamom
- 1 teaspoon of salt
- 1 egg mixed with enough water to make 1 cup and 2 tablespoons
- Sugar: 1 tbsp. + 1 tsp.
- Mixed candied fruit: 1/3 cup
- ¼ cup of softened butter
- Bread flour: 3 cups
- 1/3 cup of raisins

Instructions

- Add all ingredients, except candied fruits and raisins, to the bread machine in the manufacturer's suggested order.
- Select white bread cycle. Medium or light crust. Press start.
- Add candied fruit and raisins at the nut signal.
- Enjoy fresh bread.

10.15 Spiked Eggnog Bread

(Prep time: 10 minutes | Total time: 3 hours 10 minutes)

Ingredients

- 3 cups of bread flour
- 1 and a ¼ teaspoons of yeast
- ¾ teaspoon of salt
- Half cup of eggnog
- ¼ cup of milk
- 1 whole egg

- 2 tablespoons of sugar
- Half cup of glace cherries, cut into halves
- 2 tablespoons of butter, diced
- Half teaspoon of nutmeg

Instructions

- Place all ingredients in the bread machine, except cherries, in the suggested order by the manufacturer.
- Select basic cycle. Medium crust. Press start.
- Add cherries at the ingredient signal.
- Serve fresh bread.

10.16 Hot Buttered Rum Bread

(Prep time: 10 minutes | Total time: 3 hours 40 minutes)

Instructions

- 1 tablespoon of rum extract
- 1 whole egg
- Softened Butter: 3 tablespoons
- 3 cups of bread flour
- 1 and a ¼ teaspoons of salt
- Half teaspoon of ground cinnamon
- Bread machine: 1 teaspoon
- ¼ teaspoon of ground nutmeg
- 3 tablespoons of brown sugar, packed
- ¼ teaspoon of ground cardamom

Nuts Topping

- 1 and a half teaspoons of packed brown sugar
- 1 and a half teaspoons of pecans, finely chopped
- 1 egg yolk, beaten

Instructions

- Mix the whole egg with water to make one cup. Place in the bread machine.
- Add the rest of the ingredients to the bread machine in the suggested order by the manufacturer.
- Select sweet cycle: light or medium crust. Do not use the delay feature.
- Press start.
- Meanwhile, mix all ingredients of topping in the bowl. Before the baking cycle begins, brush the topping on the loaf.
- Enjoy fresh bread.

Chapter 11: Sweet Breads

11.1 Chocolate Chip Peanut Butter Banana Bread

(Prep time: 10 minutes | Total time: 3 hours 10 minutes)

Ingredients

- 3 whole Eggs
- Half cup of softened butter
- 1 and a half cups of mashed bananas (very ripe)
- 1 and 1/4 cups of sugar
- Half cup of vegetable oil
- 1 and a half cups of all-purpose flour
- 1 teaspoon of salt
- Half cup of plain Greek yogurt
- 1 teaspoon of vanilla
- 1 cup of peanut butter + chocolate chips
- 1 teaspoon of baking soda

Instructions

- Add all ingredients, except chocolate chips and nuts, to the bread machine in the manufacturer's suggested order.
- Select batter bread cycle. Press start.
- Add chocolate chips and nuts at the ingredient signal and take out the paddle.
- Enjoy fresh bread.

11.2 Chocolate Sour Cream Bread

(Prep time: 10 minutes | Total time: 3 hours 40 minutes)

Ingredients

- 3 and 3⁄4 cups of flour
- 3 tablespoons of butter
- 3⁄4 cup of sour cream
- 2 and a 1⁄4 teaspoons of yeast
- 1 tablespoon of sugar
- 3⁄4 cup of water
- Chocolate chips
- 1 teaspoon of salt

Instructions

- Place all ingredients into the bread machine in the suggested order by the manufacturer.
- Select basic cycle. Light crust. Press start.
- Serve fresh bread.

11.3 Nectarine Cobbler Bread

(Prep time: 10 minutes | Total time: 3 hours 40 minutes)

Ingredients

- Active dry yeast: 1 package
- Bread flour: 2 and a half cups
- Salt: 1 teaspoon
- Nutmeg: 1⁄4 tsp.
- Nectarine: 1 cup
- Gluten flour: 1 tbsp.
- Packed brown sugar: 1⁄4 cup
- Cinnamon: 1⁄4 tsp.
- Peach juice: 1/3 cup
- Whole wheat flour: half cup
- Cinnamon: 1⁄4 tsp.

- Vanilla extract: 1 tsp.
- Dried peaches: 1/3 cup, chopped
- Sour cream: 1/3 cup
- Butter: 1 tbsp.
- Baking soda: 1/8 tsp.

Instructions

- All ingredients should be at room temperature.
- Add all ingredients to the bread machine in the suggested order by the manufacturer.
- Select sweet bread cycle—press start.
- Enjoy fresh bread.

11.4 Sour Cream Maple Bread

(Prep time: 10 minutes | Total time: 3 hours 10 minutes)

Ingredients

- Melted butter: half cup
- 2 and a half cups of all-purpose flour
- Baking soda: half teaspoon
- Sugar: half cup
- Baking powder: 1 teaspoon
- Salt: half teaspoon
- 2 cups of mashed ripe bananas
- Maple syrup: 4 teaspoons
- Nutmeg: 2 teaspoons
- Sour cream: 1/4 cup
- Walnuts or pecans: 1/3 cup
- 1 teaspoon of vanilla
- Raisins: 1/3 cup
- 2 whole eggs, whisked

Instructions

- Add all ingredients, except for raisins and walnuts, to the bread machine in the manufacturer's suggested order.

- Select cake cycle. Press start. Add nuts at the ingredient signal.

- Serve fresh bread.

11.5 Barmbrack Bread

(Prep time: 10 minutes | Total time: 3 hours 10 minutes)

Ingredients

- 2 cups of bread flour

- 1 coin enclosed in foil

- Half teaspoon of salt

- Half cup of golden raisins

- Half teaspoon of ground allspice

- 1 and a half teaspoons of active dry yeast

- 1/4 cup of sugar

- 2 tablespoons of orange zest

- Half cup of currants

- 2 tablespoons of non-fat powdered milk

- 2 tablespoons of softened butter

- Water: ¾ cup + 2 tbsp.

Instructions

- Place all ingredients into the bread machine, except coin, currants, and raisins, in the manufacturer's suggested order.

- Select basic cycle. Medium crust. Press start.

- Add raisins and currants at the ingredients signal. Spray the foil coin with spray oil generously.

- Ten minutes before the baking cycle begins, place the coin under the surface. Let the bread bake.

- Enjoy.

11.6 Apple Butter Bread

(Prep time: 10 minutes | Total time: 4 hours 10 minutes)

Ingredients

- Half cup of apple butter
- 1 cup of water
- 1 tablespoon of sugar
- 2 tablespoons of vegetable oil
- 1 cup of whole wheat flour
- 2 cups of bread flour
- 1 and a half teaspoons of yeast
- 1 teaspoon of salt

Instructions

- Add all ingredients to the bread machine in the suggested order by the manufacturer.
- Select sweet cycle—press start.
- Adjust dough consistency by adding one tbsp. of flour if too sticky and one tbsp. of water, if too dry.
- Enjoy fresh bread.

11.7 Crusty Honey Bread

(Prep time: 10 minutes | Total time: 3 hours 10 minutes)

Ingredients

- 1 teaspoon of sugar
- Honey: 1 tablespoon
- 1 and 1/8 cup of warm water
- Olive oil: 1 tablespoon
- 1 package of bread machine yeast

- Salt: 1 teaspoon
- 3 cups of bread flour

Instructions

- Add all ingredients to the bread machine in the suggested order by the manufacturer.
- Select white bread cycle. Medium crust. Press start.
- Enjoy fresh bread.

11.8 Honey Granola Bread

(Prep time: 10 minutes | Total time: 3 hours 10 minutes)

Ingredients

- 2 tablespoons of butter
- 1 and 1/4 cups of water
- Bread flour: 3 cups
- Granola cereal: 3/4 cup
- 4 tablespoons of honey
- 1 and a half teaspoons of bread machine yeast
- 2 tablespoons of dry milk
- 1 teaspoon of salt

Instructions

- Add all ingredients to the bread machine in the suggested order by the manufacturer.
- Select basic cycle. Light or medium crust. Press start.
- Enjoy.

11.9 Black Bread

(Prep time: 10 minutes | Total time: 4 hours 15 minutes)

Ingredients

- 2 and 2⁄3 tablespoons of applesauce
- 1 and 1⁄3 cups of water
- 1 teaspoon of salt
- 1 teaspoon of coffee granules
- 1 and a half tablespoons of cider vinegar
- Dried onion flakes: 1 teaspoon
- 2 cups of all-purpose flour
- 2 and a half teaspoons of active dry yeast
- 1⁄4 teaspoon of fennel seed
- 1 and 1⁄3 tablespoons of dark molasses
- 1 and 1⁄3 cups of rye flour
- 2 and a half teaspoons of caraway seeds
- Oat bran: 2⁄3 cup
- 1 teaspoon of sugar
- 2 tablespoons of cocoa powder, unsweetened

Instructions

- Add all ingredients to the bread machine in the suggested order by the manufacturer.
- Select basic cycle. Press start.
- Serve fresh bread.

11.10 Apple Cider Bread

(Prep time: 10 minutes | Total time: 3 hours 40 minutes)

Ingredients

- 1 and 1/4 cup of apple cider (80 F)
- 2 tablespoons of softened butter
- 2 and 1/4 teaspoons of active dry yeast
- 3 cups of white bread flour
- 1 teaspoon of ground cinnamon
- 1 teaspoon of salt
- 2 tablespoons of packed brown sugar

Instructions

- Place all ingredients into the bread machine in the suggested order by the manufacturer.
- Select basic cycle. Light crust. Press start.
- Enjoy fresh bread.

11.11 Coffee Cake

(Prep time: 10 minutes | Total time: 3 hours 15 minutes)

Ingredients

- 1 and a half teaspoons of salt
- 3/4 cup of raisins
- Strong brewed coffee: 1 cup (70°-F)

80°

- Canola oil: 3 tablespoons
- Bread flour: 3 cups + 1 tbsp.
- 1 whole egg, whisked
- 1/4 teaspoon of ground cloves
- 1 teaspoon of ground cinnamon
- 1/4 teaspoon of ground allspice
- Sugar: 3 tablespoons
- 2 and a half teaspoons of active dry yeast

Instructions

- Coat raisins with one tbsp. of flour and set it aside.
- Add all ingredients, except raisins, to the bread machine in the suggested order by the manufacturer.
- Select basic cycle. Crust color to your liking. Press start.
- Add raisins at the ingredient signal.
- Serve fresh bread.

11.12 Pumpkin Coconut Bread

(Prep time: 10 minutes | Total time: 4 hours 10 minutes)

Ingredients

- 1 and a half teaspoons of coconut extract
- Half cup of pumpkin puree
- 1 egg yolk only
- Half cup of coconut milk, unsweetened
- 1 and a half tablespoons of olive oil
- 1/3 cup of coconut
- 1 and a half teaspoons of bread machine yeast
- 2 and a half tablespoons of sugar
- 3 cups of regular flour
- 3/4 teaspoon of salt

Instructions

- Place all ingredients into the bread machine in the suggested order by the manufacturer.
- Select sweet bread cycle. Crust to your liking. Press start.
- Enjoy fresh bread.

11.13 Vanilla Almond Milk Bread

(Prep time: 10 minutes | Total time: 3 hours 40 minutes)

Ingredients

- Olive oil: 2 tablespoons

- Honey: 2 tablespoons
- Whole wheat flour: 2 cups
- Active dry yeast: 2 and a ¼ teaspoons
- Bread flour: 1 and ¼ cups
- Vanilla almond milk: 1 and ¼ cups
- Vital gluten: 1 tablespoon
- Salt: 1 and a half teaspoons

Instructions

- Add all ingredients to the bread machine in the suggested order by the manufacturer.
- Select wheat bread cycle. Light crust. Press start.
- Enjoy.

11.14 Triple Chocolate Bread

(Prep time: 10 minutes | Total time: 3 hours 40 minutes)

Ingredients

- Vanilla extract: 1 tsp.
- Bread flour: 2 cups
- 2 tablespoons brown sugar
- 1 tablespoon margarine or butter
- Milk: 2/3 cup
- 1 teaspoon of active dry yeast
- 1 tablespoon unsweetened cocoa
- Half teaspoon of salt
- One whole egg
- Half cup of semisweet chocolate chips

Instructions

- Add all ingredients to the bread machine in the suggested order by the manufacturer.

- Select basic cycle. Press start.
- Enjoy fresh bread.

11.15 Chocolate Oatmeal Banana Bread

(Prep time: 10 minutes | Total time: 3 hours 40 minutes)

Ingredients

- 1 ounce of milk
- 2 bananas, mashed
- 1/3 cup of melted butter
- Bread flour: 2 cups
- 2 whole eggs
- Half tsp of salt
- Sugar: 2/3 cups
- Baking powder: 1.25 tsp
- Half cup of chocolate chips
- Half tsp of baking soda
- Half cup of chopped walnuts

Instructions

- Add all ingredients to the bread machine in the suggested order by the manufacturer.
- Select quick bread cycle—press start.
- Enjoy fresh bread.

Chapter 12: Ketogenic Breads

12.1 Basic Low-Carb Bread

(Prep time: 10 minutes | Total time:
3 hours 40 minutes)

Ingredients

- 1 and a half tsp of Bread Machine Yeast
- 1 and a half tbsp. of sugar
- ¼ cup of Vegetable Oil
- 1 cup of Water Warm
- 3 cups of low carb flour
- 3 tsp of Wheat Gluten

Instructions

- Spray the bread machine pan with cooking spray.
- Activate yeast in warm water with sugar. After 8-10 minutes, add to the pan.
- Add rest of the ingredients as well, as per the suggested order by the manufacturer.
- Select the low-carb cycle or basic. Press start
- Enjoy.

12.2 Almond Flour Yeast Bread

(Prep time: 10 minutes | Total time: 3 hours 40 minutes)

Ingredients

- 2 and 1/4 cups of Almond Flour
- 1 and 1/4 cups of Water
- 1/3 cup of Psyllium Husk Powder
- Ground Flax Seed: 3/4 cup

- Half cup of Wheat Gluten
- 2 tsp of Coconut Palm Sugar
- 1/3 cup of seed mix
- 6 whole Eggs, lightly whisked
- 2 tbsp. of yeast
- Extra Virgin Olive Oil: 1/3 cup
- 1 tsp of Sea Salt

Instructions

- Add all ingredients to the bread machine in the suggested order by the manufacturer.
- Select a gluten-free or basic cycle. Medium crust. Press start.
- Scrap the sides of the pan with a rubber spatula after the kneading cycle.
- Enjoy fresh bread.

12.3 Almond Milk Bread

(Prep time: 10 minutes | Total time: 3 hours 20 minutes)

Ingredients

- 1 and a half teaspoons of salt
- Unsalted butter: 1 tablespoon, slice into pieces
- 2 teaspoons of fast-rising yeast
- 3 cups of almond flour
- 1 and 1/8 cups of almond milk
- 1 tablespoon of sugar
- 1 teaspoon of xanthan gum

Instructions

- Add all ingredients to the bread machine in the suggested order by the manufacturer.

- Select basic cycle. Medium crust and Press start.
- Enjoy fresh bread.

12.4 Flaxseed Bread

(Prep time: 10 minutes | Total time: 3 hours 40 minutes)

Ingredients

- Half cup of ground flax seed
- 2 teaspoons of bread machine yeast
- 3 Tablespoon of honey

- 1 and 1/3 Cup of warm water
- 1 and a half teaspoon of salt
- 2 Tablespoon of vegetable oil
- 1 and a half cup of gluten-free flour
- 1 and 1/3 Cup of almond flour

Instructions

- Add all ingredients to the bread machine in the suggested order by the manufacturer.
- Select basic cycle. Crust to your liking. Press start.
- Serve fresh bread.

12.5 Almond Flour Bread

(Prep time: 10 minutes | Total time: 3 hours 40 minutes)

Ingredients

- 1/4 cup of ground flaxseed meal
- 4 whole eggs + 1 egg white
- Baking soda: 1 teaspoon
- Cinnamon: 1 teaspoon

- 1 tablespoon of apple cider vinegar
- 2 tablespoons of honey
- 2 tablespoons of coconut oil
- Half teaspoon of kosher salt
- 2 and a half cups of blanched almond flour

Instructions

- Add all ingredients to the bread machine in the suggested order by the manufacturer.
- Select basic cycle. Crust to your liking. Press start.
- Enjoy fresh bread.

12.6 Sandwich Bread

(Prep time: 10 minutes | Total time: 3 hours 30 minutes)

Ingredients

- 3 tablespoons of sugar
- 1/3 cup of half and half
- 3 tablespoons of softened butter
- 1 and a half teaspoons of salt
- 1 cup of milk
- 1 and a half teaspoons of instant yeast
- 3 and 3/4 cups of almond flour
- 1 tsp. of xanthan gum

Instructions

- Add all ingredients to the bread machine in the suggested order by the manufacturer.
- Select white bread cycle—press start.
- Enjoy fresh bread.

12.7 Macadamia Bread

(Prep time: 10 minutes | Total time: 3 hours 40 minutes)

Ingredients

- Very ripe bananas: ¾ cup
- 2/3 cup of warm water (110 f)
- Softened butter: 2 tablespoons
- Half cup of macadamia nuts (ground)
- 1 whole egg
- White sugar: 3 tablespoons
- 2 and ¾ teaspoons of bread machine
- 1 and ¼ teaspoons of salt
- 3 and ¼ cups of almond flour
- 1 and a 1/4 tsp of xanthan gum

For Glaze

- Slice almonds: ¼ cup
- 1 egg yolk whisked with 1 teaspoon of water

Instructions

- Add all ingredients to the bread machine in the suggested order by the manufacturer.
- Select white bread cycle—press start.
- After the rising cycle, brush with yolk glaze and sprinkle the almonds on top.
- Serve fresh bread.

12.8 Toasting Bread

(Prep time: 10 minutes | Total time: 2 hours 50 minutes)

Ingredients

- A ¼-1/3 cup of water
- 1 tsp of vinegar

- 1 cup of lukewarm milk
- half tsp of baking powder
- 1 and a half tsp of salt
- 2 and 1/4 tsp of instant yeast
- 3 and a half cups of all-purpose flour
- 2 Tbsp. of vegetable oil
- 1 and a half tsp of sugar

Instructions

- Add all ingredients to the bread machine in the suggested order by the manufacturer.
- Add less water in a warm climate and more in colder weather.
- Select basic white bread cycle. Press start.
- Before the baking cycle, take the dough out and roll it in cornmeal, although this step is optional. Place back into the machine and let it bake.
- Enjoy fresh bread.

12.9 Mediterranean Bread

(Prep time: 10 minutes | Total time: 3 hours 40 minutes)

Ingredients

- 1/3 cup of crumbled feta cheese
- 1 cup of water
- 3 and 1/4 cups of almond flour
- 1 and 1/4 teaspoons of salt
- 1 tablespoon of honey
- Extra virgin olive oil: 1 tablespoon
- 2 teaspoons of dried oregano
- 3/4 teaspoon of bread machine yeast
- 3 cloves of minced garlic
- Half cup of sliced Kalamata olive
- 1 and 1/4 tsp of xanthan gum

Instructions

- Add all ingredients to the bread machine in the suggested order by the manufacturer.
- Select basic cycle. Press start.
- Enjoy with soups

12.10 Italian Bread

(Prep time: 10 minutes | Total time: 3 hours 40 minutes)

Ingredients

- 1 and a half tsp of salt
- 4 and 1/4 cup of gluten-free whole wheat flour

- 2 Tbsp. of sugar
- 1 and a half cup of water
- 2 tsp of bread machine yeast
- 2 Tbsp. of olive oil
- 2 tsp. of xanthan gum

Instructions

- Place all ingredients into the bread machine in the suggested order by the manufacturer.
- Select whole wheat cycle. Press start.
- Serve fresh bread.

12.11 Keto Baguette

(Prep time: 10 minutes | Total time: 2 hours 40 minutes)

Ingredients

- 1 and 1/4 cups of warm water
- 1 teaspoon of salt
- 3 and a half cups of gluten-free flour
- One and a half tsp of xanthan gum
- 1 package of active dry yeast

Instructions

- Add all ingredients to the bread machine in the suggested order by the manufacturer.
- Select dough cycle. Press start.
- Take the dough out on a clean, floured surface.
- Cut into half pieces. Make a 12" long shape from each piece.
- Put on an oiled baking pan. Cover with a warm towel.
- Let it rise for one hour. Let the oven preheat to 450 F.
- Bake for 15-20 minutes, until golden brown.
- Serve fresh.

12.12 Keto Brioche Bread

(Prep time: 10 minutes | Total time: 2 hours 40 minutes)

Ingredients

- 1 and 3⁄4 cups of keto-flour
- 2 whole eggs+ 1 yolk
- 1 and 3⁄4 teaspoons of active dry yeast
- 3 tablespoons of sugar
- 3⁄4 teaspoon of salt
- Eight tablespoons of unsalted butter
- 2 tablespoons of almond flour
- 1⁄4 cup of water
- 2 tablespoons of water

Instructions

- Add all ingredients, except butter, to the bread machine in the suggested order by the manufacturer.
- Select basic bread cycle. Light crust and Press start. Cut butter into small pieces.
- After the first kneading cycle, add one tbsp. of butter at a time.
- Enjoy fresh bread.

12.13 Keto Focaccia

(Prep time: 10 minutes | Total time: 3 hours 10 minutes)

Ingredients

- 3 cups of whole wheat flour
- 1 cup of lukewarm water
- 2 teaspoons of chopped garlic
- 1 and a half teaspoons of active dry yeast
- 2 tablespoons of olive oil
- 1 tablespoon of chopped fresh rosemary

- half teaspoon of salt
- 1 and a half teaspoons of chopped fresh rosemary
- 1 tsp. of xanthan gum

Instructions

- Add all ingredients to the bread machine in the suggested order by the manufacturer.
- Select dough cycle. Press start.
- Take the dough out from the bread machine and put in a 12" pizza pan. With clean fingers, dimple the bread.
- Brush with olive oil and sprinkle fresh rosemary. Cover with wrap.
- Let the oven preheat to 400 F.
- Bake for 20-25 minutes, until golden brown.
- Serve fresh bread.

12.14 Oregano Onion Focaccia

(Prep time: 10 minutes | Total time: 3 hours 40 minutes)

Ingredients

Dough

- 3/4 cup of water
- 1 tablespoon of sugar
- 2 tablespoons of olive oil
- 1 and a half teaspoons of yeast
- 1 teaspoon of salt
- 2 tablespoons of shredded parmesan cheese
- 3/4 cup of shredded mozzarella cheese
- 2 cups of almond flour
- 3/4 tsp. of xanthan gum

Toppings

- 2 minced garlic cloves
- 3 tablespoons of butter
- 2 medium sliced onions

Instructions

- Add all ingredients of dough to the bread machine in the suggested order by the manufacturer.
- Select dough cycle. Press start.
- Meanwhile, melt butter on medium flame and sauté garlic and onion until caramelized.
- Take the dough out on an oiled baking sheet. Make the dough into 12" circles. Let it rise for half an hour until it doubles.
- Let the oven preheat to 400 F. with a wooden spoon, make a depression into the dough.
- Place topping on the dough. Bake for 15-20 minutes until golden brown.
- Enjoy fresh bread.

12.15 Zucchini Ciabatta

(Prep time: 10 minutes | Total time: 3 hours 40 minutes)

Ingredients

- 1 and a half teaspoons of Salt
- 1 and a half cups of Water
- 1 and a half teaspoons of Yeast
- One tablespoon of olive oil
- 3 and 1/4 cups of Flour
- 1 teaspoon of sugar
- Grated zucchini: half cup

Instructions

- Make sure to dry well the grated zucchini.
- Add all ingredients to the bread machine in the suggested order by the manufacturer.
- Select dough cycle. Press start.
- Once the dough cycle is completed, take the dough out. Try not to add any more flour to the dough.

- Place in a floured bowl for 15 minutes, cover with plastic wrap.
- Take out on the floured surface and half them. Make 13 by 14 oval shape. Let it rise for 45 minutes covered with a towel.
- Let the oven preheat to 425 F. dimple the dough and put it in the middle rack's oven.
- Bake for almost half an hour. During the baking process, spray with water after every 5-10 minutes.
- Enjoy fresh bread.

Chapter 13: Gluten-Free Breads

13.1 Gluten-Free White Bread

(Prep time: 10 minutes | Total time: 3 hours 40 minutes)

Ingredients

- Milk: 1 and 1/3 cup
- 2 eggs, whisked
- Vinegar: 1 tsp
- Oil: 6 tbsp.
- Whole wheat flour: 450 g
- Quick yeast: 2 tsp
- Salt: 1 tsp
- Sugar: 2 tbsp.

Instructions

- Mix the milk with vinegar and oil.
- Add all ingredients to the bread machine in the suggested order by the manufacturer.
- Select basic rapid or gluten-free cycle. Press start.
- Enjoy fresh bread.

13.2 Brown Rice Bread

(Prep time: 10 minutes | Total time: 3 hours 40 minutes)

Ingredients

- 4 cups of bread flour
- Half cup of cooked brown rice
- 1 and a half teaspoons of salt
- 1 and 1/4 cups of warm (110 F) water
- 2 and a ¼ teaspoons of bread machine yeast

- 1 teaspoon of sugar

Instructions

- Place all ingredients into the bread machine in the suggested order by the manufacturer.
- Select basic cycle. Medium crust. Press start.
- Enjoy fresh bread.

13.3 Brown Rice & Cranberry Bread

(Prep time: 10 minutes | Total time: 3 hours 40 minutes)

Ingredients

- 1/4 cup of non-fat milk powder
- 2 tbsp. of liquid honey
- 1/8 tsp of black pepper
- 1 and 1/4 cup of water
- 1 tbsp. of olive oil
- 3 cups of bread flour
- 3/4 cup of cooked brown rice
- 1 and 1/4 tsp of salt
- 2/3 cup of dried cranberries
- 1/4 cup of pine nuts
- 3/4 tsp of celery seeds
- 1 tsp of bread machine

Instructions

- Add all ingredients, except cranberries, to the bread machine in the suggested order by the manufacturer.
- Select basic cycle. Crust to your liking. Press start. Add cranberries at the signal ingredient.

- Enjoy.

13.4 Gluten-Free Peasant Bread

(Prep time: 10 minutes | Total time: 3 hours 40 minutes)

Ingredients

- 1 and a half tablespoons of vegetable oil
- 2 teaspoons of xanthan gum
- 1 and a half cups of warm water
- 1 teaspoon of cider vinegar
- 2 and a half cups of gluten-free baking flour
- 1 tablespoon of active dry yeast
- 1 teaspoon of salt
- 2 whole eggs
- 1 tablespoon of white sugar

Instructions

- Place all ingredients into the bread machine in the suggested order by the manufacturer.
- Select basic cycle. Light crust. Press start.
- Enjoy fresh bread.

13.5 Gluten-Free Hawaiian Loaf

(Prep time: 10 minutes | Total time: 3 hours 40 minutes)

Ingredients

- 3 tablespoons of oil
- 3 and a half tablespoons of honey
- 2 whole eggs
- 1 cup of pineapple juice (room temperature)

- 4 cups of gluten-free Flour
- 3 tablespoons of skim dry milk
- 1 tablespoon of fast-rising yeast

Instructions

- Add all ingredients to the bread machine in the suggested order by the manufacturer.
- Select the gluten free cycle. Dark crust. Press start.
- Enjoy fresh bread.

13.6 Vegan Gluten-Free Bread

(Prep time: 10 minutes | Total time: 1 hour 45 minutes)

Ingredients

- 1 and a half tsp of xanthan gum
- Olive oil: 2 tbsp.
- Gluten-free flour blend: 2.2 cups
- 1 tbsp. of ground flax seeds
- Warm water: 1.6 cups
- 2 and 1/4 tsp of Easy Bake yeast
- 1 tsp of sea salt

Instructions

- Add all ingredients to the bread machine in the suggested order by the manufacturer.
- Select a gluten-free cycle—press start.
- Before the baking cycle begins, brush olive oil on the loaf and sprinkle seeds.
- Enjoy fresh bread.

Chapter 14: International Breads

14.1 Italian Panettone

(Prep time: 10 minutes | Total time: 3 hours 40 minutes)

Ingredients

- Half tsp of rum
- 2 tbsp. of butter
- 2 whole eggs
- 1 tsp of lemon zest
- 1/4 tsp of salt
- 1/4 cup of granulated sugar
- 1 tsp of orange zest
- Sultana raisins: 1/4 cup
- Half tsp of anise seeds
- 2 and a half cups of all-purpose flour
- Half cup of water
- 1 and a 1/4 tsp of bread machine yeast
- 2 tbsp. of candied orange, finely diced
- 2 tbsp. of citron peel
- Toasted slivered almonds: 1/4 cup

Instructions

- Add all ingredients, except raisins, peel, and nuts, to the bread machine in the manufacturer's suggested order.
- Select basic bread cycle. Press start.
- Add remaining ingredients at the ingredient signal.
- Before the baking cycle begins, brush with melted butter and let it bake.

- Enjoy fresh bread.

14.2 Italian Bread

(Prep time: 10 minutes | Total time: 3 hours 40 minutes)

Ingredients

- 1 and a half cup of water
- 1 and a half tsp of salt
- 4 and 1/4 cup of bread flour
- 2 tsp of bread machine yeast
- 2 Tbsp. of olive oil
- 2 Tbsp. of sugar

Instructions

- Add all ingredients to the bread machine in the suggested order by the manufacturer.
- Select basic cycle. Press start.
- Serve fresh bread.

14.3 Bread of the Dead (Pan de Muertos)

(Prep time: 10 minutes | Total time: 3 hours 40 minutes)

Ingredients

- 1 and 3/4 cups of bread flour
- 3 whole eggs
- 3 Tbs. of butter
- 1/4 cup of sugar
- Half tsp. of salt
- 1/4 cup of water
- 1/4 tsp. of grated orange peel

- 1 tsp. of yeast
- 1/8 tsp. of anise

Instructions

- Add all ingredients to the bread machine in the suggested order by the manufacturer.
- Select sweet bread cycle—light crust and Press start.
- Serve fresh bread.

14.4 Mexican Sweet Bread

(Prep time: 10 minutes | Total time: 3 hours 10 minutes)

Ingredients

- 1 cup of milk
- 3 cups of bread flour
- 1 whole egg
- 1 and a half teaspoons of yeast
- 1/4 cup of sugar
- 1 teaspoon of salt
- 1/4 cup of butter
- Half tsp. of cinnamon

Instructions

- Add all ingredients to the bread machine in the suggested order by the manufacturer.
- Select sweet bread cycle—light crust and Press start.
- Serve fresh bread.

14.5 Challah

(Prep time: 10 minutes | Total time: 2 hours 30 minutes)

Ingredients

- 4 and 1/4 cups of all-purpose/bread flour
- 1 and a half cups of water

- 1 and 1/8 teaspoons of salt
- Half cup of brown sugar
- 1 tablespoon of active dry yeast
- Sesame or poppy seed
- 1 whole egg, lightly whisked
- 5 egg yolks
- 1/3 cup of oil

Instructions

- Add all ingredients to the bread machine in the suggested order by the manufacturer.
- Select dough cycle. Press start.
- Let the oven preheat to 350 F. take the dough out from the machine.
- Cut the dough into 2 pieces. Cut each piece into three parts.
- Braid the three long pieces together. Pinch the bottom and top.
- Place on an oiled baking sheet. Cover it and let it rise for half an hour.
- Before baking, brush with egg wash and sprinkle seeds on top.
- Bake for half an hour.
- Enjoy fresh bread.

14.6 Russian Black Bread

(Prep time: 10 minutes | Total time: 3 hours 40 minutes)

Ingredients

- 2 and a half cups of All-Purpose Flour
- 1 and 1/4 cups of Dark Rye Flour
- 2 Tbsp. of Cocoa Powder, Unsweetened

- 1 Tbsp. of Caraway Seeds
- Half tsp. of dried onion minced
- 1 tsp of instant crystals coffee
- Half tsp of Fennel Seeds
- 1 and a half Tbsp. of Dark Molasses
- 2 tsp of Active Dry Yeast
- 1 and 1/3 cups of Water
- 1 tsp of Sea Salt
- 3 Tbsp. of Vegetable Oil
- 1 tsp of Sugar
- 1 and a half Tbsp. of Vinegar

Instructions

- All ingredients should be at room temperature.
- Add all ingredients to the bread machine in the suggested order by the manufacturer.
- Select sweet bread cycle—press start.
- Enjoy fresh bread.

14.7 Russian Rye Bread

(Prep time: 10 minutes | Total time: 3 hours 40 minutes)

Ingredients

- Half cup of warm water + 2tbsp.
- 1 and a half tablespoons of melted butter
- 2 tablespoons of dark honey
- 1 teaspoon of salt
- 1 and 1/4 teaspoons of active dry yeast
- 3/4 cup of rye flour

- 1 and a half teaspoons of caraway seeds
- 1 and a half cups of bread flour

Instructions

- Add all ingredients to the bread machine in the suggested order by the manufacturer.
- Select basic cycle. Medium crust and Press start.
- Enjoy fresh bread.

14.8 Portuguese Corn Bread

(Prep time: 10 minutes | Total time: 4 hours 10 minutes)

Ingredients

- 1 and a half teaspoons of active dry yeast
- 1 cup of yellow cornmeal
- 1 and a half cups of bread flour
- 1 tablespoon of olive oil
- 2 teaspoons of sugar
- 1 and 1/4 cups of cold water
- 3/4 teaspoon of salt

Instructions

- Mix half of the cornmeal with cold water until it mixes well.
- Let it come to room temperature.
- Add all ingredients to the bread machine in the suggested order by the manufacturer.
- Select basic cycle. Press start.
- Enjoy fresh bread.

14.9 Amish Wheat Bread

(Prep time: 10 minutes | Total time: 3 hours 40 minutes)

Ingredients

- 1/4 cup of Canola Oil

- Whole Wheat Flour, 2 3/4 cups
- Warm water: 1.12 cups
- Half tsp of salt
- 1/3 cup of Granulated Sugar
- 1 package of active yeast
- 1 whole egg

Instructions

- Add sugar, yeast, and warm water to a bowl let it rest for 8 minutes.
- Place all ingredients into the pan of the bread machine in the manufacturer's suggested order.
- Select basic bread cycle. Light or dark crust. Press start.
- Before the second cycle of kneading starts, switch off the machine. Restart it again. It will give 2 cycles to bread to raise fully.
- Enjoy.

14.10 British Hot Cross Buns

(Prep time: 10 minutes | Total time: 3 hours 40 minutes)

Ingredients

- ¾ cup of milk
- 1 whole egg+ 1 yolk
- 6 tablespoons of sugar
- ¾ teaspoon of cinnamon
- 1/3 cup of butter

- Half teaspoon of nutmeg
- 1 tablespoon of yeast
- 1/4 teaspoon of ground cloves
- Half cup of candied fruit
- 3/4 teaspoon of salt
- 1 and a half teaspoons of grated lemon rind
- 3 cups of flour

Glaze

- Half teaspoon of lemon juice
- 1 tablespoon of milk
- Half cup of icing sugar

Instructions

- Add all ingredients, except candied fruits, to the bread machine in the manufacturer's suggested order.
- Select dough cycle. Press start.
- Add candied fruits at the ingredient signal.
- Take a 19 by 13 pan, spray with oil generously.
- Take the dough out from the machine. Slice into 18 to 24 pieces.
- Make each piece into a ball. Put all dough balls into the pan half-inch apart from each other.
- Cover them and let them rise in a warm place until doubles in size.
- Make a cross on top of buns with a knife.
- Bake at 375 F for 12 to 15 minutes.
- Meanwhile, mix all glaze ingredients.
- Drizzle over buns and serve.

14.11 Hawaiian Bread

(Prep time: 10 minutes | Total time: 3 hours 10 minutes)

Ingredients

- 2 tablespoons of vegetable oil
- 2 tablespoons of dry milk
- 2 and a half tablespoons of honey
- 1 whole egg
- 2 teaspoons of fast-rising yeast
- 3⁄4 cup of pineapple juice
- 3⁄4 teaspoon of salt
- 3 cups of bread flour

Instructions

- Add all ingredients to the bread machine in the suggested order by the manufacturer.
- Select sweet bread cycle—light crust and Press start.
- Enjoy fresh bread.

14.12 Greek Easter Bread

(Prep time: 10 minutes | Total time: 2 hours 40 minutes)

Ingredients

- Half cup of caster sugar
- 3 whole eggs, lightly whisked
- 2 tsp. Of dried yeast
- 4 and a half cups of baker's flour
- 2 teaspoons of Mahlepi
- Half cup + 1 tbsp. of butter melted
- 1/3 cup of milk
- 1/3 cup of lukewarm water
- Juice from half of an orange, grated rinds

Instructions

- Add 1 tbsp. of sugar, water, and yeast to the machine's pan. Mix lightly and let it rest for 8 minutes.

- Add the rest of the ingredients to the pan also. Select dough cycle and press start.
- Preheat the oven to 338 F. prepare a baking tray by spraying cooking oil and placing parchment paper.
- Take the dough out and cut it into three pieces. Roll the pieces into sausages shapes and pinch at one end.
- Braid the dough. Pinch the top and bottom and make a circle.
- Take three eggs and color them differently. Fit the eggs into the circled dough and let it rest for 20 minutes.
- Bake in the oven for 20 minutes after glazing with egg wash until.
- Serve.

14.13 Fiji Sweet Potato Bread

(Prep time: 10 minutes | Total time: 2 hours 15 minutes)

Ingredients

- 2 teaspoons of active dry yeast
- 1 cup of mashed sweet potatoes (plain)
- 4 cups of bread flour
- 1 and a half teaspoons of salt
- Water: 2 tablespoons + half cup
- 2 tablespoons of softened butter
- 1/3 cup of dark brown sugar
- chopped pecans
- 1 teaspoon of vanilla extract
- 2 tablespoons of dry milk powder
- 1/4 teaspoon (each) of ground nutmeg & cinnamon

Instructions

- Add all ingredients, except pecans, to the bread machine in the suggested order by the manufacturer.
- Select white bread cycle—light crust and Press start.

- Add nuts at the ingredient signal.
- Enjoy fresh bread.

14.14 Za'atar Bread

(Prep time: 10 minutes | Total time: 3 hours 40 minutes

Ingredients

- 3 and a half cups of bread flour
- 1 and 1/3 cups of water
- 1 and 1/4 teaspoons of sugar
- 2 and a half tablespoons of olive oil
- 2 tsp. of quick yeast
- 1 teaspoon of salt
- 2 and a half teaspoons of Za'atar

Instructions

- Add all ingredients to the bread machine in the suggested order by the manufacturer.
- Select quick bread cycle—medium crust and Press start.

Chapter 15: Bread & Other Bakery Products

15.1 Strawberry Jam

(Prep time: 10 minutes | Total time: 3 hours 10 minutes)

Ingredients

- 1 cup of sugar
- Half box of pectin
- 4 to 5 cups of fresh or frozen strawberries

Instructions

- Let the strawberries thaw and mash the berries, to make 3 cups. Mash as much chunky as you like, but preferably mash well.
- Add mashed berries, sugar, and pectin to the bread machine.
- Select jam cycle. Press start.
- After the jam has been made, let it cool in the machine for 30 to 45 minutes.
- Take it out into jars. Let it cool completely.
- Keep in the fridge overnight. Enjoy with freshly baked bread.

15.2 Tomato Sauce

(Prep time: 10 minutes | Total time: 3 hours 40 minutes)

Ingredients

- 1 tbsp. of olive oil
- 2 and ¾ cups of tomatoes (fresh and canned)
- Half tsp of garlic powder

- 1 tsp of sugar
- 1 tbsp. of onion powder
- Red-wine vinegar: a dash

Instructions

- Chop the tomatoes how much chunkier you like.
- Add all ingredients to the pan of the bread machine in the suggested order by the manufacturer.
- Select jam cycle and press start. Do not overfill your pan.
- Halfway through the process, with the help of a rubber spatula, scrape the sides of the pan.
- As the machine has completed the jam cycle, wait for it to cool down.
- Then blend in a blender to your desired texture.
- Adjust seasoning by adding any herbs or salt and pepper.
- Store in a jar.
- Serve with fresh bread and olive oil.

15.3 Apple pie

(Prep time: 10 minutes | Total time: 3 hours 10 minutes)

Ingredients

- 1 and 1/4 cups of apple pie filling
- Half cup of water
- 1 and a half teaspoons of salt
- 1 and a half tablespoons of butter
- 3 and 1/4 cups of flour
- 1 and a half teaspoons of yeast
- 3 tablespoons of dry buttermilk
- 1 and a half teaspoons of cinnamon

Instructions

- Add all ingredients to the bread machine in the suggested order by the manufacturer.
- Select sweet bread cycle—press start.
- Enjoy.

15.4 Blueberry Jam

(Prep time: 10 minutes | Total time: 3 hours 40 minutes)

Ingredients

- 1 Tbsp. of no sugar pectin
- 2 and a half cups of granulated sugar
- 5 cups of blueberries

Instructions

- If using frozen blueberries, let them thaw and mash them in a food processor.
- In a bowl, mix all ingredients and add to the pan of the bread machine.
- Select jam cycle and press start.
- Let it cool for half an hour in the machine. Pour into jars and let it rest for 3 hours.
- Keep in the fridge for four weeks.

15.5 Peach Jam

(Prep time: 10 minutes | Total time: 3 hours 40 minutes)

Ingredients

- 1 Tbsp. of no sugar pectin
- Ripe peaches: 4 cups, peeled and halved
- 2 cups of granulated sugar

Instructions

- Mash the ripe peaches with a masher. In a bowl, mix all ingredients and pour into the bread machine.

- Select jam or jelly cycle.
- Let the jam cool in the pan of the bread machine for half an hour.
- Pour into jars.
- Serve with fresh bread.

15.6 Grape Jelly

(Prep time: 10 minutes | Total time: 3 hours 40 minutes)

Ingredients

- 2 packets of Knox Gelatin
- 1 Tbsp. of lemon juice
- 2 cups of 100% grape juice
- 1 cup of sugar

Instructions

- Mix all ingredients in a bowl until sugar and gelatin dissolve.
- Add this into the pan of the bread machine.
- Select jam cycle.
- Let it cool for half an hour in the machine, then take it out.
- Pour into jars and serve with fresh bread.

15.7 Crab Apple Jelly

(Prep time: 10 minutes | Total time: 3 hours 40 minutes)

Ingredients

- 2 packets of Knox Gelatin
- 4 cups of Crabapple Juice
- 2 cups of sugar

Instructions

- Juice the apples by a juice or with a blender, add apples and water to blender and pulse and make it 4 cups. Add water to make 4 cups. Strain the juice.
- In a bowl, add all ingredients until gelatin and sugar dissolves.

- Select jam cycle and press start.
- Let it cool for half an hour in the machine, then take it out.
- Pour into jars and serve with fresh bread.
- Keep in the fridge for four weeks.

15.8 Pizza Dough

(Prep time: 10 minutes | Total time: 1 hour 40 minutes)

Ingredients

- 1 and a half tablespoons of vegetable oil
- 1 and a half teaspoons of salt
- 1 and a half teaspoons of active dry yeast
- 3 and 3/4 cups of bread flour
- 1 and a half cups of water
- 1 tablespoon + 1 teaspoon of sugar

Instructions

- Add all ingredients to the bread machine in the suggested order by the manufacturer.
- Select dough cycle. Press start.
- Let the oven preheat to 400 F.
- Take the dough out and roll it into one inch thick.
- Drizzle oil and let it rest for 10-15 minutes.
- Add pizza sauce and toppings of your choice.
- Bake for 20-25 minutes.
- Enjoy the fresh pizza.

15.9 Milk & Honey Bread

(Prep time: 10 minutes | Total time: 2 hours 10 minutes)

Ingredients

- 3 cups of bread flour
- Milk: 1 cup + 1 tbsp.
- 3 tablespoons of melted butter
- 2 teaspoons of active dry yeast
- 1 and a half teaspoons of salt
- 3 tablespoons of honey

Instructions

- Add all ingredients to the bread machine in the suggested order by the manufacturer.
- Select basic cycle. Medium crust and Press start.
- Enjoy fresh bread.

15.10 Soft Pretzels

(Prep time: 10 minutes | Total time: 3 hours 40 minutes

Ingredients

- 1 tablespoon of packed brown sugar
- 1 and a half cups of water
- 2 teaspoons of active dry yeast
- 3 and a half cups of flour

- 1 teaspoon of kosher salt
- Kosher salt
- 1/3 cup of baking soda
- 8 cups of water

Instructions

- Add the first 5 ingredients into the pan of the bread machine as per the manufacturer's suggested order.

- Select the dough cycle—press start.

- Take the dough out on a floured, clean surface.

- Let the oven preheat to 475 F.

- Cut dough into 12-14 pieces. Make each piece long into a 15" rope.

- Make into a pretzel shape. Seal the edges by pinching them.

- Place these pretzels onto baking sheets.

- In a large pot, boil the water with baking soda. Let it simmer.

- Add 2-3 pretzels to the pot and let them boil for 2 minutes.

- Take out the pretzels and let them cool and sprinkle with salt.

- Place on baking sheets and bake for 8-12 minutes.

- Enjoy soft pretzels.

Chapter 16: Oven Recipes to Bread Machine Conversion

The bread machine can label a 1-pound, 1.5 pounds, or 2-pound loaf. What it means is the "flour capacity." Review the manufacturer's booklet of the bread machine to calculate any individual bread machine's flour capability. You can check if the manufacturer's booklet calls for 3-4 cups of flour regularly, then it is your bread machine's capacity. Now you can convert oven recipes to bread machine recipes.

These are general flour capacities that yield a certain pound of bread loaf:

- The bread machine that yields 1-pound uses 2 or 2-3/4 cups of flour

- Bread machine that yields 1.5 pound uses 3-4 cups of flour

- Bread machine that yields 2-pound use 4 to 5 and a half cups of flour

Here are some measurements to help you convert the oven to bread machine recipes:

- Reduce the amount of yeast to 1 tsp for a 1.5-pound bread machine and 1 and 1/4 tsp. for a two-pound machine.

- Reduce the flour to three cups for a 1.5-pound bread machine and 4 cups for a 2-pound bread machine.

- Reduce the other ingredients as well, along with flour and yeast.

- If a recipe calls for 2 or different kinds of flour, add the flour quantities and use it to decrease the formula. The total amount of flour used can be either 3 -4 cups based on the bread's size.

- Use 1-3 tbsp. of gluten flour in a bread machine with all-purpose flour, or only use bread flour, which is a better option. If you are using any rye flour, must combine with 1 tbsp. of gluten flour if even the base is bread flour.

- All ingredients should be at room temperature and added to the bread machine in the manufacturer's suggested order.

- Add any nuts, raisins, dried fruits to the ingredient signal, or as the manufacturer's booklet specifies.

- If you are using only dough cycle, try to handle the dough with a little more flour after taking out from the machine, so it will be easy to handle.

- Use the whole-grain cycle if the bread machine has one, for whole-wheat, rye, and any grain flour.

- Always try to keep the recipe or any additional changes made to the recipe safe for future references.

- Use the sweet bread cycle with a light crust for rich and sweet bread.

16.1 Conversion Tables

Here are some conversion tables to help you measure recipes accurately.

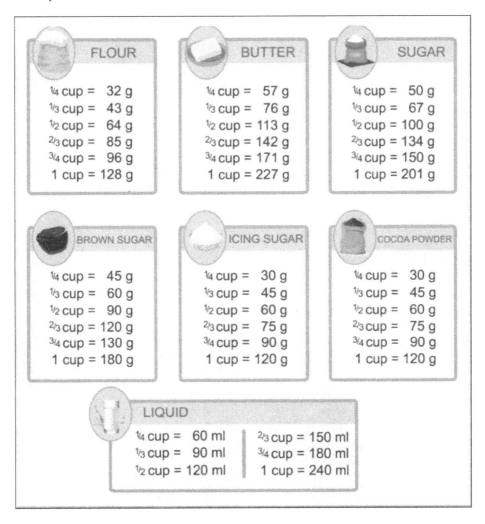

FLOUR

¼ cup = 32 g
⅓ cup = 43 g
½ cup = 64 g
⅔ cup = 85 g
¾ cup = 96 g
1 cup = 128 g

BUTTER

¼ cup = 57 g
⅓ cup = 76 g
½ cup = 113 g
⅔ cup = 142 g
¾ cup = 171 g
1 cup = 227 g

SUGAR

¼ cup = 50 g
⅓ cup = 67 g
½ cup = 100 g
⅔ cup = 134 g
¾ cup = 150 g
1 cup = 201 g

BROWN SUGAR

¼ cup = 45 g
⅓ cup = 60 g
½ cup = 90 g
⅔ cup = 120 g
¾ cup = 130 g
1 cup = 180 g

ICING SUGAR

¼ cup = 30 g
⅓ cup = 45 g
½ cup = 60 g
⅔ cup = 75 g
¾ cup = 90 g
1 cup = 120 g

COCOA POWDER

¼ cup = 30 g
⅓ cup = 45 g
½ cup = 60 g
⅔ cup = 75 g
¾ cup = 90 g
1 cup = 120 g

LIQUID

¼ cup = 60 ml
⅓ cup = 90 ml
½ cup = 120 ml
⅔ cup = 150 ml
¾ cup = 180 ml
1 cup = 240 ml

CUPS	TBSP	TSP	ML
1	16	48	250
3/4	12	36	175
2/3	11	32	150
1/2	8	24	125
1/3	5	16	70
1/4	4	12	60
1/8	2	6	30
1/16	1	3	15

If you want to double the recipes:

Original Recipe	Double Recipe
1/8 tsp	1/4 tsp
1/4 tsp	1/2 tsp
1/2 tsp	1 tsp
3/4 tsp	1 1/2 tsp
1 tsp	2 tsp
1 Tbsp	2 Tbsp
2 Tbsp	4 Tbsp or 1/4
1/8 cup	1/4 cup
1/4 cup	1/2 cup
1/3 cup	2/3 cup
1/2 cup	1 cup
2/3 cup	1 1/3 cups
3/4 cup	1 1/2 cups
1 cup	2 cups
1 1/4 cup	2 1/2 cups
1 1/3 cup	2 2/3 cups
1 1/2 cup	3 cups
1 2/3 cup	3 1/3 cups
1 3/4 cup	3 1/2 cups

Conclusion

Everybody is occupied in this busy day and age, but no one has time to bake bread from scratch, but with a bread machine, you only have to add precisely measured ingredients, and it will bake you fresh bread. The bread machine is easy to use. If one doesn't have the time to practice and have little training, but you also want fresh bread, this really is the machine for you. The bread machine can easily turn you into a baker. You will save money, time, be in charge of the food (the food that goes into your body), and eat fresh food. The bread maker does all the labor of kneading the dough and avoids the trial and error involved with the dough's readiness. To combine and knead the bread dough, one can use a stand mixer or a food processor. But you are offered the choice of completing the baking by the bread maker. So, it's a handy appliance that saves time.

Making the bread allows you to control over the products, as opposed to buying prepared bread. The bread machines are enjoyed by many, solely for the diet element. You get to select the ingredients, monitor or use substitutes for starch, milk, and other components with a bread machine. You will ensure the family a no-preservative product with a bread machine. Many people enjoy their machines for bread and jams and will not be without one. As gluten-free bread is often best when baked in the machine, many gluten-free diets consider this an indispensable appliance. For some, it appears like the excitement of baking fresh bread from scratch wears off easily. The entire thing is rendered so much simpler by the bread machine. Place the ingredients into the bread maker, push start, select the cycle you want, and that's all one has to do. The kitchen remains tidy, and waiting for the fresh bread to be ready is all that's you have left to do.

The schedule becomes critical if you bake bread regularly and despite the rigorous routine that most of us maintain and know so well. There are many benefits of using a bread machine. Most bread machines would have built-in times to avoid mixing, enable to rise, punch down the dough, and so on. Bread Machines will bake bread as well, clearly, but mixers can't. With its many benefits, jams, jellies, and sauces may also be made.

Bread machines are very useful. For all the reasons, I would certainly suggest it. The pros outweigh the cons, and you can enjoy delicious freshly baked bread with many flavors any time you want.

Recipe Index

Instant Vortex Air Fryer Cookbook for Beginners

A Complete Guide with 200+ Scrumptious and Delicious Recipes to Cook From Instant Vortex Air Fryer and 30 day Meal Plan To Make A Healthy Routine

By

MEGAN BUCKLEY

Introduction

Air Frying is the trend and, with two new, finely designed Vortex Air-fryers, Instant Pot has stepped into the air-fryer market. Before purchasing, this is you should learn about it.

Two excellent new products, the Instant Vortex 6 Qt Air-fryer & the Instant Pot Vortex 10 Quart Oven Air-fryer, were recently launched by Instant Pot.

What's an air-fryer?

They are famous, so you can use 95 percent less oil & fat than deep frying to create fast, simple meals. Basically, they are little convection ovens that pump heat and air using a fan so that the food crisps and cooks easily without a bunch of added fat.

Air-fryer tips you need to get started,

- Preheat the air-fryer.
- Don't overcrowd the air-fryer basket.
- Avoid cooking sprays.

- Keep your air-fryer clean.

- Use the recipe cooking and prep times as a guide.

Instant Vortex 6 qt air-fryer

It is simple to use, and its cleaning is easy. It comes with a Guide and a Protection Guidance Manual for Maintenance. The cooking tray slips into the bottom of the basket of the air-fryer.

It was quick to move around and lightweight. Instant Pot suggests that you have at least 5" of room around the appliance.

Smart Programs, including preset temperatures and cooking times, are included in the Vortex. There are 6 Smart Applications in the Vortex Plus. You should adapt the Smart Programs to your very own settings.

For chips, chicken nuggets, cauliflower wings and more, Air Fried.

Bake cookies and pastries that are light and soft, scalloped potatoes and more.

Beef, pork, vegetable dishes, fish and more are roasted.

Heat it without drying out or overcooking to prepare leftovers.

Broil for immediate top-down cooking, melt the cheese around nachos, French onion soup.

Dehydrate it.

When air frying, you can change the time or temperature without stopping the cooking. To rotate the dial to the correct cooking period or temperature, hit the Time or Temp button and push the dial before it clicks.

Instant vortex purchase guide of air-fryer

Deciding which one is correct for you may be challenging.

The Instant Vortex 6 Quart Air-fryer's quick cleanup, lightweight, and simple architecture.

There are many amazing features in the Instant Vortex Air-fryer Oven. The glass oven door is great to have because the progress of the cooking can be seen. It's more flexible.

Tips to clean the air-fryer

Deep frying the food is messy, which leaves many grimy dishes, dirty pans and a coating of grease on everything around the Fryer. Air-fryers, usually, are relatively cleaner. The cooking basket is completely enclosed, eliminating the splattering and grease, oil, and fat in the food poured down into the oil pan below it. It does not mean there's no need for cleaning. The air-fryer must be cleaned after using it

every time.

Instructions

- Unplug from the electric socket and make sure it's cool down.
- Clean the outside of the air-fryer with a wet cloth.
- Clean the tray, pan and basket with dishwashing soap and warm water. All the air-fryer's components, which can be removed, can be used in the dish-washer, so put them in a dish-washer if preferred not to clean them by using hand.
- Clean with hot water and tissue or sponge within the air-fryer.
- Gently clean it off with a soft brush if there is food sticking to the heating unit above the food basket.
- Before placing them into the air-fryer, check if the basket, pan and tray are safe.

Tips

- Please don't use any kitchen utensils in it to scrape the stuck-on food. The air-fryer parts are covered with a coating(non-stick) that is very easy to clean. Always

  use a sponge to remove the leftover foodstuffs stuck in the drip pan or the basket.

- If the food gets stuck onto the pan and the basket, leave them completely in soap and hot water. It will soften food and make it very easy to remove.

- When cooking many batches, keep waiting until the last batch is completed, then clean the air-fryer.

Storing the air-fryer properly

Once the air-fryer is clean, ensure to store it safely. Then wait for almost 30 mins for it to cool down, then put it away. Please make sure it is in an upright posture and not plugged into a wall socket as you store it. If there is a convenient space for the cables, before moving the air-fryer, tuck the cords into it.

Air-fryer Maintenance

Your air-fryer needs some simple maintenance, beyond routine washing, to ensure that it does not get broken or begin to work improperly. It involves:

Before any use, check the cables. Never plug in a socket with a bent or frayed cable. Severe injuries or even death may be caused. Before using your air-fryer, make sure the cords are clean and damage-free.

Before you start cooking, check that the machine is clean and clear from any dust. Check the interior whether it has been a long time since you have used your air-fryer. It could have collected some dust. If the pan basket has some food waste, wash it out before you start cooking.

Before you start cooking, ensure the air-fryer is put upright on a level floor.

Be sure that the air-fryer is not located against a wall or other device. To properly vent steam and hot air when frying, air-fryers need at least 4 inches of space behind and 4 inches of space above. Placing it in a confined space will overheat the Fryer.

Before each use, examine each part visually, including the basket, pan and handle. Call the maker if you notice any defective parts, and have them fixed.

Features and functions

How do air-fryers work?

The air-fryer isn't a fryer. That's just like oven-fried. It doesn't cook food as slow cooking or pan-frying would.

They don't need to preheat most models, which saves so much time, and they cook food fast. They won't fire up the kitchen how the oven will work in warmer climates and hot weather.

What should be looked for in an air-fryer?

A single brand like Instant Pot would not dominate sales of air-fryers, unlike pressure cookers. If you're in the hunt for the right air-fryer for you, there are a few specifications and variables you can bear in mind.

Loading: For loading and unloading the food, some models have front drawers, while others have a flip-top lid. For simplicity and protection, the specialists recommend drawer-style versions.

The simplicity of usage: Are the controls easy to understand and operate? Maybe you want everyone in your household to use an air-fryer. Detaching and cleaning the basket should also be simple.

Controls. Temps up to 400 degrees Fahrenheit F can be set for most models, although others have only one temp setting. Many people prefer to have a reheat button for leftovers and presets for fish and chicken foods.

Functionality can create a difference. Is it possible to pause cooking to turn or stir up your food? You have to reset the time and temp on certain versions.

Size. For one or two persons, most countertop versions are large enough. You'll need to make more than one batch or purchase a bigger model if you're preparing with more, which may take up a lot of counter space. A toaster oven and an air-fryer are combined in some versions, so you can save some space if you substitute your toaster oven.

Tips for storing leftovers

How to Safely Reheat Leftovers?

First, to avoid bacterial development, cool the leftovers to 40 degrees Fahrenheit within 2 hours. 165 degrees Fahrenheit is the safe temp for reheating leftover foods, so having a food thermometer ready to guarantee that you kill any unhealthy

bacteria is a smart idea. Using whatever gadget you choose, you can heat leftovers to this healthy temperature: stovetop, refrigerator, freezer, toaster oven, or air-fryer. Generally, it is often smart to cover leftovers before reheating to maintain moisture and guarantee that the food heats during the whole process. Only make sure that the cover is secure with the device you want. While you're reheating previously frozen leftovers such as pancakes or a fruit pie, any thawed unconsumed portions are healthy to refreeze.

Troubleshooting

If the air-fryer does not work, here are the steps are taken.

1. Try Unplugging

As we know, turning it off and on again with something remotely technological will also make it function again, at times in life with seemingly complicated machinery that has started functioning again by using such a method.

Make sure to unplug the air-fryer for a decent time to make sure it resets fully. 10 mins are supposed to do the trick. It is also only likely to function if it is a digital air-fryer. An old-style analog dial air-fryer is not affected by such a method.

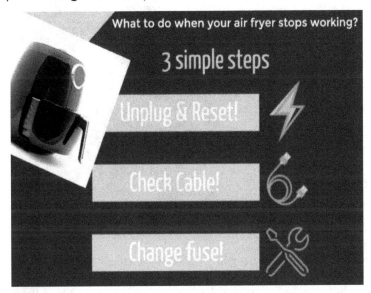

Steps to go through if your air-fryer isn't heating up.

2. Check the power cable

You don't want the shame of getting your nice shiny air-fryer back to the store only to discover out the power cord wasn't properly connected. So, inspect the power cord to make sure the wall socket and your air-fryer are correctly attached. It seems simple, but it is a problem many times.

You also want to exclude the risk of a defective cable, rather than the air-fryer itself. Asking your air-fryer maker to give out a replacement cable is even better than a brand new air-fryer!! Swapping out the power cable is the easiest way to verify if the fault is with the cable or the air-fryer itself. Hopefully, a similar wire is there in your house. You will learn that most household appliances use a similar cable design. Of course, for long periods, utilizing another cable is not recommended, merely to verify your existing cable's integrity for warranty reasons.

3. Check the fuse

You will want to adjust the fuse if you don't have the same power cable to test out.

And if not all connectors in the first place have a fuse. To figure out whether the air-fryer plug has a fuse, see the photos below.

It likely has a fuse inside of the socket that looks like this.

UK type plug looks like above.

However, if your plug looks like this, it probably doesn't have a fuse.

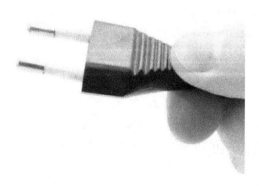

European plug looks like above.

Another way to verify whether your plug does not appear like one of these is to see if your plug is one continuous piece or held together with screws. This likely implies that if it has screws, it can be opened and insert a fuse inside.

And then, if you've never seen a fuse previously and want to know what to look for, that's how a fuse looks.

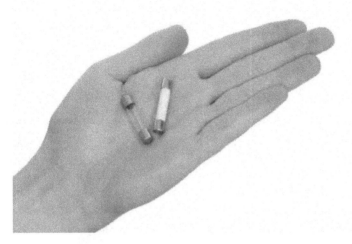

If you discover that you have a plug with a fuse, you can find that changing it will get your air-fryer running again. Only because of a blown fuse you don't need to have your air-fryer returned.

Chapter No. 1: Fast Food for Good Health

Is there such a thing as fast food being healthy?

The reality is that while you eat daily at fast food outlets, it's incredibly challenging to adopt a balanced diet. Usually, fast food is filled with calories, salt, and unnecessary fat in one meal for a whole day, frequently enough. It often happens to be deficient in nutrients and almost entirely missing in fiber, fruits and vegetables.

It doesn't mean that you have to completely avoid fast food. Fast food will always hit the spot while you are starving and on the run. It is affordable, delicious, and, most of all, convenient. Though it's all right to satisfy an appetite now and then, you can't make it a daily routine to keep safe. The key is balance, both in the frequency of fast-food franchises and what you order while you are at the restaurant.

When you're looking at your weight or fitness, fast food menus are tricky. It is a struggle to find a healthy, well-balanced lunch at most fast-food restaurants. But there are still options that are healthier than any of those that you can make. It will help you keep healthy with the following suggestions.

- Aim to keep the whole meal at just below 500 calories. For every fast food meal, the typical adult consumes 836 calories-and underestimates what they consume by 175 calories. Don't guess then. Many chains post nutritional statistics both on their blogs and at the venue of the franchise. Take advantage of this data.

- Go for diets that are lower in fat and higher in fiber and protein. Look for things like fiber, whole wheat, and high-quality protein with more positive stuff.

- When you want a health boost, carry your add-on items. And if you buy carefully, having enough fiber and other essential vitamins and nutrients from a fast-food menu can be pretty difficult. It would help if you held nutritious sides and toppings, including dried fruits, nuts and seeds, sticks of carrot, pear or apple slices, and cottage cheese or yogurt.

Making healthier fast food choices

If you prepare ahead by checking the nutritional manuals that most franchises share on their sites, creating healthy fast food decisions is easier. But if you don't have the time to plan, you can still make better decisions by adopting those common sense rules.

Healthier fast food ordering guidelines

Many fast-food dinners, in the guise of a single-serve, deliver sufficient food for several meals. Stop super-sized and value-sized items, and when it comes to sandwiches, burgers, and sides, go for the smallest size. On the children's menu, you can also find more appropriate portions.

Emphasis on lean meats that are grilled. Stop things that are breaded and fried,

such as crispy chicken sandwiches and fillets of breaded fish. Instead, choose turkey, lean ham, chicken breast or lean roast beef. Typically, grilled skinless chicken is your best choice. Read the instructions carefully on the menu. Foods labeled deep-fried, scalloped, pan-fried, basted, creamy, batter-dipped, breaded, crispy are usually unhealthy fats, high in calories and sodium. Same with items in Alfredo or cream sauce.

Don't be scared of a certain order. With a few tweaks and substitutions, several food products can be made better. For instance, you may inquire about keeping the sauce or dressing or serving it on the side. Or you may order your hamburger's wheat bun or your sandwich's whole-grain bread.

Do not assume that the only choice is often healthy-sounding meals. For example, a diet minefield, smothered in high-fat dressing and fried toppings, is a lot of fast-food salads. This is where it will make a big difference to learn the facts on a diet before you buy.

Fast Food Recipes

1. Air-fryer Popcorn Chicken

Cook Time: 8 mins, Prep Time: 10 mins, Difficulty: Easy, Serving: 4

Ingredients

- 3 tbsps powdered sugar

- 1 tsp garlic powder

- 1 tbsp paprika

- 1 tsp black pepper

- 1/2 cup cornstarch
- 1 lb boneless chicken breasts
- Cooking spray
- 3/4 tsp kosher salt, divided half-cup whole buttermilk
- 4 ounces cornflakes (crushed)

Instructions

1. Mix powdered sugar, cornstarch, pepper, paprika and garlic powder in a deep dish. Drizzle chicken with salt. Dredge in a cornstarch mixture, shake off extra. In buttermilk, dip chicken, leaving excess to slip off. Shake the cornflakes with the chicken to cover.

2. Spray the air-fryer basket gently with the cooking spray. In the basket, put half of the chicken in a single layer and spray it with cooking spray. Cook until cooked through and lightly browned, about 8 mins, turning chicken midway through cooking time, at 400 degrees Fahrenheit. Take the chicken from the air-fryer basket and apply 1/8 tsp. Repeat the procedure with the remaining bits of salt and chicken.

2. Air-Fryer Chicken Nuggets

Cook Time: 12 mins, Prep Time: 10 mins, Difficulty: Easy, Serving: 4

Ingredients

- ¼ tsp garlic powder
- ¼ tsp ground pepper
- ¼ cup whole buttermilk
- ¼ cup cornstarch
- ¼ tsp kosher salt
- Cooking spray
- 2 ounces cornflakes, properly crushed
- 1 tbsp confectioners' sugar

- 8 ounces boneless, chicken breast, cut these into 1-inch pieces

Instructions

1. spray the basket of an air-fryer with cooking spray.

2. Mix cornstarch, pepper, sugar and garlic powder in a deep dish. Put the buttermilk in another deep dish and cornflakes in a third deep dish. Sprinkle chicken with salt. Put the chicken in the cornstarch mixture, shaking off extra, then put in the buttermilk, allowing extra to drain off. Shake the chicken in the cornflakes to cover.

3. Spray the chicken with cooking spray; Put in the already prepared basket. Cook at 400 degrees Fahrenheit until cooked through and golden brown for almost 9 mins, turning midway through cooking time.

3. Air-Fryer Quinoa Arancini

Cook Time: 8 mins, Prep Time: 10 mins, Difficulty: Easy, Serving: 3

Ingredients

- 1 3/4 cups cooked quinoa
- 1 package (9 ounces) quinoa
- 2 large eggs, lightly beaten
- 1/4 cup shredded Parmesan cheese
- 1 tbsp olive oil
- 1 cup seasoned bread crumbs, divided
- 1/2 tsp salt
- 2 tbsps minced fresh basil
- 1/8 tsp pepper
- Cooking spray
- 2 tsps dried basil
- 1/2 tsp garlic powder

- 6 cubes part-skim mozzarella cheese
- Warmed pasta sauce, optional

Instructions

1. Preheat the air-fryer to 375 degrees Fahrenheit. Prepare quinoa according to the instructions on the package. Stir in 1 egg, Parmesan cheese, 1/2 cup bread crumbs, basil, oil and seasonings.

2. Divide into 6 portions. Shape each portion to cover completely around a cheese cube, and a ball is formed.

3. Put the rest of the egg and 1/2 cup bread crumbs in different deep bowls. Dip the balls in egg, then put in bread crumbs. Put on a greased tray in the air-fryer basket; spray with cooking spray. Cook until crisp or golden brown for almost 8 mins.

4. If needed, serve with a pasta sauce.

4. Air-fryer grilled cheese sandwich

Cook Time: 5 mins, Prep Time: 5 mins, Difficulty: Easy, Serving: 1

Ingredients

- 2 slices cheddar cheese
- 1 tsp butter
- 2 slices bread
- 2 slices turkey (optional)

Instructions

1. Preheat the air-fryer to 350 degrees Fahrenheit.

2. Spread the butter on one side of the bread. Add turkey, cheese if using and cover with a different piece of bread, buttered on the other side.

3. Put the sandwich inside the Air-fryer. Set the time for almost 5 mins. Turn midway.

4. The grilled cheese sandwich should look toasty and with lots of melted cheese.

5. Serve and enjoy.

5. Vegan Veggie Balls In The Air-fryer

Cook Time: 12 mins, Prep Time: 5 mins, Difficulty: Easy, Serving: 4

Ingredients

Kitchen Gadgets:

- Air-fryer

- Meatball Maker

- Air-fryer Grill Pan

- Tea Towel

- Blender

Recipe Ingredients:

- 2 tsp Garlic Puree

- 70 g Carrot

- 1 tsp Chives

- 100 g Sweet Potato

- 90 g Parsnips

- 2 tsp Oregano

- 1 tsp Paprika

- 1 cup Gluten-Free Oats

- 1 tsp Mixed Spice

- Salt & Pepper

- ½ Cup Desiccated Coconut

- Metric – Imperial

Instructions

1. Put the cooked vegetables into a clean towel and squeeze out any extra water.

2. Put them in a large bowl and add the seasoning. Mix well and shape into medium-sized balls.

3. Put them in the fridge for almost 2 hours so that they firm up a little.

4. In a blender, mix the gluten-free oats and coconut and mix until it resembles the rough flour. Pour into a small bowl.

5. Roll the veggie balls in the above mixture and then put them in the grill pan in the air-fryer.

6. Cook for 10 mins at 400 degrees Fahrenheit. Cook and roll over for another 2 mins at the same temp on the other side.

7. Remove and serve.

6. Crispy Air-fryer Eggplant Parmesan

Cook Time: 25 mins, Prep Time: 15 mins, Difficulty: Easy, Serving: 4

Ingredients

- 3 tbsp grated parmesan cheese
- 1 large eggplant
- 1 tsp Italian seasoning mix
- 3 tbsp whole wheat flour
- Olive oil spray
- 1/2 cup wheat bread crumbs
- Salt to taste
- 1/4 cup grated mozzarella cheese
- Fresh parsley to garnish
- 1 egg

- 1 tbsp water

- 1 cup marinara sauce

Instructions

1. Slice eggplant into ½ inch slices. Rub some salt on each side of the slices and leave it for at least 15 mins.

2. Simultaneously take a small bowl, mix an egg with flour and water to make the batter.

3. Take a medium shallow plate mix bread crumbs, Italian seasoning blend, parmesan cheese, and salt. Mix properly.

4. Now add the batter to each eggplant cut evenly. Roll the buttered slices in the breadcrumb mixture to cover it properly on all the sides. See the tips section to do this procedure perfectly.

5. Put breaded eggplant pieces on a dry and clean flat plate and sprinkle oil on them. See the tips section for more details.

6. Preheat the Air-fryer to 360 degrees Fahrenheit. Then put the eggplant pieces on the wire mesh, cook for almost 8 min.

7. Top the fried slices with almost 1 tbsp of marinara sauce and gently spread mozzarella cheese(fresh) on it. Cook the eggplant pieces for another 2 min or until the cheese on it melts.

8. Serve warm with your favorite pasta.

7. Air-fryer Parmesan Truffle Oil Fries

Cook Time: 40 mins, Prep Time: 10 mins, Difficulty: Easy, Serving: 6

Ingredients

- 1 tsp paprika

- 3 large russet potatoes

- Salt and pepper

- 1 tbsp parsley chopped

- 2 tbsp white truffle oil
- 2 tbsp parmesan shredded

Instructions

1. Put the sliced potatoes in a big bowl with cold water.

2. Allow the potatoes in the water to soak for almost 30 mins or an hour.

3. Place the fries onto a surface and dry them properly with paper towels. Cover them with seasonings and 1 tbsp of the white truffle oil.

4. Add half of the fries to the Air-fryer basket. Set the temperature to 380 degrees Fahrenheit and cook for almost 20 mins. Set a timer for almost 10 mins, stop and shake the basket when the timer stops.

5. If the fries need more cooking or to be crisper, allow cooking for more time. If the fries look crisp before 15 mins, remove them.

6. Cook the remaining half when the first half completes.

7. Add the rest of the parmesan and truffle oil to the fries upon removing them immediately from the Air-fryer.

8. Top with parsley and serve.

8. Easy Air-fryer Crispy Crunchy Sweet Potato Fries

Cook Time: 25 mins, Prep Time: 5 mins, Difficulty: Easy, Serving: 6

Ingredients

- 2 tsps garlic powder
- 2 big sweet potatoes
- 1 tbsp olive oil
- 1 1/2 tbsp cornstarch
- Salt and pepper
- 2 tsps paprika

Instructions

Fry Cutter Instructions

1. Use a fry cutter to cut the sweet potatoes to provide more shaped fries.

Air-fryer

2. Put the sliced potatoes in a big bowl with cold water. Leave the sweet potatoes to soak in the water for almost an hour.

3. Remove the potatoes from water and let them dry completely. Drizzle the cornstarch entirely.

4. Sprinkle in the garlic powder, paprika, pepper and salt.

5. Put the fries in the air-fryer basket and sprinkle with olive oil. Do not overcrowd the basket. Fry in batches if required. If white spots of cornstarch are seen on the fries, sprinkle the area with olive oil.

6. Adjust the temperature to 380 degrees Fahrenheit and cook for almost 25 mins. Set a timer for almost 10 mins and stop and shake the basket when the timer stops. It is up to you. If you prefer crispy fries, leave them longer and be sure to check on them.

7. Cool before serving.

9. Easy Air-fryer Pepperoni Pizza

Cook Time: 8 mins, Prep Time: 2 mins, Difficulty: Easy, Serving: 1

Ingredients

- 1/8th cup cheddar cheese
- 1 tbsp chopped parsley
- 8 slices pepperoni
- 2 tbsp pizza sauce or marinara
- 1 whole-wheat pita
- 1/8th cup mozzarella cheese (shredded)
- Olive oil spray

- 1/4th cup mozzarella

Instructions

1. Sprinkle the sauce on the pita bread, then put the shredded cheese and pepperoni on top.

2. Spray olive oil spray on the top of the pizza.

3. Put in the Air-fryer for almost 8 mins at 400 degrees Fahrenheit. Check-in on the pizza after 7 min, to ensure it does not overcook.

4. Remove the pizza from the Air-fryer. A spatula can be used for it.

5. Cool before serving.

Crispy Crust Instructions

6. Spray a side of the pita bread with olive oil for a crisp crust. Put in the Air-fryer for almost 4 mins at 400 degrees Fahrenheit. It will allow the pita to crisp entirely on one side.

7. Remove the bread from the Air-fryer. Flip the pita over to the less crisp side. This side should be face-down in the Air-fryer.

8. Sprinkle the sauce throughout, then load the shredded cheese and pepperoni on top.

9. Put the pizza in the Air-fryer for almost 4 mins until the cheese on it has melted. Cook for an additional min for desired texture.

10. Remove the pizza from the Air-fryer. A spatula can be used for it.

11. Cool before serving.

10. Sweet Potatoes Au Gratin

Cook Time: 1 hr 5 mins, Prep Time: 15 mins, Difficulty: Easy, Serving: 6

Ingredients

- 2 lbs sweet potatoes
- 1 tbsp butter

- 1/4 cup heavy whipping cream

- 1 tsp onion powder

- 1/4 cup shredded parmesan cheese

- 2 garlic cloves minced

- 1 cup shredded cheddar cheese

- 4 oz cream cheese

- 1/2 cup shredded mozzarella cheese

- Salt and pepper

Instructions

1. Preheat the air-fryer to 350 degrees Fahrenheit.

2. Add the butter and heat a saucepan on medium-high heat.

3. When the butter is melted, put some garlic and cook for almost 2 mins until fragrant.

4. Add in the whipping cream, cream cheese, 1/2 cup shredded cheddar cheese and Parmesan Reggiano, Stir. Add in the salt, onion powder and pepper to taste. Adjust the flavor as needed.

5. Stir until the cheese has melted.

6. Remove and set aside.

7. Arrange the sweet potato slices in rows on a baking dish. Sprinkle the cheese sauce on it.

8. Sprinkle the rest of the mozzarella and 1/2 cup of shredded cheddar throughout the pan.

9. Cover with foil and cook for almost 30 mins.

10. Remove the foil and cook an additional 25 mins until the potatoes are soft.

11. For a crisp top, turn on the Broil function on the air-fryer for a couple of mins. Broil for almost 3 mins until the crisp top.

12. Cool for almost 30 mins then serve.

11. Mediterranean Paleo Burgers In The Air-fryer

Cook Time: 15 mins, Prep Time: 3 mins, Difficulty: Easy, Serving: 2

Ingredients

- 2 tbsp Fried Onions
- Sweet Potato Fries
- ¼ Small Onion
- 2 tsp Oregano
- 350 g Mixed Mince
- 1 tsp Garlic Puree
- 2 Fried Eggs
- 1 tsp Parsley
- Salt and Pepper
- ½ tsp Rosemary
- 1 tsp thyme

Instructions

1. Dice and peel the ¼ of an onion.
2. Put the garlic, the mince and the onion into a large bowl with the seasoning and whisk well.
3. Make it into hamburger shapes.
4. Cook in the air-fryer for almost 15 mins at 360 degrees Fahrenheit.
5. Serve with sweet potato fries, a fried egg and some fried onions.

12. Air-fryer Burgers

Cook Time: 12 mins, Prep Time: 5 mins, Difficulty: Easy, Serving: 4

Ingredients

- 1 tbsp Soft Cheese
- 500 g Minced Pork
- 500 g Minced Beef
- 2 tsp thyme
- ½ Small Onion
- 2 tsp Oregano
- 1 tsp Garlic Puree
- Salt & Pepper

Instructions

1. Dice and peel the onion and put it into a mixing bowl with the rest of the burger

   patty ingredients.

2. Mix well with hands.

3. Add in the cheese and mix more.

4. Use a cutter to slice into burger shapes.

5. Put into the air-fryer basket and cook for almost 12 mins at 360 degrees Fahrenheit.

6. Add the burger bun cover and serve.

13. Perfect Personal Pizzas in an Air-fryer

Cook Time: 10 mins, Prep Time: 5 mins, Difficulty: Easy, Serving: 1

Ingredients

- 1 Stonegate Mini Naan
- 2 tbsp shredded pizza cheese
- 2 tbsp jarred pizza sauce
- 6 or 7 mini Pepperoni

Instructions

1. Top shredded pizza cheese, pizza sauce and mini pepperoni over the mini naan.

2. Put the topped pizza into the basket of an air-fryer.

3. Set the air-fryer to about 375 degrees Fahrenheit. Fry the pizza for almost 7 mins- or until starting to brown and cheese is completely melted.

4. Serve immediately.

14. Air-fryer Scallops | Tomato Basil Scallops

Cook Time: 10 mins, Prep Time: 5 mins, Difficulty: Easy, Serving: 2

Ingredients

- 1 tsp Minced Garlic
- 1/2 tsp Kosher Salt
- 1/2 tsp Ground Black Pepper
- 3/4 cup Whipping Cream
- 1 tbsp Tomato Paste
- Cooking Oil Spray
- 1 12 oz Frozen Spinach
- 1 tbsp chopped fresh basil
- 8 jumbo sea scallops
- Salt and pepper

Instructions

1. Spray a heatproof pan (7-inch), and Put the spinach in a single layer at the bottom.

2. Spray each side of the scallops with vegetable oil, sprinkle a little more pepper and salt on them, and Put scallops in the heatproof pan on the top of spinach.

3. Take a small bowl, mix the tomato paste, cream, garlic, basil, pepper and salt, and pour over the scallops and spinach.

4. Set the air-fryer to 350 degrees Fahrenheit for almost 10 mins until they are cooked through to an internal temp of 130 degrees Fahrenheit and the sauce

   is bubbling and hot.

5. Serve immediately.

15. Air-fryer Korean Tacos

Cook Time: 10 mins, Prep Time: 10 mins, Difficulty: Easy, Serving: 6

Ingredients

Marinade

- 2 tsps Minced Ginger

- 1 cup Onion, sliced

- 2 tbsps Gochujang

- 1 tbsp Dark Soy Sauce

- 2 tsps sugar or 1 tsp Truvia

- 1/2 tsp Kosher Salt

- 1.5 lbs sirloin beef (thinly sliced)

- 2 tbsps Sesame Oil

- 2 tsps Minced Garlic

- Vegetables and Meat

- 2 tbsp Sesame Seeds

For Serving

- 1/2 cup Kimchi

- 12 flour tortillas

- 1/4 cup Cilantro (chopped)

- 1 head Romaine Lettuce Leaves
- 1/2 cup Green Scallions(Chopped)

Instructions

1. Put sliced onions, sliced beef, and green onions into a plastic zip-lock bag. Add soy sauce, gochujang, garlic, ginger, sesame oil, sesame seeds and sweetener. Press the bag properly to get the sauce and meat to combine well.

2. Leave the beef to marinate for almost 30 mins or put in the refrigerator for up to 24 hours.

3. Put the veggies and meat into the air-fryer basket. Set air-fryer to 400 degrees Fahrenheit for almost 12 mins, shaking midway through.

4. To serve, put meat in the tortillas, top with Cilantro, green onions and kimchi.

5. Serve napkins for this messy but very delicious meal.

16. Air-fryer hamburger

Cook Time: 10 mins, Prep Time: 5 mins, Difficulty: Easy, Serving: 1

Ingredients

- 4 burger buns (gluten-free)
- Tomatoes lettuce
- 1 lb 450g ground beef
- Salt
- 4 slices of cheese
- Ground black pepper
- Mayo
- Garnishes

Instructions

1. Preheat the air-fryer to 350 degrees Fahrenheit.

2. Mix the salt, black pepper and beef in a bowl.

3. Make the mixture into 4 burger patties.

4. Sprinkle the air-fryer basket, add in the patties.

5. Cook for almost 12 mins and turn them midway through cooking.

6. 1 minute before they are cooked, remove the air-fryer basket. Top each burger with cheese, put it back in the air-fryer and heat till done.

7. Make the burgers and serve.

17. Cajun Fried Okra with Creamy Chili Sauce

Cook Time: 8 mins, Prep Time: 10 mins, Difficulty: Easy, Serving: 6

Ingredients

*   Okra

*   1 cup cornmeal

*   ½ cup buttermilk

*   2 tsps House Seasoning

*   1 cup purpose flour

*   3 tbsp Thai sweet chili sauce

*   Oil for spraying

*   ¼ tsp Cajun seasoning

*   Creamy Chili Sauce

*   2 lbs fresh okra (1/2 inch)

*   1 cup mayo

*   1/3 tsp ground red pepper

*   1 tbsp garlic chili sauce

Instructions

1. Take a medium bowl, mix flour, House Seasoning, Cajun seasoning and cornmeal. Put the buttermilk in a tiny bowl. Put okra in buttermilk, then put in cornmeal mixture. Put on a baking sheet wrapped with parchment paper. Cool battered okra in the fridge for almost 30 mins.

2. Working in 10 batches, spray okra with oil and put in the air-fryer basket. Set temp to 400 degrees Fahrenheit, and cook for almost 5 mins. Toss okra properly, sprinkle with oil, and cook for almost 5 mins. Do the same and cook for almost 3 mins more. Repeat with the rest of the okra.

3. Serve warm with Chili Sauce.

4. To make the chili sauce, combine Thai sweet chili sauce, garlic chili sauce, mayonnaise and red pepper in a tiny bowl, and mix well.

5. Cover and cool until ready for serving.

18. Air-fryer falafel burger recipe

Cook Time: 15 mins, Prep Time: 3 mins, Difficulty: Easy, Serving: 2

Ingredients

- 400 g Can Chickpeas
- 140 g sugar-free Oats
- 1 Small Red Onion
- 28 g Cheese
- 1 Small Lemon
- 4 tbsp Soft Cheese
- 28 g Feta Cheese
- 1 tbsp Garlic Puree
- 3 tbsp Greek yogurt
- 1 tbsp parsley
- 1 tbsp coriander

- Salt & Pepper
- 1 tbsp Oregano

Instructions

1. Put in a blender or food processor all the garlic, the seasonings, the red onion, lemon rind and the drained chickpeas. Mix until coarse but not smooth.

2. Mix them in a bowl with the hard cheese, ½ the soft cheese and the feta.

3. Make them into burger shapes.

4. Roll them in sugar-free oats until all of the chickpea mixture is covered.

5. Put them in the Air-fryer inside the Air-fryer baking pan and cook for almost 8 mins at 360 degrees Fahrenheit.

6. Make the burger sauce. In a mixing bowl, add the Greek Yoghurt, the rest of the soft cheese and some extra pepper and salt. Mix until it is fluffy and nice. Add the juice of the lemon and mix.

7. Put the falafel burger inside the buns with garnish.

8. Load up with the burger sauce and sauce.

19. Best ever air-fryer vegan lentil burgers

Cook Time: 30 mins, Prep Time: 10 mins, Difficulty: Easy, Serving: 4

Ingredients

- 4 Vegan Burger Buns
- 1 Large Onion peeled and diced
- 100 g Black Beluga Lentils
- 100 g White Cabbage
- 1 tbsp Garlic Puree
- 300 g Sugar-Free Oats
- 1 Large Carrot peeled & grated

- Fresh Basil properly cleaned & chopped
- Salt & Pepper
- 1 tsp Cumin

Instructions

1. Start by putting your sugar-free oats and putting them in the blender. Blitz until it resembles flour.

2. Put the mixture in a saucepan. Cover with water until it is well covered. Cook on medium heat for almost 45 mins.

3. Simultaneously, put the vegetables into the Instant Pot and steam them for almost 5 mins using the steam function.

4. Drain the lentils and put them in a large bowl with the oats and the steamed vegetables.

5. Add the seasoning and make it into burgers.

6. Put the burgers in the Air-fryer and cook for almost 30 mins at 356 degrees Fahrenheit.

7. Serve with vegan mayonnaise and salad garnish.

20. Air-fryer Persian Joojeh Kababs

Cook Time: 20 mins, Prep Time: 15 mins, Difficulty: Easy, Serving: 3

Ingredients

- 1 tbsp Oil
- 1/4 cup onion (chopped)
- 1/2 tsp Ground Black Pepper
- 1 tsp Kosher Salt
- 1 tsp Turmeric
- 1/2 tsp Smoked Paprika
- 1/2 lbs chicken breasts

- 1/4 cup Greek Yogurt
- 2 tbsp saffron water

Instructions

Joojeh Kabobs

1. Put the chicken in a big bowl.

2. Put Greek yogurt, paprika, onion, salt, oil, and black pepper in a small blender container and process until you get a smooth mixture.

3. Pour this mixture over the chicken.

4. Add saffron water and turmeric and mix until the chicken is well-covered with

   the marinade.

5. Leave the chicken to marinate for almost 30 mins or put in the refrigerator for up to 24 hours.

6. Remove the chicken from the marinade, and put it in the air-fryer basket.

7. Set the air-fryer to 370 degrees Fahrenheit for almost 15 mins, flipping it midway through.

8. Test with a thermometer to ensure the cooked chicken has reached an internal temp of 165 degrees Fahrenheit, then serve.

9. These kababs are served with plain white rice with butter and a drizzle of saffron water.

21. Air-fryer Potato Wedges

Cook Time: 22 mins, Prep Time: 10 mins, Difficulty: Easy, Serving: 4

Ingredients

- 2 large Russet Potatoes
- ½ cup flour
- 1 large egg

- ½ tsp paprika
- ½ tsp garlic powder
- 1 ½ tbsp Seasoned Salt
- 1 tbsp milk
- Oil for Spraying
- ½ tsp ground black pepper

Instructions

1. Clean and dry Russet potatoes. Slice into wedges, put aside.

2. Mix milk and egg in a big bowl. Mix russet potatoes in the egg mixture until potatoes are entirely covered. Put aside.

3. Mix paprika, flour, seasoned salt, black pepper and garlic powder in a medium bowl.

4. Take a wedge of russet potato out of the egg mixture and put it in the flour mixture, covering every side. Shake off any extra flour. Put this on the bottom of a greased Air-fryer basket.

5. Repeat with the rest of the wedges, making sure the wedges are on the basket's bottom in a single layer.

6. Sprinkle the wedges with cooking oil, covering the flour spots.

7. Close the Air-fryer basket and cook the wedges at 360 degrees Fahrenheit for almost 11 mins. Open basket, spray the flour spots seen on the wedges, and then turn the wedges over. Now spray this side of the potato wedges. Close the Air-fryer basket and cook for almost 11 mins again.

8. Serve the wedges with ketchup and enjoy.

22. Taco bell crunch wrap

Cook Time: 20 mins, Prep Time: 15 mins, Difficulty: Easy, Serving: 1

Ingredients

- 2 lbs ground beef
- 1 1/3 c water
- 12 oz nacho cheese
- 6 large flour tortillas
- 2 Prep Time Taco Seasoning
- 2 cups Mexican blend cheese
- 3 Roma tomatoes
- 6 tostada shell
- 2 c lettuce, shredded
- Cooking Spray
- 2 cup sour cream

Instructions

1. Combine all the ingredients.
2. Preheat the air-fryer to 400 degrees Fahrenheit.
3. Cook beef in a pan on the stove until thoroughly cooked or no longer pink.
4. Add 1 1/2 cups of water and 2 Prep Time of the taco seasoning and bring to a boil.
5. Reduce the boil and allow the mixture to thicken.
6. Fill the middle of each flour tortilla with 4 tbs of nacho cheese, 2/3 cup of beef, 1/3 cup sour cream, 1 tostada shell, 1/6th of the tomatoes, 1/3 cup of lettuce and 1/3 cup cheese.
7. Flood the edges up, over the middle. It will look like a pinwheel.

8. Repeat 2 and 3 with the rest of the wraps.

9. Sprinkle the air-fryer basket or rack with oil.

10. Put seam side down in the air-fryer.

11. Again, sprinkle with oil.

12. Cook for almost 2 mins or until crisp or golden brown.

13. Gently flip by using a spatula and spray again.

14. Cook for almost 2 mins more and repeat with the rest of the wraps.

15. Leave for a few mins to cool and enjoy.

23. Air-fryer Blooming Onion

Cook Time: 20 mins, Prep Time: 10 mins, Difficulty: Easy, Serving: 4

Ingredients

- 1 tbsp buttermilk

- 3 tbsp mayonnaise

- 1/2 tsp Cajun seasoning

- 1 yellow or white onion

- 3/4 cup panko bread crumbs

- Olive oil

- 1 tbsp ketchup

- 1 tsp prepared horseradish
- 2 eggs, beaten
- 1/2 cup flour

Instructions

1. Slice the top of the onion (the pointed end) to make a flat surface.
2. Slice the onion into 4 wedges, then slice each wedge in half. Repeat until wedges are about 1/4 inch thick.
3. Gently remove the layers.
4. Mix Cajun seasoning with flour in a medium bowl. Mix buttermilk and eggs in another medium bowl. Then put Panko bread crumbs into a 3rd bowl.
5. Dredge onion in the flour and shake off the extra. Put into the egg mixture, covering evenly. Then roll into Panko breadcrumbs, then flip to ensure complete coverage of the coating all around breadcrumbs.
6. Put the crusted onion into the air-fryer basket. Sprinkle the entire onion with oil. Put a foil piece over the onion.
7. Set the air-fryer to 390 for almost 10 mins. Remove the foil and cook for almost 10 mins again until crisp or brown. Your cook time depends on the size of the onion.
8. Mix dipping sauce ingredients.
9. Serve with the blooming onion and enjoy.

24. Air-fryer buttermilk biscuits

Cook Time: 20 mins, Prep Time: 10 mins, Difficulty: Easy, Serving: 3

Ingredients

- 1 tbsp baking powder
- 1 1/2 cup purpose flour
- 1 tsp salt

- 2/3 cup buttermilk
- 1/3 cup vegetable shortening
- 1 tsp sugar

Instructions

1. Start by adding the flour to a large mixing bowl.
2. Add a tsp of salt, a tbsp baking powder, a tsp of sugar, buttermilk and vegetable shortening. Mix well together.
3. Then place the batter onto a flat, floured surface.
4. Roll out the dough.
5. Slice the dough with a biscuit cutter.
6. Then put the parchment paper into the air-fryer. Sprinkle with the cooking spray (non-sticky).
7. Then put the biscuits onto the paper.
8. Set the time for almost 4 mins. After 4 mins, flip & cook for almost 2 mins more.
9. Serve after brushing the biscuits with the melted butter.

25. Chili's boneless Buffalo wings

Cook Time: 23 mins, Prep Time: 5 mins, Difficulty: Easy, Serving: 4

Ingredients

- 1 tsp black pepper
- 2 cups flour
- 2 boneless chicken breasts
- 1 cup milk
- 1/2 tsp cayenne
- 1 egg

- 3 tsp salt
- 2 tbsp butter
- 1/2 tsp paprika
- 1/2 cup Buffalo Sauce

Instructions

1. Preheat Air-fryer for 4 mins to 360 degrees Fahrenheit.
2. Take a bowl, mix all spices and flour.
3. Take another bowl whisk together milk and egg.
4. Slice chicken into 2 pieces.
5. Put chicken pieces into egg/milk mixture and then into the flour mixture.
6. Repeat this step, so the chicken is fully coated.
7. Cook in the air-fryer for almost 23 mins, turning chicken over after almost 15 mins. (Cook in the deep fryer for almost 6 mins).
8. Leave the chicken on a plate while you prepare the sauce.
9. Combine butter and hot sauce in a bowl and cook for almost 30-sec increments, stirring until butter is fully melted.
10. Put the chicken in a container with a lid or a ziplock bag and drizzle the sauce over the chicken. Shake properly until the chicken is coated.
11. Serve with celery sticks and ranch dressing.

26. Chipotle burrito bowl

Cook Time: 20 mins, Prep Time: 4 hrs, Difficulty: Medium, Serving: 6

Ingredients

- 1 lb Boneless Chicken Thighs
- 1 cup Monterrey Jack Cheese
- 1/2 cup Pico De Gallo
- 6 cups Chopped Romaine Lettuce

- 1/2 cup Sour Cream
- 1/4 cup Chipotle Adobo Sauce
- 1/2 cup Guacamole

Instructions

1. Marinate the chicken thighs in adobo sauce for almost 4 hours or less.

2. Set air-fryer to 400 degrees Fahrenheit for almost 20 mins. Midway through, flip chicken by using kitchen tongs. Make sure the chicken reaches an internal temp of almost 165 degrees Fahrenheit, then remove it.

3. Remove chicken from air-fryer and leave for almost 5 mins. Slice chicken into small pieces.

4. Make burrito bowl with chicken, lettuce, cheese, pico de gallo, sour cream, guacamole and any other topping to taste.

27. Air-fryer Fried Chicken

Cook Time: 25 mins, Prep Time: 4 mins, Difficulty: Easy, Serving: 4

Ingredients

- 1 tsp seasoning salt
- 1 egg (beaten)
- 1/2 cup purpose flour
- 1 1/2 tbsp Cajun
- 4 small chicken thighs
- Cooking spray

Instructions

1. Preheat the Air-fryer to 390 degrees Fahrenheit.

2. Mix the salt, flour and Cajun.

3. Spray the chicken with cooking spray after dredging in the ingredients and shaking off the extra flour.

4. Put the 4 chicken thighs into the bottom of the Air-Fryer. Cook for almost 25 mins or until the chicken reaches 180 degrees Fahrenheit.

5. Remove and serve.

28. Mozzarella sticks

Cook Time: 20 mins, Prep Time: 15 mins, Difficulty: Easy, Serving: 3

Ingredients

- 12 piece 1-ounce mozzarella sticks
- 1/2 cup unbleached purpose flour
- 2 large eggs
- 1/4 tsp salt
- 1 tbsp grated Parmesan cheese
- 1/2 cup plain bread crumbs
- 1/4 tsp Italian seasoning
- 1 tsp garlic powder

Instructions

1. Start by slicing the mozzarella sticks in half.

2. Put the mozzarella sticks on parchment paper, placed them on a baking sheet (that will store in the freezer).

3. Put the baking sheet (with the mozzarella sticks and parchment paper) into the freezer for almost 25 mins.

4. After almost 25 mins, Put the flour in one bowl, take another bowl and put the eggs and beat. Take another bowl, mix the cheese, bread crumbs and seasonings. Mix well. Then put the frozen mozzarella stick into the egg, flour and bread crumb mixture. While doing this, put them back on the parchment paper-lined baking sheet.

5. Freeze them again for almost 1 hour.

6. NOW–Preheat the air-fryer to 400 degrees Fahrenheit.

7. Spray the air-fryer basket with non-stick cooking spray.

8. Please do not overcrowd the air-fryer basket.

9. Spray the mozzarella sticks while they are in the air-fryer until it gets a nice golden color.

10. Set the time for almost 5 mins at 400 degrees Fahrenheit.

11. Remove, serve and enjoy.

29. Wingstop Fries

Cook Time: 25 mins, Prep Time: 5 mins, Difficulty: Easy, Serving: 2

Ingredients

- 1 tbsp Swerve Granular (12g)
- Wingstop Fries Seasoning
- 1/8 tsp Salt
- 1/2 tsp Black Pepper
- 1/2 tsp Paprika
- 1/2 tbsp Swerve Brown (6g)
- 2 Russet Potatoes (400g)
- 1/4 tsp Salt
- 1/4 tsp Garlic Powder
- 1/2 tbsp Olive Oil (8g)
- 1/4 tsp Chili Powder

Instructions

1. Wash and dry 3 potatoes (about 400 g in total).

2. Begin by slicing the end of every potato to make a flat surface. Put the sliced side down and cut the potato vertically into 5 pieces. Then cut lengthwise, and it's done.

3. Add the sliced potatoes to a big bowl and sprinkle with olive oil and salt. Toss to coat every potato slice.

4. Put the fries in the air-fryer and cook at 400 degrees Fahrenheit for almost 25 mins, shaking midway through.

5. While the fries cook, mix the seasoning ingredients in a small bowl. Sprinkle with the seasoning. Toss the fries until coated.

30. Air-fryer Fried Pickles

Cook Time: 20 mins, Prep Time: 15 mins, Difficulty: Easy, Serving: 4

Ingredients

- 3/4 cup panko bread crumbs
- 1 tsp paprika
- 1 jar pickle slices (32 oz.)
- 1/2 tsp salt
- 1 egg
- 1 tsp dried oregano
- 1 tsp garlic powder
- Ranch for dipping
- 1/4 tsp. pepper

Instructions

1. Preheat air-fryer at 400 degrees Fahrenheit. Sprinkle the basket with cooking spray.

2. Take a bowl, mix oregano, panko, paprika garlic powder, pepper and salt. Take another bowl, mix the egg. Put aside.

3. Pat pickle chips dry with paper towels. Put pickle chips first in egg and then in the breadcrumb mixture. Put pickles in the air-fryer and cook for almost 5 mins (in batches).

4. Serve with sauce and enjoy.

Chapter No.2: Breakfast Recipes

1. Air-fryer apple fritters

Cook Time: 8 mins, Prep Time: 15 mins, Difficulty: Easy, Serving: 15

Ingredients

- 1-1/2 cups of purpose flour
- 1/4 cup of sugar
- 2 tsps baking powder
- 1-1/2 tsps ground cinnamon
- 1/2 tsp salt
- 2/3 cup of 2% milk
- 2 large eggs, room temp
- 1 tbsp lemon juice
- 1-1/2 tsps divided vanilla extract
- 2 medium chopped and peeled Honeycrisp apples

- 1/4 cup of butter

- 1 cup of confectioners' sugar

- 1 tbsp 2% milk

- Cooking spray

Instructions

1. Line the air-fryer basket with parchment paper; spray with a cooking spray. Preheat the air-fryer to 400 degrees Fahrenheit.

2. Take a big bowl, mix flour, baking powder, sugar, cinnamon and salt. Add milk, lemon juice, eggs and 1 tsp vanilla extract; stir just until it gets moist. Fold in the apples.

3. Drop dough by 1/4 cupful's 2-inches (in batches). Put into air-fryer basket. Spritz with a cooking spray. Cook until crispy and golden brown for almost 6 mins. Turn over; continue to air fry until golden brown for almost 2 mins.

4. Take a small saucepan, melt butter in it over medium-high heat. Cook until butter starts to brown and foamy for almost 5 mins. Cool slightly after removing from heat. Add 1 tbsp milk, confectioners' sugar and remaining 1/2 tsp vanilla extract to browned butter; whisk until smooth. Drizzle over the fritters, then serve.

2. Air-fryer Breakfast Toad-in-the-Hole Tarts

Cook Time: 8 mins, Prep Time: 15 mins, Difficulty: Easy, Serving: 4

Ingredients

- 1 sheet frozen puff pastry

- 4 tbsps shredded Cheddar cheese

- 4 tbsps diced cooked ham

- 4 eggs

- 1 tbsp chopped fresh chives

Instructions

1. Preheat the air-fryer to 400 degrees Fahrenheit.

2. Put a pastry sheet on a surface and cut it into 4 squares.

3. Put 2 pastry squares in the air-fryer basket and cook for almost 8 mins.

4. Remove basket from the air-fryer. Use a metal tbsp to press each square gently to form an indentation. Put 1 tbsp of Cheddar cheese and 1 tbsp ham in each hole and pour 1 egg on top of each.

5. Return basket to air-fryer. Cook when done, about 6 mins more. Remove tarts from the basket and let cool for 5 mins. Repeat with remaining pastry squares, ham, cheese and eggs.

6. Garnish tarts with chives.

3. Air-fryer breakfast sweet potato skins

Cook Time: 23 mins, Prep Time: 7 mins, Difficulty: Medium, Serving: 4

Ingredients

- 2 tsp. olive oil
- 4 eggs
- 1/4 cup whole milk
- 2 green onions (sliced)
- salt and pepper
- 4 slices cooked bacon
- 2 medium sweet potatoes

Instructions

1. Clean the sweet potatoes and add 3 to 4 cuts to the potatoes. Microwave for 6 to 8 mins, depending on the size of potatoes until they become soft.

2. Slice the potatoes in half lengthwise by using an oven mitt. Scoop out the flesh of the potato, leaving only 1/4 inch around their edges.

3. Brush the olive oil over potato skins and sprinkle it with sea salt. Put the skins in the Air-fryer basket and cook at 400 degrees Fahrenheit for almost 10 mins.

4. Simultaneously, add the eggs, salt, pepper and milk to a nonstick pan. Cook this over medium heat while constantly stirring it until liquid eggs become invisible.

5. Top 1/4 of the scrambled eggs and 1 slice of crumbled bacon for each fried potato skin. Cover with shredded cheese and cook until the cheese is melted, or for 3 mins.

6. Serve after topping it with green onion.

4. Air-fryer easy bourbon bacon cinnamon rolls

Cook Time: 10 mins, Prep Time: 25 mins, Difficulty: Easy, Serving: 4

Ingredients

- 3/4 cup bourbon
- 1/2 cup pecans(chopped)
- 2 tbsps maple syrup
- 1 tsp minced fresh ginger root
- 1 tube cinnamon rolls with icing
- 8 bacon strips
- Powered by Chicory

Instructions

1. Take a shallow dish and Put bacon in it; add the bourbon. Cool and seal overnight. Remove the bacon and let dry; remove bourbon.

2. Take a large pan, cook bacon over medium heat(in batches) until brown or nearly crisp but still pliable. Remove the paper towels. Remove all except 1 tsp drippings.

3. Preheat the air-fryer to 350 degrees Fahrenheit. Make the dough in 8 even roll. Unroll rolls into long strips; pat dough to form 6x1-inches strips.

Put 1 bacon strip on every strip of dough, trim the bacon as needed; reroll, and form a spiral. Pinch both ends to seal. Repeat with the rest of the dough. Put 4 rolls on an ungreased tray in the air-fryer basket; cook for almost 5 mins. Turn rolls over and cook until it gets golden brown, about 4 mins.

4. Simultaneously, combine maple syrup and pecans. Take another bowl, mix ginger with the contents of the icing packet. Heat remaining bacon drippings over medium heat in the same pan. Add the pecan mixture; cook, stirring until toasted for almost 3 mins.

5. Sprinkle half the icing over cinnamon rolls; top with half the pecans. Repeat the same procedure to make the next batch.

5. Air-fryer French toast sticks

Cook Time: 10 mins, Prep Time: 20 mins, Difficulty: Easy, Serving: 6

Ingredients

- 6 slices of Texas toast
- 4 large eggs
- 1 cup whole milk
- 2 tbsp sugar
- 1 tsp vanilla extract
- 1/4 tsp cinnamon
- 1 cup crushed cornflakes
- Confectioners' sugar
- Maple syrup
- Powered by Chicory

Instructions

1. Cut every piece of bread into thirds; put in an ungreased dish. Take a large bowl, milk, whisk eggs, vanilla, sugar and cinnamon. Pour over

bread for 2 mins, turning once. Cover bread with cornflake crumbs on each side.

2. Put in a greased baking pan. Freeze until firm, about 45 mins. Move to an airtight container or freezer bag and cool it by storing it in the freezer.

3. Preheat the air-fryer to 350 degrees Fahrenheit. Put whatever number you want on a greased tray in the air-fryer basket. Cook for almost 3 mins. Turn; cook until crispy or golden brown, 2-3 mins longer. It can be sprinkled with confectioners' sugar.

4. Serve with syrup.

6. Air-fryer red potatoes

Cook Time: 10 mins, Prep Time: 10 mins, Difficulty: Easy, Serving: 8

Ingredients

- 2 tbsps olive oil

- 1 tbsp minced fresh rosemary

- 2 garlic cloves, minced

- 1/2 tsp salt

- 1/4 tsp pepper

- 2 pounds small unpeeled red potatoes

- Powered by Chicory

Instructions

1. Preheat the air-fryer to 400 degrees Fahrenheit. Drizzle oil on potatoes. Sprinkle with garlic salt, rosemary and pepper; toss slowly to coat.

2. Put on an ungreased tray in the air-fryer basket. Cook until potatoes are brown and tender for almost 12 mins.

7. Air-fryer puff pastry Danishes

Cook Time: 10 mins, Prep Time: 25 mins, Difficulty: Easy, Serving: 5

Ingredients

- 1/4 cup sugar
- 2 large egg yolks
- 2 tbsps purpose flour
- 1 tbsp water
- 1 package frozen puff pastry
- 1/2 tsp vanilla extract
- 1 package cream cheese
- 2/3 cup seedless raspberry jam

Instructions

1. Preheat the air-fryer to 325 degrees Fahrenheit. Beat cream cheese, flour, sugar and vanilla until it gets smooth; beat in an egg's yolk.

2. Mix remaining egg yolk and water. On a floured surface, unfold every sheet of puff pastry; roll into a square. Cut every into nine squares.

3. Top every square with 1 tbsp cream cheese and 1 tsp jam. Put 2 opposite corners of the pastry over filling, sealing with the yolk. Brush tops with the rest of the yolk mixture.

4. In batches, put in a single layer on a greased tray in the air-fryer basket. Cook until brown for almost 10 mins.

5. Serve warm. Refrigerate leftovers.

8. Air-fryer ham & cheese breakfast bundles

Cook Time: 10 mins, Prep Time: 35 mins, Difficulty: Easy, Serving: 4

Ingredients

- 1/8 tsp pepper
- 4 large eggs
- 1/4 cup chopped fully cooked ham
- 1/8 tsp salt
- 1/4 cup shredded provolone cheese
- 2 tsps seasoned bread crumbs
- 5 sheets phyllo dough
- 1/4 cup butter(melted)
- 2 tsps minced chives
- 2 ounces cream cheese
- Powered by Chicory

Instructions

1. Preheat the air-fryer to 325 degrees Fahrenheit. Put phyllo dough(1 sheet) on a surface; brush it with butter. Layer with 4 more phyllo sheets, brush each layer. Cut the layered sheets in half(crosswise), remaining half(lengthwise).

2. Put each stack in a 4-oz greased jar. Put a slice of cream cheese on each one. Split an egg into each cup carefully. Top with ham, bacon, bread crumbs and chives; sprinkle with salt and pepper. Bring together the phyllo above the filling; pinch to seal and form packages.

3. In an air-fryer basket, Put the ramekins on the tray; brush with the remaining butter. Cook until the brown is crispy, 10-12 mins.

4. Serve warm.

9. Air-fryer candied bacon

Cook Time: 18 mins, Prep Time: 5 mins, Difficulty: Easy, Serving: 12

Ingredients

- 1/4 cup white miso paste
- 6 tbsp honey or maple syrup
- 1 tbsp rice wine vinegar
- 1 tbsp butter
- 8 ounces thick-cut bacon

Instructions

1. Preheat the air-fryer to 390 degrees Fahrenheit.

2. Take a small saucepan. Butter is then melted over normal heat. Then increase it to medium-high and add the miso paste, rice wine vinegar and honey. Stir until all the ingredients are combined completely and put the mixture to a boil. Set aside by Removing it from the heat.

3. The maple glaze is brushed over bacon.

4. Put the bacon in the air-fryer in a single layer and fry for almost 4 mins on every side. Take a pastry brush, brush a layer of the miso glaze over a side of bacon and air fry for 1 more min. It should be sticky and crispy when it's done.

5. Candied the bacon on parchment paper.

10. Cheesy breakfast egg rolls

Cook Time: 10 mins, Prep Time: 30 mins, Difficulty: Medium, Serving: 12

Ingredients

- 1/2 cup shredded sharp cheddar cheese
- 1/2 cup shredded Monterey Jack cheese
- 1 tbsp chopped green onions

- 4 large eggs
- 1 tbsp 2% milk
- 1/4 tsp salt
- 1/8 tsp pepper
- 1 tbsp butter
- 12 egg roll wrappers
- 1/2 pound bulk pork sausage
- Cooking spray
- Maple syrup or salsa, optional

Instructions

1. Take a small pan(non-sticky), put the sausage over normal heat until it is no longer pink for almost 6 mins, breaking into crumbles; drain it. Stir in green onions and cheeses; put aside. Pan is then cleaned.

2. Take a small bowl, whisk eggs, salt, milk and pepper until it gets blended in the same pan, heat butter over normal heat. Put in the egg mixture; stir, and cook until the eggs are thick and no liquid remains. Stir in sausage.

3. Preheat the air-fryer at 400 degrees Fahrenheit. Put 1/4 cup of filling just under the middle of the wrapper. Fold the lower corner over the filling; moisten the remaining sides of the wrapper with water. Fold the side corners over the filling into the middle. Roll the egg firmly, pressing to secure the tip. Repeat this.

4. Arrange egg rolls in batches on a greased tray in the air-fryer basket in a single layer; spritz with cooking spray. Cook for almost 4 mins, until lightly browned. Turn; spritz with spray for cooking. Cook until crisp and golden brown for almost 4 mins longer.

5. Serve with maple syrup or salsa if needed.

12. Low-carb breakfast casserole

Cook Time: 15 mins, Prep Time: 10 mins, Difficulty: Medium, Serving: 6

Ingredients

- 8 whole eggs
- 1 lb ground sausage

- 1 diced green bell pepper

- 1/2 cup shredded cheese

- 1 tsp fennel seed

- 1/4 cup diced white onion

- 1/2 tsp garlic salt

Instructions

1. Put in the pepper and onion and cook along with the ground sausage until the sausage is cooked and the veggies are soft.

2. Using the Air-fryer pan, spray the pan with cooking spray(non-sticky).

3. Put the ground sausage on the bottom of the air-fryer pan.

4. Top with cheese.

5. Put the beaten eggs evenly over the sausage and cheese.

6. Add garlic salt and fennel seed over the eggs.

7. Put the rack in the Ninja Foodie, and then put the pan on top.

8. Set to Air Crisp for almost 15 mins at 390 degrees Fahrenheit.

9. If you are using the air-fryer, Put the plate directly into the basket of the air-fryer and cook for almost 15 mins at 390 degrees Fahrenheit.

10. Carefully remove and serve.

12. Air-fryer Donuts

Cook Time: 5 mins, Prep Time: 10 mins, Difficulty: Easy, Serving: 6

Ingredients

- 2 tsp cinnamon

- olive oil spray

- 4 tbsp butter (melted)

- 1/2 c. granulated white sugar

- 16 oz cold, flaky jumbo biscuits

Instructions

1. Take a shallow dish, combine the cinnamon and sugar, and set aside.

2. Take the biscuits out from the dish, separate them and put them on a surface flat enough. Slice holes out of the middle of every biscuit by Using a small round biscuit cutter.

3. Gently coat the air-fryer basket with coconut oil or olive oil spray. Please do not use the nonstick spray because it can destroy the coating on the basket.

4. Put 4 donuts in a single layer in the air-fryer basket. Make sure they are not in contact.

5. Air Fry at 360 degrees Fahrenheit for almost 5 mins or until crispy or lightly browned.

6. Remove donuts from the Air-fryer, Roll in cinnamon sugar to coat, then dip in melted butter.

7. Immediately serve.

13. Air-fryer Breakfast Sausage

Cook Time: 10 mins, Prep Time: 10 mins, Difficulty: Easy, Serving: 5

Ingredients

- 2 tsp dry rubbed sage
- 2 tsp garlic powder
- 2 tsp fennel seeds
- 1 tsp paprika
- 1 lb ground turkey
- 1 tsp sea salt
- 1 lb ground pork

- 1 tbsp maple syrup

- 1 tsp dried thyme

Instructions

1. Mix the turkey and pork in a large bowl. Take a small bowl, mix the remaining ingredients: fennel, salt, sage, paprika, garlic powder and thyme. Pour spices into the meat and mix completely.

2. Spoon into balls (almost 2-3 tbsp of meat), and make them into patties. Put inside the air-fryer. It will be done in 2 different batches.

3. Set the temperature of the air-fryer to 370 degrees Fahrenheit, and cook for almost 10 mins. Remove and repeat with the rest of the sausage.

14. Wake up Air-fryer avocado boats

Cook Time: 5 mins, Prep Time: 10 mins, Difficulty: Easy, Serving: 4

Ingredients

- 2 plum tomatoes, seeded and diced

- 2 tbsps chopped fresh cilantro

- 1 tbsp finely diced jalapeno (optional)

- 1 tbsp lime juice

- 4 eggs

- 1/2 tsp salt

- 1/4 cup diced red onion

- 1/4 tsp black pepper

- 2 avocados, halved and pitted

Instructions

1. Scoop the pulp of the avocado out of the skin by using a spoon, keeping the shell intact. Take a medium bowl and diced avocado in it. Toss with tomato, jalapeno, onion, cilantro, salt, lime juice, and pepper. Cover and cool avocado mixture until ready to use.

2. Preheat the air-fryer to 350 degrees Fahrenheit.

3. Put them on a ring of foil to ensure that the avocado shells do not rock when cooking. Roll two 3-inch-wide strips of aluminum foil into shapes of rope, and form each into a 3-inch circle. In an air-fryer basket, put each avocado shell on a foil ring. Break 1 egg into every avocado shell and cook for almost 7 mins or until done.

4. Remove from the basket; top with salsa with avocado and serve.

15. Quick Air-fryer breakfast pockets

Cook Time: 10 mins, Prep Time: 10 mins, Difficulty: Easy, Serving: 2

Ingredients

- One box puff pastry sheet
- 5 eggs
- 1/2 cup bacon
- 1/2 cup cheddar cheese
- 1/2 cup sausage crumbles

Instructions

1. Cook eggs as normal scrambled eggs. While you cook, Add meat to the egg mixture, if needed.

2. Put puff pastry sheets on a cutting board and cut out pieces with a knife or cookie cutter, making sure they are all the same.

3. Spoon meat, egg and cheese combos onto half of the pastry.

4. Cover the mixture with a slice of pastry and press the sides together with a fork to seal.

5. For a shiny, smooth pastry, spray it with spray oil, but it's optional.

6. In the air-fryer basket, put breakfast pockets and cook at 370 degrees Fahrenheit for almost 10 mins.

7. Carefully observe and review for desired done-ness every 3 mins.

16. Air-fryer breakfast potatoes

Cook Time: 25 mins, Prep Time: 15 mins, Difficulty: Medium, Serving: 2

Ingredients

- 1/2 tsp paprika
- 1/4 onion
- 1 green bell pepper
- 2 garlic cloves
- 1 tbsp olive oil
- 1/4 tsp pepper
- 1/2 tsp salt
- 1 1/2 pounds potatoes

Instructions

1. Clean potatoes and bell pepper.

2. Dice the potatoes and put them in water for almost 30 mins. After 30 mins, pat dry.

3. Chop bell pepper, onion and potatoes. Mince garlic.

4. Take a large bowl and mix the ingredients in it. Put in the air-fryer.

5. Cook in the air-fryer at 400 degrees Fahrenheit for almost 10 mins. Shake and cook for 10 mins more. Shake again and cook for 5 mins more. The total cook time will be almost 25 mins.

6. Serve.

17. Breakfast Egg Rolls Air-fryer

Cook Time: 10 mins, Prep Time: 15 mins, Difficulty: Easy, Serving: 3

Ingredients

- 2 Tbsp milk
- Salt
- Pepper
- 1/2 cup cheddar cheese
- 2 sausage patties
- 6 egg roll wrappers
- 2 eggs
- 1 Tbsp olive oil
- water

Instructions

1. Cook the sausage in a small pan. Remove and cut into bite-sized pieces.

2. Mix milk, eggs, a pinch of salt and pepper. Over medium/low pressure, apply 1 tsp of oil or a tiny pat of butter to the plate. Pour in the mixture of eggs and cook for a few mins, often mixing to produce scrambled eggs. Stir the sausage in.

3. Put egg roll wrapper on a work surface with points. Put about 1 tsp of cheese. Top with a mixture of the egg.

4. Wet a pastry brush and brush every edge of the egg roll wrapper. It will seal it.

5. Fold the egg roll wrapper up and over the filling at the bottom stage, attempting to keep it as close as you can. Then, fold the sides together to make an envelope-looking shape. Last, tie the whole wrapping around the top. Place the

   side of the seam down and begin assembling the remaining rolls.

6. Preheat the air-fryer to 400 degrees Fahrenheit for almost 5 mins.

7. Brush rolls with spray or oil them. Put in a preheated basket. Set to 400 degrees Fahrenheit for almost 8 mins.

8. After 5 mins, turn the egg rolls over. Take egg rolls to the air-fryer again for 3 mins.

9. Serve and enjoy.

18. Air-fryer-egg in a hole

Cook Time: 10 mins, Prep Time: 5 mins, Difficulty: Easy, Serving: 1

Ingredients

- 1 egg
- salt and pepper
- 1 piece of toast

Instructions

1. Spray the air-fryer safe pan with cooking spray(non-sticky).

2. Put a piece of bread down inside the air-fryer safe pan.

3. Make a hole with a cookie cutter and remove the bread.

4. Crack open the egg into the bread's hole.

5. Air Fry at 330 degrees Fahrenheit for almost 6 mins, then flip the egg using a spatula, and air fry for another 4 mins.

19. Air-fryer sausage breakfast casserole

Cook Time: 20 mins, Prep Time: 6 mins, Difficulty: Medium, Serving: 10

Ingredients

- 1 lb ground breakfast sausage
- 1 red bell pepper diced
- 1 yellow bell pepper diced

- 1/4 cup sweet onion diced
- 1 lb hash browns
- 4 eggs
- 1 green bell pepper diced

Instructions

1. Foil line the basket of the air-fryer.
2. Put the hash browns on the bottom.
3. Top it with the uncooked sausage.
4. Evenly put the peppers and onions on top.
5. Cook at 355 degrees Fahrenheit for almost 10 mins.
6. Open the air-fryer and mix up the casserole, if desired.
7. Crack every egg in a bowl, then pour on top of the casserole.
8. Cook on 355 degrees Fahrenheit for another 10 mins.
9. Serve with pepper and salt to taste.

20. Air-fryer French toast sticks recipe

Cook Time: 12 mins, Prep Time: 5 mins, Difficulty: Easy, Serving: 12

Ingredients

- 2 tbsp butter
- 2 eggs (gently beaten)
- 1 pinch salt
- 1 pinch cinnamon
- 1 pinch nutmeg
- 1 pinch ground cloves
- 4 pieces bread
- 1 tsp icing sugar

Instructions

1. Preheat the Airfryer to 356 degrees Fahrenheit.

2. Take a bowl, slowly beat together 2 eggs, a few heavy shakes of cinnamon, a sprinkle of salt, and small pinches of both ground cloves and nutmeg.

3. Butter each side of bread slices and cut into pieces.

4. Dredge every strip in the mixture of egg and put in Air-fryer (in 2 batches).

5. After 2 mins of cooking, take out the pan, spray the cooking spray over the bread.

6. Once coated the strips, flip and spray the other side as well.

7. Take a pan to the fryer and cook for almost 4 more mins, checking after 2 mins to ensure they are not burning.

8. When it is cooked and bread is crispy or brown, take it out from Air-fryer and serve.

21. Air-fryer sweet potato hash

Cook Time: 15 mins, Prep Time: 10 mins, Difficulty: Easy, Serving: 6

Ingredients

- 2 slices bacon, cut into small pieces
- 2 tbsps olive oil
- 1 tbsp smoked paprika
- 1 tsp sea salt
- 1 tsp ground black pepper
- 2 large sweet potato
- 1 tsp dried dill weed

Instructions

1. Preheat the air-fryer to 400 degrees Fahrenheit.

2. Put the sweet potato, salt, olive oil, bacon, paprika, pepper, and dill in a large bowl. Put the mixture into the preheated air-fryer. Cook for almost 16 mins. Check and stir after almost 10 mins and then after every 3 mins until browned and crispy.

22. Air-fryer Bacon

Cook Time: 15 mins, Prep Time: 5 mins, Difficulty: Easy, Serving: 11

Ingredient

- ½ (16 ounces) package bacon

Instructions

1. Preheat the air-fryer to 390 degrees Fahrenheit.

2. Put bacon in the air-fryer basket in a single layer; some of the overlaps are okay.

3. Fry for almost 8 mins. Flip and continue cooking until bacon is brown and crisp, for about 7 mins. Move cooked bacon to a dish lined with paper towels to absorb excess grease.

4. Serve and enjoy.

23. Air-Fried Cinnamon and Sugar Doughnuts

Cook Time: 8 mins, Prep Time: 15 mins, Difficulty: Medium, Serving: 12

Ingredients

- 2 ½ tbsps butter
- 2 large egg yolks
- 2 ¼ cups purpose flour
- 1 ½ tsps baking powder
- 1 tsp salt
- ½ cup sour cream

- ⅓ cup white sugar

- 1 tsp cinnamon

- ½ cup white sugar

- 2 tbsps butter, melted

Instructions

1. Press butter and 1/2 cup white sugar together in a bowl until crumbly. Add egg

   yolks in the mixture and stir until well mixed.

2. Sift baking powder, flour, and salt into another bowl. Put 1/2 the sour cream and 1/3 of the flour mixture into the sugar-egg mixture; stir until combined. Mix in the sour cream and remaining flour. Cool the dough until ready to use.

3. Mix cinnamon and 1/3 cup sugar in a bowl.

4. Roll the dough to a 1/2-inch thickness on a well-floured work surface. Break the dough into 9 wide circles; cut a tiny circle from the middle of each large circle to build the shape of a doughnut.

5. Preheat the air-fryer to 350 degrees Fahrenheit.

6. Brush the melted butter over both sides of the doughnuts.

7. Put half doughnuts into the basket of the air-fryer; cook for almost 8 mins. Brush cooked donuts with the rest of the melted butter and dip into the cinnamon-sugar mixture immediately. Repeat with the rest of the doughnuts.

24. Air-fryer Breakfast Frittata

Cook Time: 8 mins, Prep Time: 15 mins, Difficulty: Easy, Serving: 2

Ingredients

- 4 eggs, lightly beaten

- ½ cup shredded Cheddar-Monterey Jack cheese blend

- 2 tbsp red bell pepper
- 1 green onion, chopped
- ¼ pound breakfast sausage
- 1 pinch cayenne pepper
- cooking spray

Instructions

1. Combine sausage, Cheddar-Monterey Jack cheese, eggs, onion, bell pepper and cayenne in a large bowl and mix to combine.
2. Preheat the air-fryer to 360 degrees Fahrenheit. Spray a cake pan with cooking spray.
3. Put the egg mixture in the cake pan already prepared.
4. Cook in the air-fryer until frittata is done, for almost 20 mins.

25. Air-fryer tofu

Cook Time: 15 mins, Prep Time: 15 mins, Difficulty: Easy, Serving: 4

Ingredients

- Black firm tofu
- 2 tbsp Soy sauce
- 1 tbs Olive oil
- 1 tbsp Sesame oil
- 1 Garlic clove

Instructions

1. Push the tofu for at least 14 mins, using either a hardpan or placing it on top, enabling the moisture to drain away. When done, bite-sized chunks of tofu are cut and moved to a dish.
2. In a tiny cup, combine all the leftover ingredients. Drizzle and throw over the tofu to coat. Let the tofu marinate for 15 more minutes.

3. Heat the air-fryer to 374 degrees Fahrenheit. In a single layer, apply tofu blocks to the Air Fryer bowl. Cook for 15 minutes, frequently shaking the pan to facilitate frying. Before transferring a rack to them, let the muffins cool a bit in the baking pan to cool completely.

26. Tex-Mex Air-fryer Hash Browns

Cook Time: 30 mins, Prep Time: 15 mins, Difficulty: Medium, Serving: 4

Ingredients

- 1 tbsp olive oil
- 1 red bell pepper
- 1 small onion
- 1 jalapeno
- ½ tsp olive oil
- ½ tsp taco seasoning mix
- ½ tsp ground cumin
- 1 ½ pounds potatoes
- 1 pinch salt and black pepper

Instructions

1. Soak the potatoes in cold water for almost 20 mins.

2. Preheat the air-fryer to 320 degrees Fahrenheit. Drain the potatoes, dry them with a towel (it should be clean), and put them in a large bowl. Put 1 tbsp olive oil over the potatoes and toss to coat. Add them to the preheated air-fryer basket. Cook for almost 18 mins.

3. Put bell pepper, jalapeno and onion in the bowl already used for the potatoes. Sprinkle in salt, 1/2 tsp olive oil, ground cumin, taco seasoning and pepper. Toss to coat.

4. Move potatoes from the air-fryer to the vegetable mixture bowl. Put the empty basket in the air-fryer and increase the temperature to 356 degrees Fahrenheit.

5. Toss the contents of the bowl easily to combine the potatoes equally with the vegetables and season. Move the mixture to the basket. Shake the basket, cook for 6 minutes and finish cooking until the potatoes are browned and crispy, around 5 more mins.

6. Serve immediately.

27. Easy Air-fryer French toast

Cook Time: 10 mins, Prep Time: 15 mins, Difficulty: Easy, Serving: 4

Ingredients

- Parchment paper
- 2 eggs, lightly beaten
- 4 slices thick bread (staled slightly)
- 1 tsp vanilla extract
- ¼ cup milk
- 1 tsp cinnamon
- 1 pinch nutmeg

Instructions

1. Cut every slice of bread to build sticks of bread. Cut a tiny piece of parchment paper to place at the bottom of the air-fryer basket.

2. Preheat the air-fryer to 365 degrees Fahrenheit.

3. Take a bowl, add the eggs, milk, vanilla extract, cinnamon, and nutmeg until well mixed. Dip each slice of bread into a mixture of eggs to ensure that each piece is well dipped. To remove excess fluid, shake each breadstick and place it in a single layer in the air-fryer basket. To avoid overcrowding the fryer, cook in batches, if possible.

4. Cook for almost 5 mins, turn bread pieces and cook again for almost 5 mins.

28. Air-fryer Sausage Patties

Cook Time: 8 mins, Prep Time: 10 mins, Difficulty: Easy, Serving: 5

Ingredients

- 1 serving nonstick cooking spray
- 1 package sausage patties

Instructions

1. Preheat the air-fryer to 400 degrees Fahrenheit.

2. Put sausage patties in a single layer into the air-fryer basket, working in batches, if needed.

3. Cook in the preheated air-fryer for almost 5 mins. Take the basket out, turn sausage over, and cook until a thermometer (instant-read) inserted into the patty center reads 160 degrees Fahrenheit, about 3 mins more.

29. Air-fried banana cake

Cook Time: 8 mins, Prep Time: 15 mins, Difficulty: Easy, Serving: 4

Ingredients

- ⅓ Cup brown sugar
- 3 ½ tbsps butter
- 1 banana, mashed
- 1 egg
- 2 tbsps honey
- 1 cup self-rising flour
- Cooking spray

- ½ tsp ground cinnamon
- 1 pinch salt

Instructions

1. Use a cooking spray to spray a tiny fluted tube pan.

2. Set the air-fryer temperature to 320 degrees Fahrenheit.

3. Take a bowl and beat butter and sugar together using an electric mixer until it gets creamy. Combine egg, banana and honey in another bowl. Whisk banana mixture into butter mixture until smooth.

4. Sift salt, cinnamon and flour into the mixture of banana-butter. Mix batter until smooth. Move to the prepared pan; By using the back of a spoon, level the surface.

5. Put the cake pan in the air-fryer basket. Slide the basket into the air-fryer and set the timer for almost 30 mins. Bake until a toothpick put into the cake comes out clean.

30. Crispy air-fryer breakfast burritos

Cook Time: 10 mins, Prep Time: 40 mins, Difficulty: Easy, Serving: 1

Ingredients

- 2 tbsp avocado oil
- 1 tbsp arrowroot powder
- 2 tsps paprika
- 1 tsp garlic powder
- 1/2 tsp onion powder
- 7–8 burrito size (10 inches) tortillas
- 1 pound russet
- 1 tsp salt
- 1/2 tsp black pepper
- 1 cup shredded cheddar cheese

- 1 pound breakfast seasoned ground pork

- 1 (4 ounces) can dice green chilies

- 8 large eggs, whisked

- 2 tbsp milk of choice

- 1/2 tsp salt & pepper

- Hot sauce, salsa, sour cream

Instructions

1. Bring the potatoes together: Preheat the oven to 425 degrees Fahrenheit. Take a silicone baking liner, place the diced potatoes on it. Pour oil, paprika, arrowroot powder, onion powder, garlic powder, salt and pepper on top of the potatoes and mix until the potatoes are thinly coated. Put in the oven and roast it for almost 30 mins in all, stirring halfway through the potatoes. Prepare the other fillings as the potatoes boil in the oven.

2. Make the ground sausage: Over medium, prepare, heat a nonstick plate. To split the meat into tiny pieces when it heats, incorporate ground pork and use a wooden spoon or spatula. Cook the beef, stirring regularly, for around 6-7 mins or until it is cooked through. Apply the green chilies, then whisk until they are combined.

3. Make your eggs: reduce the heat to medium-low. In a medium dish, combine the milk, salt and pepper with the eggs. Cook the meat in the same pan and apply 1 tbs of butter or ghee. Add the eggs to the pan until they have warmed. Holding the heat low, begin using a spatula to transfer the eggs until they thicken and cook through. Switch off the air-fryer and transfer the eggs to a cup.

4. Assemble burritos: Use your tortillas, fried ground sausage, scrambled eggs, and shredded cheddar cheese to prepare a burrito assembly station. For each burrito number, apply * up to* 1 and 1/2 cups of filling. Roughly use 1/2 cup beef, 1/3 cup potatoes, 1/4 cup scrambled eggs,

and a big pinch of shredded cheese with each burrito. The burritos should not overfill.

5. Wrap burritos: Wrap and cover tortillas in a tight and safe burrito that keeps all the filling inside (see pictures above to help). Phase 1: Draw each end of the filling over the sides of the tortilla until secure. Phase 2: Draw the bottom of the tortilla up and over the filling with your thumbs, covering the sides that you folded over in Step 1. Phase 3: Tuck the underside of the tortilla you folded into the burrito in Step 2, tucking the sides from the tortilla's top and bottom as well. Phase 4: Arrange the burrito such that it protects the tucked sides and bottom over the remaining exposed tortilla.

6. Fry the burritos in the air: Placing 2 burritos carefully into the air-fryer basket. Fry for 6-10 minutes at 350F, or until the burritos are crispy and golden brown. Pamper yourself with salsa, ice cream, chili sauce, etc.

7. Prepare & reheat the freezer: Obey the recipe through phase 5 and place the burritos for up to 4 days in an airtight jar in the fridge. Air fried cold burritos with

   325F avocado spray oil spritz for 14-16 minutes or until brown and crispy golden.

8. Prep & reheat freezer: Follow the recipe through phase 5, then let the burritos cool thoroughly on the counter for at least 30 minutes. Place burritos in an airtight jar in the freezer for up to 3 months (wrap them individually if you prefer). For 30 minutes, air fried frozen burritos with a spritz of avocado spray oil at 250F, then raise the temperature to 350F and air fry for 2-3 more minutes until golden brown and crispy.

Chapter No. 3: Snacks and Appetizers

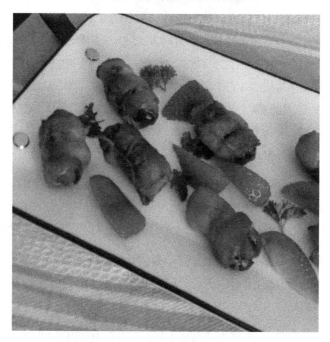

1. Prosciutto wrapped brie

Cook Time: 25 mins, Prep Time: 10 mins, Difficulty: Medium, Serving: 6

Ingredients

- 4 ounces Prosciutto, thinly sliced
- 2 tbsps Sugar-Free Preserves
- 1 Double Brie Cheese Wheel, small

Instructions

1. Put four slices of the Prosciutto in a 5-inch pan.

2. Put the other two slices the other way.

3. Cut the Brie in half, spread 1 tbs of sugar-free preserves on half, then put the rest back on and spread preserves on the top of it.

4. Six slices of bacon are used to Cover the Brie.

5. Bake at 400 degrees Fahrenheit for almost 20 mins, then broil for almost 3 mins.

6. Fig or raspberry preserves are used to make this dish.

7. Peach Chutney or Cranberry Chutney can be used in place of the preserves.

8. Prosciutto Wrapped Brie can be enjoyed with some bread, some low carb crackers, or even just eaten with a spoon or fork.

9. Do not try this with bacon, else only fresh bacon or overcooked Brie would be open. Both of them have somewhat different cooking times.

10. To make this happen in an air-fryer, set the air-fryer to 350 degrees Fahrenheit and carefully monitor it. The cheese is likely melting until you see the prosciutto crisping up. To keep the cheese in place, you would need to bring it into a small pan.

2. Queso fundido

Cook Time: 25 mins, Prep Time: 10mins, Difficulty: Medium, Serving: 12

Ingredients

- 4 ounces Mexican-style chorizo, casings removed

- 1 cup (149 g) diced tomatoes

- 1 tbs (1 tbs) Minced Garlic

- 1 cup (160 g) onions, chopped

- 2 cups grated Oaxaca cheese or Mozzarella

- 2 (2) jalapenos, diced

- 2 tsps (2 tsps) Ground Cumin

- ½ half and half

Instructions

1. Take a pan, mix the ground cumin, jalapenos, onion, garlic, tomatoes and chorizo. Put pan in the air-fryer basket.

2. Set the air-fryer to 400 degrees Fahrenheit for almost 15 mins or until cooked properly. Midway through cooking, stir the mixture with a spoon to break up the sausage.

3. Add the half and half and cheese and stir again.

4. Set the air-fryer to 320 degrees Fahrenheit for almost 10 mins until the cheese has melted.

5. Serve with chips or tortillas.

6. Cut the onions in half and use cherry tomatoes instead of normal tomatoes to help eliminate carbs.

3. Sweet and salty snack mix

Cook Time: 12 mins, Prep Time: 10 mins, Difficulty: Easy, Serving: 10

Ingredients

- 3 tbsp butter melted
- 1 tsp salt
- 1 cup pepitas pumpkin seeds
- 2 cups granola
- 2 cups sesame sticks
- 1 cup cashews
- 2 cups crispy corn puff cereal Kix or Corn Pops
- 2 cup mini pretzel crisps
- ½ cup honey

Instructions

1. Combine the butter, honey and salt. Stir until combined.

2. Take a large bowl, combine the sesame sticks, pepitas, cashews, corn puff cereal, and granola and pretzel crisps. The honey mixture is poured over the top and toss to combine.

3. Preheat the air-fryer to 370 degrees Fahrenheit.

4. Air fry the mixture in 2 batches. Put half the mixture in the air-fryer basket and air-fry for almost 12 mins, or until the mixture of snacks is lightly toasted. Throughout the process, toss the basket often to cooks evenly and doesn't get too dark on top.

5. Take a baking sheet, switch the snack mix and let it cool down. Put in an airtight jar for up to one week or package in gift bags for holiday gifts.

4. Air-fryer Tater Tots

Cook Time: 15 mins, Prep Time: 20 mins, Difficulty: Medium, Serving: 4

Ingredients

- 2 tsps all-purpose flour

- Cooking oil

- Optional spices/seasoning

- Salt and pepper

- 1 tsp garlic powder

- 1/4 tsp thyme

- 1 1/2 pounds russet potatoes

- 1 tsp smoked paprika

Instructions

1. Take a saucepan or pot and fill it 3/4 of the way with cold water, bring to a boil and add a pinch of salt. Add more water to cover the potatoes.

2. Add the potatoes and simmer for almost 6-12 mins. Pierce the potatoes on the outside and make sure that the inside of the potatoes is still firm.

3. Take the potatoes out from the water. Dry and allow them to cool. Wait about 10 mins for this procedure.

4. When the potatoes are cooled, use the cheese grater and grate the potatoes. Squeeze the remaining water from the potatoes.

5. Put the grated potatoes and the flour and seasonings in a bowl. Russet potatoes are bland. Make sure to taste the salt.

6. Stir to combine. The hands are used to create tots with the mixture. Larger or smaller tots can be made as you wish.

7. Spray the tots with cooking oil on both sides. Put the tots in an air-fryer. Air fry for 10 mins at 400 degrees Fahrenheit.

8. Open and flip the tots. Cook for an extra 5 mins or until the perfect crisp is reached by the tots.

5. Crispy Artichoke Hearts with Horseradish Aioli

Cook Time: 45 mins, Prep Time: 15 mins, Difficulty: Hard, Serving: 2

Ingredients

- 2 tbsps Olive Oil
- 1/2 tsp Homemade Seasoned Salt
- 1/4 tsp Black Pepper coarsely ground
- 3 cups frozen artichoke hearts
- 1 tbs lemon juice fresh squeezed

Instructions

1. Preheat the oven to 425 degrees Fahrenheit, the cookie sheet is lined on parchment paper.

2. Open the packet of frozen artichoke hearts; drizzle in lemon juice and olive oil; shake well to coat hearts. Sprinkle with black pepper and seasoned salt, toss it again to evenly mix.

3. Arrange seasoned artichoke hearts on a parchment-lined cookie sheet in a single layer and bake at 425 for 45 mins in the middle of the oven, stirring multiple times during baking, until slightly brown.

4. 4. Remove from the oven, and when they cool, the hearts will crisp up more. Move to a plate and serve with a dip of chilled horseradish sauce.

6. German Currywurst recipe

Cook Time: 12 mins, Prep Time: 5 mins, Difficulty: Easy, Serving: 4

Ingredients

- 2 tbsp vinegar
- 2 tsps curry powder
- 1/2 tsp Truvia, or 1 tsp sugar
- ¼ tsp cayenne pepper
- ½ cup diced onion
- 1 cup canned tomato sauce
- 1 pound bratwurst
- 2 tsps sweet paprika

Instructions

1. Take a 6 x 3 container, mix cayenne pepper, curry powder, vinegar, sugar, paprika, and tomato sauce. Stir the mixture in onions.

2. Cut the bratwurst into 1 inch thick pieces on the diagonal. Put bratwurst into the tomato sauce and stir the mixture well.

3. Place the pan in the air-fryer basket.

4. Set the air-fryer to 400F for 12 mins until the sausage is cooked and the sauce is bubbling.

7. Greek baked feta psiti

Cook Time: 10 mins, Prep Time: 5 mins, Difficulty: Easy, Serving: 4

Ingredients

- 2 tbsps olive oil
- 1 tbs crushed red pepper
- 1 tbsp Dried Oregano
- 2 tbsps Honey or Choczero Syrup for Keto
- 8 ounces Feta cheese in a block

Instructions

1. Cut the feta block (at the equator) in half and then cut every thinner slice half to yield 4 even pieces.
2. Put these on a serving dish.
3. Spread the cheese with olive oil, spread the oil evenly by using a silicone basting brush. Then sprinkle the oregano and red pepper flakes.
4. Top with honey. Spread the honey around evenly by using a silicone basting brush.
5. Put the dish in the air-fryer basket.
6. Set the air-fryer to 400 degrees Fahrenheit for almost 10 mins.
7. When done, take it out, spread any oil and honey using the same brush that has rendered to the bottom, and serve.

8. Air-fryer French toast sticks

Cook Time: 8 mins, Prep Time: 12 mins, Difficulty: Easy, Serving: 12

Ingredients

- 1 cup milk
- 5 large eggs
- 1 tsp. vanilla extract
- 1/4 cup granulated sugar
- 1 tbsp cinnamon

- 4 tbsp butter, melted
- Maple syrup, optional
- 12 slices Texas Toast

Instructions

1. Cut every bread slice into thirds.
2. Take a bowl, add the milk, butter, eggs, and vanilla. Whisk until combined.
3. Take a separate bowl, add the sugar and cinnamon.
4. Dip every breadstick into the mixture of eggs quickly.
5. Sprinkle the mixture of sugar onto both sides.
6. Put into the air-fryer basket and cook at 350 degrees Fahrenheit for almost 8 mins or until it gets crispy.
7. Take out from the basket and allow it to cool. According to taste, serve with maple syrup.

9. Bacon-wrapped avocado wedges

Cook Time: 15 mins, Prep Time: 15 mins, Difficulty: Medium, Serving: 12

Ingredients

- 12 bacon strips
- 1/2 cup mayonnaise
- 2 to 3 tbsps Sriracha chili sauce
- 1 to 2 tbsps lime juice
- 1 tsp grated lime zest
- 2 medium ripe avocados
- Powered by Chicory

Instructions

1. Preheat the air-fryer to 400 degrees Fahrenheit. Cut every avocado in half; remove the pit and peel. Cut each half into one third.

2. Wrap 1 bacon slice around every avocado wedge. If needed, work in batches, put wedges in a fryer basket in a single layer and cook until bacon is cooked through for almost 15 mins.

3. Simultaneously, take a small bowl, stir together mayonnaise, lime juice, sriracha sauce and zest.

4. Serve wedges with chili sauce.

10. Air-fryer ravioli

Cook Time: 10 mins, Prep Time: 20 mins, Difficulty: Easy, Serving: 12

Ingredients

- 1/4 cup shredded Parmesan cheese
- 2 tsps dried basil
- 1/2 cup all-purpose flour
- 2 large eggs, lightly beaten
- Cooking spray
- Fresh minced basil, optional
- 1 package (9 ounces) frozen beef ravioli
- 1 cup marinara sauce, warmed
- 1 cup seasoned bread crumbs
- Powered by Chicory

Instructions

1. Preheat the air-fryer to 350 degrees Fahrenheit. Take a shallow bowl, Parmesan cheese mix, basil and bread crumbs.

2. Put eggs and flour in separate shallow bowls. Coat both sides by Dipping ravioli in flour; shake off the mixture. Dip in eggs, then in a mixture of crumbs, pat it to help coat properly adhere.

3. Put ravioli on a greased tray in a single layer in the air-fryer basket (in batches); spritz with cooking spray. Cook until golden brown for almost 4 mins. Then spritz with cooking spray. Cook until golden brown for almost 4 mins longer. According to taste, sprinkle with additional Parmesan cheese and basil.

4. Serve warm with marinara sauce.

11. Air-fryer crumb-topped sole

Cook Time: 10 mins, Prep Time: 10 mins, Difficulty: Easy, Serving: 4

Ingredients

- 3 tbsps grated Parmesan cheese, divided
- 2 tsps mustard seed
- 4 sole fillets (6 ounces each)
- 1 cup soft bread crumbs
- 1 green onion, finely chopped
- 1/4 tsp pepper
- 1/2 tsp ground mustard
- 2 tsps butter, melted
- 3 tbsp reduced-fat mayonnaise
- Cooking spray
- Powered by Chicory

Instructions

1. Preheat the air-fryer to 375 degrees Fahrenheit. Combine mayonnaise, mustard seed, 2 tbsp cheese and pepper; spread over the tops of fillets.

2. Put fish on a greased tray in a single layer in the air-fryer basket. Cook until fish flakes with a fork easily, for almost 5 mins.

3. Simultaneously, take a small bowl, combine bread crumbs, ground mustard, onion and remaining 1 tbs cheese; stir in butter. Spoon the mixture over fillets, pat slowly to adhere, spritz the topping with cooking spray. Cook until it turns golden brown for almost 3 mins longer. If desired, sprinkle with green onions.

12. Air-fryer Greek breadsticks

Cook Time: 15 mins, Prep Time: 20 mins, Difficulty: Medium, Serving: 16

Ingredients

- 2 tbsps pitted Greek olives
- 1 package frozen puff pastry, thawed
- 1 carton spreadable spinach and artichoke cream cheese
- 2 tbsps grated Parmesan cheese
- 1 large egg
- 1 tbs water
- 2 tsps sesame seeds
- 1/4 cup marinated quartered artichoke hearts
- Refrigerated tzatziki sauce, optional
- Powered by Chicory

Instructions

1. Preheat the air-fryer to 325 degrees Fahrenheit. Place olives and artichokes in a food processor; cover and pulse until they get finely chopped. On a floured board, unfold a pastry sheet; place half the cheese over half of the pastry. Place half the artichoke mixture on top of that. Sprinkle the Parmesan cheese with half of it. Fold the plain half over the filling; press to seal softly.

2. Again do the same with the remaining pastry, artichoke mixture, cream cheese and Parmesan cheese. Whisk water and egg; brush over tops. Sprinkle with sesame seeds. Cut every rectangle into 16, 3/4-inches-wide strips. Twist several times.

3. Arrange the breadsticks in batches on a greased tray in an air-fryer basket in a single layer. Cook until it gets golden brown and crispy for almost 15 mins. If needed, serve warm with tzatziki sauce.

13. Crispy, Homemade Air-fryer Onion Rings

Cook Time: 10 mins, Prep Time: 15 mins, Difficulty: Medium, Serving: 4

Ingredients

- 1 1/2 cup panko breadcrumbs
- 1 cup buttermilk
- 1 egg (beaten)
- 1 cup flour
- 1 tsp smoked paprika
- 1 large Vidalia onion (peeled)
- 1 tsp garlic powder
- Salt and pepper
- Cooking oil spray
- Optional dipping sauce
- 1/3 cup mayo

- 1 1/2 -2 tbsps ketchup 1-2 tbsps creamy horseradish
- 1/2 tsp smoked paprika
- 1/2 tsp oregano
- Salt and pepper to taste

Instructions

1. Cooking oil is sprayed over the air-fryer basket.

2. Cut both sides of the onion stems. Cut the onion into rounds that are around 1/2 inch thick. There are unsafe onions. When chopping, be patient and use a mandolin if necessary. Before you slice, try to stabilize the onion.

3. Take a bowl large enough and add the flour to dredge onions. Season the flour with smoked paprika, salt, garlic powder and pepper according to taste.

4. Add the egg and buttermilk to seasoned flour. Beat and stir the mixture to combine.

5. Take a separate bowl large enough and add the panko breadcrumbs, which help dredge the onions properly

6. Dredge the sliced onions and then the panko breadcrumbs in the flour buttermilk mixture. Have your hands handy with a wet kitchen towel. They're

   starting to get sticky.

7. Take a plate and put the onion rings. Freeze the onion rings for 15 mins after breading the onions. It is optional, although strongly recommended, move. It helps maintain the intact breading.

8. Put the onions in an air-fryer. Don't leave them stacked. If required, cook in batches.

9. Spray with cooking oil.

10. Cook at 370 degrees Fahrenheit for almost 12 mins. Flip if necessary.

14. Air-fryer bacon wrapped chicken bites

Cook Time: 8 mins, Prep Time: 10 mins, Difficulty: Easy, Serving: 10

Ingredients

- 10 slices center-cut bacon
- Duck sauce
- 1.25 lbs, 3 boneless chicken breast, cut in 1-inch chunks (30 pieces)

Instructions

1. Preheat the air-fryer.
2. Wrap bacon around every piece of chicken and put a toothpick in it to secure it.
3. Air fry in an even layer at 400 degrees Fahrenheit for almost 8 mins(in batches), turning halfway until the bacon is browned and the chicken is cooked.
4. Blot on a paper towel.
5. Serve right away.

15. Air-fryer New York style egg rolls

Cook Time: 15 mins, Prep Time: 15 mins, Difficulty: Medium, Serving: 12

Ingredients

- 12 Egg Roll Wrappers
- 1 Egg
- 1 Oil Mister
- 1 cup Simple Sweet 'N Sour Sauce Recipe
- 4 cups Instant Pot Egg Roll Bowls
- 1 cup Hamburger Hamlet Secret Apricot

Instructions

1. Make a Dipping Sauce so that it has a chance for the flavors to mix. Take a small bowl, crack an egg in it and then whisk.

2. Use Egg Wash to Lightly moisten the Wrapper edges. To compact the filling, take a good one-third cup of Egg Roll filling and squeeze out excess liquid. Place the filling just slightly below the wrapper center.

3. Tuck underfilling and fold bottom point overfilling. Fold all sides in to make sure the first flap holds to them. Close up firmly and cover the wrapper with Egg Wash. Repeat until you have finished all the Egg Rolls.

4. Place the Egg Rolls Through the greased Air-fryer Basket. Spray the egg rolls generously with grease.

5. Cook for almost 10 mins at 390 degrees Fahrenheit, shaking the basket and turning halfway through, if necessary.

16. Air-Fryer Chickpea Fritters with Sweet-Spicy Sauce

Cook Time: 5 mins, Prep Time: 15 mins, Difficulty: Easy, Serving: 12

Ingredients

- 1 tbs honey
- 1/2 tsp salt
- 1/2 tsp pepper
- 1/2 tsp crushed red pepper flakes
- 2 tbsp sugar
- 1 can chickpeas
- 1 tsp ground cumin
- 1/2 tsp salt
- 1/2 tsp garlic powder
- 1/2 tsp ground ginger
- 1 large egg

- 1/2 tsp baking soda
- 1/2 cup chopped fresh cilantro
- 2 green onions, thinly sliced

Instructions

1. Preheat the air-fryer to 400 degrees Fahrenheit. Take a small bowl, combine the 1st 6 ingredients, cool by putting them in the refrigerator until serving.

2. Place seasonings and chickpeas in a food processor; process the mixture until finely ground. Add baking soda and egg; pulse until completely blended. Move

   to a bowl; stir in green onions and cilantro.

3. Put rounded tbsps mixture of beans onto a greased tray in the air-fryer basket(In batches). Cook until lightly browned, 5-6 mins. Serve with sauce.

17. Air-fryer taquitos

Cook Time: 15 mins, Prep Time: 20 mins, Difficulty: Medium, Serving: 10

Ingredients

- 1/2 cup dry bread crumbs
- 3 tbsp taco seasoning
- 1 pound lean ground beef (90% lean)
- 2 large eggs
- 10 corn tortillas (6 inches), warmed
- Cooking spray
- Optional: Salsa and guacamole

Instructions

1. Preheat the air-fryer to 350 degrees Fahrenheit. Take a large bowl, mix bread, crumb eggs and taco seasoning. Add beef; mix thoroughly and slowly.

2. Spoon 1/4 cup beef mixture down of each tortilla's center. Roll up tightly and put toothpicks in it to secure. Arrange taquitos in batches on a greased tray in the air-fryer basket in a single layer; spritz with cooking spray. Cook for almost 6 mins; turn and cook until meat is cooked through and taquitos are crispy and golden brown.

3. Remove the toothpicks, then serve. If desired, serve with guacamole and salsa.

18. Baked zucchini sticks

Cook Time: 25 mins, Prep Time: 10 mins, Difficulty: Medium, Serving: 4

Ingredients

- 4 medium, 7 oz each zucchini

- 3 large egg whites

- 1/4 tsp kosher salt

- Fresh black pepper

- 1 cup seasoned bread crumbs

- 1 tbsp Romano cheese (grated)

- 1/4 tsp garlic powder

- Cooking spray

- 1/2 cups quick marinara sauce

Instructions

1 Air-fryer the Zucchini Sticks.

2 Preheat the air-fryer 400 degrees Fahrenheit. Air fry in a single layer for almost 14 mins(in batches), turning halfway until it turns golden.

3 Serve and enjoy.

19. Air-fried ratatouille, Italian-style

Cook Time: 25 mins, Prep Time: 25 mins, Difficulty: Hard, Serving: 4

Ingredient

- 1 zucchini, cut into cubes
- 1 medium tomato, cut into cubes
- ½ large red bell pepper, cut into cubes
- ½ onion, cut into cubes
- 1 fresh cayenne pepper, diced
- 5 sprigs fresh basil, stemmed and chopped
- Sprigs fresh oregano stemmed and chopped
- ½ small eggplant, cut into cubes
- 1 clove garlic, crushed
- Salt and ground black pepper to taste
- 1 tbs olive oil
- 1 tbs white wine
- 1 tsp vinegar
- ½ large yellow bell pepper, cut into cubes

Instructions

1. Preheat the air-fryer to 400 degrees Fahrenheit.
2. Take a bowl and put eggplant, bell peppers, zucchini, tomato, and onion. Add cayenne pepper, pepper, oregano, basil, garlic, and salt. Mix to distribute all the things evenly. Drizzle in wine, oil and vinegar, mix for vegetable coating.
3. Pour the vegetable mixture into the baking dish and put it into the air-fryer basket. Cook for almost 8 mins. Stir; cook for an additional 8 mins. Stir again and begin to cook until crispy, stirring for another 15 minutes.

Switch the air-fryer off, keeping the dish inside. Leave to relax before serving for 5 mins.

20. Air-fryer acorn squash slices

Cook Time: 15 mins, Prep Time: 15 mins, Difficulty: Medium, Serving: 4

Ingredients

- 2/3 cup packed brown sugar

- 1/2 cup butter, softened

- Medium acorn squash

- Powered by chicory

Instructions

1 Preheat the air-fryer to 350 degrees Fahrenheit. Slice the squash lengthwise in half; cut and discard the seeds. Cut crosswise into 1/2-in each portion. Slices; discard ends. Arrange squash in a single layer (in batches) on a greased tray in an air-fryer basket. Cook until only warm, 5 minutes on each side.

2 Combine the butter and sugar; scatter on the squash. Cook for 3 minutes longer.

Chapter No.4: Poultry Recipes

1. Air-fryer Jalapeno Popper Stuffed Chicken

Cook Time: 12 mins, Prep Time: 10 mins, Difficulty: Easy, Serving: 12

Ingredients

- 125 g cream cheese
- 3 cloves garlic, minced
- 1/2 tsp onion powder
- 1/2 tsp chili powder
- 1/4 tsp fresh ground pepper
- 12 chicken thighs, boneless and skinless
- 1 tsp salt
- Oil Mixture
- 4 tbsp avocado oil
- 1/4 tsp chili powder

- 1/4 tsp onion powder
- 6 jalapenos, seeded and cut lengthwise

Instructions

1. Take a medium bowl, mix the cream cheese, onion powder, chili powder, salt, and pepper. Put aside.

2. The stem is removed from the jalapenos, slice them lengthwise, and take out the seeds.

3. A butter knife is used to add the cheese cream to every jalapeno halves as if you are placing butter on bread. The cream cheese mixture is Divided up between every jalapeno halves.

4. Roll out a chicken thigh piece, so it becomes as flat as possible. Put a jalapeno popper on the chicken piece and roll it up. Put a toothpick in it to hold it.

5. Repeat the procedure until all the ingredients are used up.

6. Take a small bowl, mix the ingredients used for the mixture of oil.

7. Brush the mixture of oil on each side of every piece of chicken.

8. Preheat oven to 400 degrees Fahrenheit.

9. Put the chicken pieces on a baking sheet and bake for almost 20 mins, flipping

   the chicken midway through cooking.

10. Place the chicken in the air-fryer basket in a single layer. If they don't all fit, do multiple batches.

11. Set the temp to 380 degrees Fahrenheit and the timer to almost 12 mins. Flip the chicken midway through the cooking time.

12. Store leftovers for cooling in the fridge for almost 4 days.

2. Crispy Air-fryer Chicken Breast

Cook Time: 10 mins, Prep Time: 10 mins, Difficulty: Easy, Serving: 4

Ingredients

- ½ cup bread crumbs (dried)
- ¼ tsp dried chili powder
- ¼ tsp ground black pepper
- ½ tsp paprika
- ¼ tsp garlic powder
- 1 tbsp olive oil
- 2 big boneless chicken breasts
- ¼ tsp cayenne pepper
- ¼ tsp onion powder
- ½ tsp salt

Instructions

1. Put the chicken breasts in a big bowl and spray with oil. Make sure that they're well coated.
2. Take a shallow dish, mix the spices with the dried bread crumbs until well mixed.
3. Coat every chicken breast in the bread crumbs, and move it to the air-fryer basket.
4. Air fry in the air-fryer at 390 degrees Fahrenheit for almost 12 mins. After the first 7 mins, Open the air-fryer, turn the chicken to the other side, and then begin to cook. (Cook for approximately 3 mins, depending on the size of the chicken used).
5. Spray oil over the boneless, skinless chicken breasts, and season with your favorite seasonings.
6. Put the seasoned chicken breasts in the Air-fryer basket and air fry for almost 15 mins flipping midway through kitchen tongs.

7. When the cooking time is over, quickly remove the chicken from the air-fryer to dry out. Allow 5 mins to rest before serving.

3. Air fried turkey

Cook Time: 30 mins, Prep Time: 10 mins, Difficulty: Medium, Serving: 4

Ingredients

- Salt

- Pepper

- Sage

- Turkey breast

- Poultry seasoning

- Olive oil

- Seasonings are optional.

Instructions

1. Spray the turkey breast with olive oil, rub seasonings on the entire turkey breast and put it in the air-fryer basket.

2. Set your air-fryer to 325 degrees Fahrenheit (set the dial to the correct time).

3. Set the timer for almost 30 mins.

4. Flip the turkey breast after the timer went off and set the timer for another 15-30 mins.

5. Make sure the inner temp is 180 degrees Fahrenheit, let it sit for almost 15 mins,

6. slice and serve.

4. Air-fryer teriyaki chicken drumsticks

Cook Time: 20 mins, Prep Time: 30 mins, Difficulty: Easy, Serving: 6

Ingredients

- 6 chicken drumsticks
- 1 cup teriyaki sauce

Instructions

1. It is the easiest recipe ever. Mix the drumsticks with teriyaki sauce in a large size bag with a ziplock. Let marinate for almost 30 mins.

2. Preheat the air-fryer to 360 degrees Fahrenheit. Put drumsticks in a layer in the air-fryer basket and cook for almost 20 mins. Shake the basket during the cooking. Do this a few times.

3. Garnish with chopped green onions and sesame seeds.

5. Crispy air-fryer chicken wings recipe

Cook Time: 35 mins, Prep Time: 8 mins, Difficulty: Medium, Serving: 4

Ingredients

- 2 tsp Gluten-free baking powder
- 3/4 tsp Sea salt
- 1/4 tsp Black pepper
- 2 lb Chicken wings

Instructions

1. Take a large bowl, toss the wings with sea salt, baking powder and black pepper.

2. Grease the 2 racks of the air-fryer oven.

3. Put the chicken wings onto the racks or be in a single layer. (When using a basket, cook in 2 batches).

4. Put the basket or racks into the air-fryer and cook for almost 15 mins at 250 degrees Fahrenheit.

5. Flip over the wings and change the trays so that the top is on the bottom and vise-versa. Increase temp to 430 degrees Fahrenheit. Cook for almost 20 mins, until chicken wings, are crispy and done.

6. Air-fryer Peanut Chicken

Cook Time: 20 mins, Prep Time: 15 mins, Difficulty: Medium, Serving: 4

Ingredients

- 1/4 cup Creamy Peanut Butter
- 1 tbsp Sriracha Sauce
- 1 tbsp Soy Sauce
- 2 tbsp Thai sweet chili sauce
- 1 pound Bone-in Skin-on Chicken Thighs
- 2 tbsps lime juice
- 1 tsp Minced Garlic
- 1 tsp Minced Ginger
- 1/2 tsp Kosher Salt, to taste
- 1/2 cup hot water
- 5-6 tsps Cilantro
- 1/4 cup Chopped Green Scallions
- 2-3 tbsps crushed peanuts

Instructions

1. Mix soy sauce, peanut butter, sriracha, lime juice, sweet chili sauce and salt. Put in hot water and mix until you have a smooth mixture.

2. Put the chicken in a bag with a zip-top. Put in half of the sauce and stir until the chicken is well coated. If there is time, allow the chicken to marinate for almost 30 mins or up to 24 hours by putting it in the refrigerator.

3. Take the chicken from the bag and keep as much of the marinade as possible with it. In the air-fryer basket, put the coated chicken.

4. Set the air-fryer to 350 degrees Fahrenheit for almost 22 mins or until the chicken thighs are heated 165 degrees Fahrenheit at their thickest part.

5. Garnish with onion, cilantro and peanuts.

6. Serve with the remaining sauce for dipping.

7. Brazilian chicken

Cook Time: 25 mins, Prep Time: 5 mins, Difficulty: Medium, Serving: 4

Ingredients

- 1 tsp Dried Oregano
- 1 tsp Dried Parsley
- 1 tsp Turmeric
- 1 tsp Kosher Salt
- 1/2 tsp Coriander Seeds
- 1/2 tsp Whole Black Peppercorns
- 1/2 tsp Cayenne Pepper
- 1 tsp cumin seeds
- 1/4 cup lime juice
- 2 tbsps Oil
- 1.5 pounds chicken drumsticks

Instructions

1. Take a clean coffee grinder, blend the cumin, parsley, peppercorns, oregano, turmeric, coriander seeds, kosher salt and cayenne pepper.

2. Take a medium bowl, mix the ground spices with the oil and lime juice. Add the chicken drumsticks and turn them, coating well with the marinade. Allow the chicken to marinade for almost 30 mins or up to 24 hours by putting it in the refrigerator.

3. When ready to cook, put the chicken legs into the air-fryer basket, skin side up.

4. Set your air-fryer to 390 degrees Fahrenheit for almost 25 mins for the meaty chicken legs. Midway through, turn the chicken legs over.

5. A thermometer is used to make sure that the chicken has reached an inner temp of 165 degrees Fahrenheit.

6. Remove and serve with plenty of napkins.

8. Tandoori Chicken - Air-fryer

Cook Time: 15 mins, Prep Time: 1 hr 25 mins, Difficulty: Medium, Serving: 4

Ingredients

- 1 tbsp Oil
- 2 tbsp Cilantro leaves
- 5 Chicken Drumsticks
- 4 Lemon wedges
- 1/4 cup Yogurt thick
- 1 tbsp Garlic paste
- 1 tbsp Ginger paste
- 1/2 tsp Turmeric
- 1 tsp Ground Cumin
- 1 tsp Red Chili powder
- 1 tbsp Dried Fenugreek leaves
- 1 tsp salt
- 1/2 tsp Masala (Garam)
- 1 tbsp Lime juice

Instructions

1. Make 3 to 4 slits on every drumstick.

2. Mix all ingredients for the marinade.

3. Apply the chicken drumsticks evenly and let them marinate for almost 1 hour by putting them in the refrigerator (can keep it cool in the refrigerator for up to 10 hours).

4. Remove marinated chicken from the refrigerator when ready to cook. Put in a single layer in the pan or basket of the air-fryer. Baste it with a little cooking oil.

5. Cook in air-fryer at 360 degrees Fahrenheit for almost 10 mins. Baste with oil and flip over the chicken. Then cook for another 5 mins.

6. Put on a serving plate.

7. Serve with sliced onion and lemon wedges.

9. Basic Air-fryer Chicken Breasts

Cook Time: 11 mins, Prep Time: 4 mins, Difficulty: Easy, Serving: 2

Ingredients

- 1 tbsp olive oil
- 1 pinch salt
- 1 tsp garlic powder
- 2 chicken breasts
- 1 tsp paprika

Instructions

1. Rub the olive oil onto the chicken breasts, then cover them with garlic powder, salt and paprika mixture.

2. Put into the air-fryer, ensure there is little space between them.

3. Set the air-fryer to 400 degrees Fahrenheit and cook for almost 7 mins then flip the chicken and cook for another 4 mins.

10. Air-fryer Chic-fil Chicken Nuggets

Cook Time: 14 mins, Prep Time: 10 mins, Difficulty: Medium, Serving: 4

Ingredients

- 1 cup pickle juice
- 1 large egg
- 3 tbsp milk
- 3/4 cup all-purpose flour
- 3 tbsp corn starch
- 2 tbsp powdered sugar
- 1 1/2 tsp salt
- 3/4 tsp paprika
- 1/4 tsp black pepper
- 1/4 tsp garlic powder
- 1/4 tsp onion powder
- oil for spraying
- 2 6 oz chicken breast

Instructions

1. Put pickle juice and chicken pieces in a plastic bag. Close the bag and put it for cooling in the refrigerator for almost 30 mins.

2. Simultaneously, take a shallow bowl mix together milk and egg.

3. Take another bowl, whisk together flour, paprika, corn starch, garlic powder, salt, onion powder and black pepper. Set Aside.

4. Remove pieces of chicken from the refrigerator. Grease the Air-fryer basket with some oil. Coat the chicken parts in the mixture of the milk, then coat them in the mixture of the flour, then shake off any extra flour and place it in the basket. Repeat until the air-fryer basket's bottom is full. Be sure that none of the pieces overlap or are touched.

5. Close the air-fryer basket and cook at 360 degrees Fahrenheit for almost 12 mins, flipping midway. Spray any flour spots during flipping.

6. After almost 12 mins, increase the heat to 400 degrees Fahrenheit and cook for an additional 2 mins.

7. Remove and serve with any favorite dipping sauce.

11. Buffalo chicken egg rolls

Cook Time: 10 mins, Prep Time: 15 mins, Difficulty: Easy, Serving: 12

Ingredients

- 1.5 cups Shredded Chicken
- 1/2 cup Buffalo Wing Sauce
- 4 oz. Cream Cheese softened
- 1/2 cup Blue Cheese Crumbles
- 1/2 cup Cheddar Cheese shredded
- 12 Egg Roll Wrappers
- 2 Green Onions finely chopped
- Blue Cheese Dressing optional

Instructions

1. Take a large bowl, mix blue cheese crumbles, buffalo wing sauce, cream cheese and cheddar cheese until combined well. Stir in chopped green and onions shredded chicken. Mix them well.

2. Assemble egg rolls utilizing around 2 tsps of filling for each egg roll, following the egg roll packaging directions.

3. Put egg rolls in the air-fryer basket, leave a little space b/w the egg rolls. Spray with cooking spray (non-sticky).

4. Cook in the air-fryer at 370 degrees Fahrenheit for almost 10 mins, flipping midway through cook time.

5. Serve the dish hot with blue cheese dressing.

12. State Fair Air-fryer Chicken Tender "hot dogs" (with homemade soy-free hot dog buns!)

Cook Time: 15 mins, Prep Time: 15 mins, Difficulty: Easy, Serving: 1

Ingredients

- 1 cup of Buttermilk
- 1½ cup of Gluten-Free Breadcrumbs
- 1 tsp of Celery Salt
- ½ tsp of Garlic Powder
- ½ tsp of Onion Powder
- ¼ tsp of cayenne
- ½ tsp of crushed black pepper
- 3 tbsps of Honey
- 2 tsp of Yellow Mustard
- 2 tsp of Stoneground Mustard
- 1.25 lb. of Chicken Tenderloins
- ¼ cup of diced Red Onion
- 8 Homemade Gluten-free Hot Dog Buns

Instructions

1. Soak the chicken tenders in buttermilk for almost 15 mins.
2. Take a bowl, combine the breadcrumbs, garlic powder, celery salt, cayenne, onion powder and black pepper. Whisk it well.
3. Pick up a chicken tender, remove the extra buttermilk & dip in the breadcrumbs. Keep it aside on a different plate.
4. Repeat with the rest of the tenders.
5. Put a few pieces, in a single layer, in the slightly greased air-fryer basket. Spray the cooked tenders lightly.

6. Air fry at 370 degrees Fahrenheit for almost 15 mins, flipping at the midway mark.

7. Repeat with every prepared chicken tenders.

8. While they are air frying, take a small bowl, combine yellow mustard, honey and whisk it well.

9. To serve: Cut open the hot dog buns lengthwise that are warm.

10. Put in the air-fried chicken tender and top with the honey mustard ready and the red onion diced.

11. Serve immediately.

12. Air-fryer Cornish hen

Cook Time: 25 mins, Prep Time: 5 mins, Difficulty: Medium, Serving: 2

Ingredients

- Salt
- Black pepper
- Paprika
- 1 Cornish hen
- Coconut spray or olive oil spray

Instructions

1. Rub the spices on Cornish hen. Spray the Air-fryer basket with olive or coconut oil spray.

2. Place the Cornish hen in the Air-fryer at 390 degrees Fahrenheit for almost 25 mins. Turn midway through.

3. Take it out carefully and serve.

14. Air-fryer Cheesy Chicken Tenders

Cook Time: 30 mins, Prep Time: 15 mins, Difficulty: Medium, Serving: 3

Ingredients

- 1/4 tsp. paprika
- Olive Oil as Cooking Spray
- 1/2 tsp onion powder
- 2 lbs. Boneless Chicken Tenders (thawed)
- 2 cups 2% Milk
- 2 cups cheese crackers

Instructions

1. Take a bowl, soak the chicken tenders cover them with milk for almost one hour. It can be soaked all day or overnight while you are working.

2. Take a food chopper and Pulverize the crackers in it.

3. Put the crushed cheese crackers into a large size resealable bag.

4. Add the crackers with the seasonings and shake to mix.

5. Drain the chicken tenders.

6. Put about 2 to 3 tenders with the cracker mixture in the bag at a time and shake them to cover.

7. Put these coated tenders into the Air-fryer basket.

8. Spritz each one with the cooking spray.

9. Set the temp to 400 degrees Fahrenheit.

10. Set the timer for almost 12 mins and then cook.

11. After the first 12 mins, check the tenders, turn over, and spray this side with the cooking spray.

12. Continue to cook for another 15 mins and check every 3 mins.

13. Check the inner temp, which should be 165 degrees Fahrenheit.

14. Serve with any favorite dipping sauce and enjoy.

15. Air-fryer Rotisserie Chicken

Cook Time: 40 mins, Prep Time: 2 mins, Difficulty: Medium, Serving: 4

Ingredients

- Kitchen Towel

- Medium Freezer Bag

- Whole Chicken

- 1 tbsp Paprika

- 2 tsp thyme

- Kitchen Tongs

- 1 Chicken Cube

- Salt & Pepper

- 1 tbsp Olive Oil

- 1 tbsp Paprika

- 1 tsp Celery Salt

- Large Bowl

- Salt and Pepper

- Metric – Imperial

Instructions

1. Take a freezer bag and put all of the brine ingredients in it. Add the entire chicken then, once it is completely coated, pour some cold water. Zip it back and then cool it overnight.

2. Take the chicken from the bag, remove the brine stock, take the giblets out and let the whole chicken dry with a kitchen towel.

3. Take a small bowl and rub the chicken in it.

4. In the air-fryer, place the whole chicken and rub the chicken rub and the olive oil into whole visible flesh.

5. Keep cooking the chicken for almost 20 mins at 360 degrees Fahrenheit.

6. Flip over with tongs after 20 mins, then apply the remaining oil and chicken rub to the chicken's other side.

7. Now, cook at the above temp for another 20 mins.

8. Serve warm.

16. Air-fryer Turkey Meatballs

Cook Time: 16 mins, Prep Time: 15 mins, Difficulty: Medium, Serving: 4

Ingredients

- 150 g Cooked Vegetables
- 1 tbsp Greek Yoghurt
- 30 g Soft Cheese
- 30 g Leftover Turkey
- 0.5 Cup Couscous
- 30 ml Turkey Stock
- 20 g Desiccated Coconut
- 1 tbsp Cumin
- 1 tbsp Moroccan Spice

- 1 tbsp Coriander
- Salt & Pepper
- Metric – Imperial

Instructions

1. If you don't have anything already prepared, cook the couscous. See for recipe notes.

2. Mix the turkey leg meat, soft Greek yogurt cheese, turkey stock, and seasoning. Put the cooked vegetables in the blender. Blend for a few mins or before a thick pate resembles the mixture.

3. Take a mixing bowl, remove the blender components, stir in the couscous and combine properly.

4. Convert the mixture into small balls and roll in the desiccated coconut.

5. Put in the Air-fryer for 16 mins at 360 degrees Fahrenheit and then serve.

6. If serving at a party, put on sticks for a nice party piece.

17. Air-fryer Nashville hot chicken

Cook Time: 10 mins, Prep Time: 30 mins, Difficulty: Easy, Serving: 6

Ingredients

- 2 pounds chicken tenderloins
- 1 cup all-purpose flour
- 1/2 tsp pepper
- 1 large egg
- 1/2 cup buttermilk
- 2 tbsp hot pepper sauce, divided
- Cooking spray

- 1/2 cup olive oil
- 2 tbsp cayenne pepper
- 2 tbsp dill pickle juice, divided
- 1 tsp salt
- 2 tbsps dark brown sugar
- 1 tsp paprika
- 1 tsp chili powder
- 1/2 tsp garlic powder
- Pickle slices
- Powered by Chicory

Instructions

1. Take a bowl or a deep plate, combine1 tbsp hot sauce, 1 tbsp pickle juice and 1/2 tsp salt. Put chicken and flip it over to coat. Put in a fridge after covering for an hour.

2. Preheat the air-fryer at 375 degrees Fahrenheit. Take a bowl, mix the rest of the salt, flour and pepper. Take another bowl, whisk buttermilk, egg, 1 tbsp hot sauce and the rest of the 1 tbsp pickle juice. To coat all sides, dip the chicken in flour; shake off the excess. Dip this in the egg mixture, then in the flour mixture again.

3. In batches, arrange chicken in one layer on a well-greased tray in the air-fryer basket; spray with cooking spray. Keep cooking until crispy or golden brown for almost 6 mins. Turn it over and spray with cooking spray. Keep cooking until crispy or golden brown, for almost 6 mins longer.

4. Mix oil, brown sugar, cayenne pepper and seasonings; pour over the hot chicken and coat it by tossing.

5. Serve with some pickles.

18. Basil pesto chicken

Cook Time: 15 mins, Prep Time: 10 mins, Difficulty: Easy, Serving: 4

Ingredients

- 1/2 cup Onion, sliced
- 1/4 cup Red Bell Pepper, sliced
- 1/4 cup Bell Peppers, sliced
- 1/2 cup Cherry Tomatoes
- 1/2 cup pesto
- 1/4 cup Half and Half
- 1/4 cup shredded parmesan cheese
- 1 pound Boneless Skinless Chicken Thighs
- 1/2-1 tsp Red Pepper Flakes

Instructions

1. Grease a heatproof pan and put it aside.
2. Take a medium bowl, mix pesto, parmesan cheese, cream and pepper flakes. Add the chicken and turn to cover the sauce properly.
3. Put the chicken and sauce into the greased pan.
4. Scatter the peppers, onions and tomatoes on top.
5. Put the pan in the air-fryer basket. Set the air-fryer to 360 degrees Fahrenheit for almost 15 mins until the chicken is well cooked.

19. Crumbed chicken tenderloins (air fried)

Cook Time: 12 mins, Prep Time: 15 mins, Difficulty: Easy, Serving: 4

Ingredients

- ½ cup dry bread crumbs
- 2 tbsps vegetable oil
- 1 egg

- 8 chicken tenderloins

Instructions

1. Preheat the air-fryer to 350 degrees Fahrenheit.

2. Whisk an egg in a small bowl.

3. Mix oil bread crumbs in another bowl until the mixture becomes crumbly and loose.

4. Dip every chicken tenderloin into a bowl of an egg; shake off any remaining residual egg. Dip the chicken into a crumb mixture, making sure it is fully and evenly covered. Put the chicken tenderloins into the basket of the air-fryer. Cook until it is no longer pink in the center for almost 12 mins. A thermometer inserted into the center (instant-read) should read at least 165 degrees Fahrenheit.

20. Garlic Parmesan Chicken Wings Recipe (Air-fryer & Oven)

Cook Time: 30 mins, Prep Time: 10 mins, Difficulty: Medium, Serving: 3

Ingredients

- 1/2 tsp Garlic Powder
- 1/2 tsp Onion Powder
- 1/2 tsp Natural Ancient Sea Salt
- 1 tsp Onion Powder
- 1/2 tsp Smoked Paprika
- 1/2 tsp Black Pepper
- 1 tsp Garlic Powder
- 1/4 cup butter, melted
- 1/2 cup grated parmesan
- 1 tbsp Baking Powder
- 1.5 lbs Chicken Wings
- Garlic Parmesan Wings Sauce

- 1/4 tsp Black Pepper
- Chicken Wings
- 1 tsp Dried Parsley

Instructions

1. Take the chicken wings from the fridge and pat them off (removing most of the moisture).

2. Whisk the garlic powder, paprika, sea salt, onion powder, black pepper and baking powder in a ramekin or small dish.

3. Spray seasoning mixture on the chicken wings and toss to cover.

4. Put wings in the air-fryer in a layer.

5. Using the programmed chicken air-fryer settings to 400 degrees Fahrenheit and cook for almost 30 mins. Set the timer for 15 mins, flip the wings, then test the wings at intervals of 5 mins until the skin is appropriately crisp. It needs to turn them around halfway through to get the wings crispy easily.

6. Combine all of the ingredients for the sauce by mixing them in a tiny bowl.

7. Shake the wings in a mixture of garlic parmesan.

8. Serve immediately.

21. Chicken Jalfrezi Air-fryer Chicken Jalfrezi

Cook Time: 15 mins, Prep Time: 10 mins, Difficulty: Medium, Serving: 4

Ingredients

- 1 cup (160 g) onions, chopped
- 2 cups (298 g) Chopped Bell Peppers
- 2 tbsps (2 tbsps) Oil
- 1 tsp (1 tsp) Kosher Salt

- 1 tsp (1 tsp) Turmeric
- 1 tsp (1 tsp) Garam Masala
- 1/2-1 tsp (0.5 tsp) Cayenne Pepper
- 1 pound (453.59 g) Boneless Skinless Chicken Thighs
- 1/4 cup (61.25 g) tomato sauce
- 1 tbsp (1 tbsp) Water
- 1 tsp (1 tsp) Garam Masala
- 1/2 tsp Kosher Salt
- 1/2 tsp Cayenne Pepper

Instructions

1. Take a large bowl, mix chicken, garam masala, oil, peppers, salt, turmeric, onions and cayenne.

2. Put the vegetables and chicken in the air-fryer basket.

3. Set the air-fryer for 360 degrees Fahrenheit for almost 15 mins. Stir and toss midway cooking.

4. Simultaneously, prepare the sauce. Take a little bowl, combine garam masala, tomato sauce, water, garam masala and cayenne.

5. Microwave for almost 1 minute. Stir and Remove. Microwave for another 1 minute. Set aside.

6. If the chicken is fried, place the chicken and vegetables in a big bowl after removing them from heat. To cover the chicken and vegetables equally with the sauce, spill the prepared sauce over them and toss. Rice, naan, or side salad are served with it.

22. Air-fryer Asian-glazed boneless chicken thighs

Cook Time: 30 mins, Prep Time: 5 mins, Difficulty: Medium, Serving: 4

Ingredients

- 2 1/2 tbsp vinegar(balsamic)

- 1 tbsp honey
- 3 cloves garlic
- 1/4 cup soy sauce
- 1 tsp hot sauce (Sriracha)
- 1 tsp fresh grated ginger
- 32 ounces 8 boneless
- 1 scallion, green only sliced for garnish

Instructions

1. Take a small bowl, mix the balsamic, garlic, soy sauce, honey, sriracha, ginger, and whisk them properly.

2. Pour half (1/4 cup) of the marinade into a large chicken dish, cover all the meat,

   and marinate for at least 2 hours or as long as overnight.

3. Reserve the rest of the sauce for later.

4. Preheat the air-fryer to 400 degrees Fahrenheit.

5. Remove and move the chicken from the marinade to the air-fryer basket.

6. Cook 14 mins in batches, turning midway in the center before cooked through.

7. Simultaneously, put the rest of the sauce in a small pot and cook over medium-low heat until it reduces slightly and thickens for almost 2 mins.

8. To serve, top with scallions and drizzle the sauce over the chicken.

23. Un-fried chicken

Cook Time: 55 mins, Prep Time: 15 mins, Difficulty: Hard, Serving: 4

Ingredients

- Black pepper and Kosher Salt

- 1 1/2 cups multi-grain panko breadcrumbs

- 1 lemon

- 1 tbsp lemon zest

- 1 tbsp hot sauce

- 1 tsp red pepper flakes

- 3 tbsps grated Parmesan

- 4 skinless, boneless chicken breasts

- 1 cup buttermilk

Instructions

1. In a deep bowl, mix the hot sauce, butter and milk. Season the salt and black

   pepper with the chicken and soak it in the buttermilk mixture.

2. In a deep bowl, combine the parmesan, breadcrumbs, lemon zest, red pepper flakes and one pinch of salt and black pepper each. Remove the buttermilk mixture from the chicken, let the excess fall off, and dredge until evenly covered in the breadcrumb mixture. On a nonstick baking dish, lay the bits flat and leave them in a refrigerator, uncovered, for 30 mins.

3. Preheat the oven to 400 degrees Fahrenheit. Bake the chicken for 20 to 25 mins until it's only cooked through. Divide the chicken into 4 dishes and press the lemon on the chicken.

24. Chicken Stuffed with Prosciutto and Fontina

Cook Time: 10 mins, Prep Time: 10 mins, Difficulty: Easy, Serving: 2

Ingredients

- Salt

- 2 boneless chicken breast halves

- Freshly ground black pepper

- 4 tbsps unsalted butter

- 2 tbsps olive oil

- 1 cup sliced portabella mushrooms

- 4 ounces fontina cheese

- ½ cup dry wine

- 3 sprigs rosemary

- 1 bunch arugula

- ½ lemon

Instructions

1. Put the chicken breast in wax paper sheets, using a rolling pin or mallet, then make thin.

2. Cover each stick of fontina cheese with one slice of prosciutto and place half of every chicken breast in its middle. Wrap chicken around cheese and prosciutto. Season the rolls of chicken with black pepper and salt.

3. Take a heavy pan, heat 1 tbsp of olive oil and 2 tbsps of butter. Quickly brown chicken rolls over medium heat for almost 3 mins per side. Put the rolls of chicken in the air-fryer basket. Adjust the temp to 350 degrees Fahrenheit, and cook for almost 7 mins. Place the chicken rolls on a cutting board and leave for 5 mins. Cut rolls into 6 slices at an angle.

4. Reheat pan, add rest of the butter, mushrooms, rosemary and wine; season with pepper and salt; and cook for almost 10 mins.

5. Take a large bowl, shake arugula leaves in the rest of the olive oil, salt, lemon juice, and pepper.

6. Arrange mushrooms and chicken on dressed arugula bed.

Chapter No.5: Red Meat Recipes

1. Air-fryer Party Meatballs

Cook Time: 15 mins, Prep Time: 5 mins, Difficulty: Easy, Serving: 4

Ingredients

- ¾ Cup Tomato Ketchup
- 1 tbsp Tabasco
- 21/2 tbsp Worcester Sauce
- 1 lb Mince Beef
- ¼ Cup Vinegar
- 1 tbsp Lemon Juice
- ½ Cup Brown Sugar
- ½ Tsp Dry Mustard
- 3 Gingersnaps crushed
- Metric – Imperial

Instructions

1. Take a big whisking bowl, put on the seasonings and whisk well so that everything is coated evenly.

2. Add the mince to the small bowl and whisk well.

3. Form into medium-sized meatballs and put them into the Air-fryer.

4. Cook them for almost 15 mins on 375 degrees Fahrenheit heat or until brown and crispy and cooked in the center.

5. Put them on sticks, then serve.

2. Air-fryer ground beef wellington

Cook Time: 20 mins, Prep Time: 30 mins, Difficulty: Medium, Serving: 2

Ingredients

- 1/2 cup chopped fresh mushrooms

- 2 tsps all-purpose flour

- 1/4 tsp pepper, divided

- 1/2 cup half-and-half cream

- 1 tbsp butter

- 1 big egg yolk

- 2 tbsps chopped onion

- 1/4 tsp salt

- 1/2 pound minced beef

- 1 tube (4 ounces) refrigerated crescent rolls

- 1 big egg

- 1 tsp dried parsley flakes

- Powered by Chicory

Instructions

1. Preheat the air-fryer at 300 degrees Fahrenheit. Take a saucepan and heat the butter over medium-high heat. Add mushrooms; cook and mix for 5-6 mins, until soft. Add flour and 1/8 of a tsp of pepper when mixed. Add cream gradually. Carry to a boil; cook and stir until thickened, about 2 mins. Remove and set aside from the heat.

2. In a bowl, combine egg yolk, 2 tbsps mushroom sauce, salt, onion, and 1/8 tsp pepper. Crumble beef over mixture and whisk properly. Form it into 2 loaves. Unroll and divide the crescent dough into 2 rectangles; press the perforations to close. Put each rectangle with the meatloaf. Bring together the edges and press to seal. Brush the beaten egg if desired.

3. Put Wellingtons on a greased tray in a single layer in the air-fryer basket. Cook until crisp or brown and a thermometer inserted into meatloaf reads 160 degrees Fahrenheit for almost 22 mins.

4. Simultaneously, warm the remaining sauce over low heat; stir in parsley.

5. Serve sauce with Wellingtons.

3. Air-fryer steak fajitas

Cook Time: 10 mins, Prep Time: 15 mins, Difficulty: Easy, Serving: 6

Ingredients

- 1/4 cup lime juice
- 1/2 cup diced red onion
- 1 jalapeno pepper (seeded and minced)
- 2 big tomatoes (seeded and chopped)
- 3 tbsps minced fresh cilantro
- 3/4 tsp salt, divided
- 2 tsps ground cumin, divided
- 1 beef flank steak (about 1-1/2 pounds)
- 1 big onion, halved and sliced

- 6 whole-wheat tortillas (8 inches), warmed

- Sliced avocado and lime wedges

Instructions

1. Take a small bowl and put the first 5 ingredients; stir in 1 tsp cumin and 1/4 tsp salt. Leave until serving.

2. Preheat the air-fryer to 400 degrees Fahrenheit. Sprinkle steak with the rest of the salt and cumin. Put on a greased tray in the air-fryer basket. Cook until the meat reaches desired doneness (for medium-rare, an instant thermometer should read 135 degrees Fahrenheit; medium, 140 degrees Fahrenheit, 6-8 mins per side. Remove from basket and leave for 5 mins.

3. Simultaneously, put the onion on the tray in the air-fryer basket. Cook until crisp for almost 3 mins, stirring once. Cut steak across the grain.

4. Serve in tortillas with salsa and onion. If needed, serve with lime wedges and avocado.

4. Air-fryer keto meatballs

Cook Time: 10 mins, Prep Time: 30 mins, Difficulty: Easy, Serving: 4

Ingredients

- 1 big egg

- 2 tbsps heavy whipping cream

- 1/2 cup shredded mozzarella cheese

- 1/2 cup grated Parmesan cheese

- 1 garlic clove, minced

- 1 pound lean ground beef

SAUCE:

- 1 can tomato sauce with basil, garlic and oregano

- 2 tbsp prepared pesto

- 1/4 cup heavy whipping cream

Instructions

1. Preheat the air-fryer to 350 degrees Fahrenheit. Take a big bowl, combine the first 5 ingredients. Add beef; whisk gently but thoroughly. Slice into 1-1/2-inches balls. Put on a greased tray in a single layer in the air-fryer basket; cook until browned and cooked through, 8-10 mins.

2. Simultaneously, take a small saucepan, whisk the sauce ingredients; heat through. Serve with meatballs. Freeze cooled keto meatballs in the freezer containers. To use, partially thaw them in the refrigerator overnight. Preheat the air-fryer to 350 degrees Fahrenheit. Again heat until completely heated for almost 5 mins.

3. Make the sauce as directed.

5. Jamaican Jerk Meatballs In The Air-fryer

Cook Time: 14 mins, Prep Time: 3 mins, Difficulty: Easy, Serving: 4

Ingredients

Kitchen Gadgets:

- Meatball Maker

- Air-fryer

Jamaican Meatball Ingredients:

- 1 tbsp jerk dry rub

- 1 kg Chicken Mince

- 100 g Breadcrumbs

- Jamaican Sauce Ingredients:

- 1 tsp Jerk Dry Rub

- 4 tbsp Honey

- 1 tbsp Soy Sauce

Instructions

1. Put the chicken into a big bowl along with the jerk seasoning and the breadcrumbs and whisk well. Make into meatball shapes by using a meatball press.

2. Put the Jamaican Jerk Meatballs into the air-fryer and cook for almost 14 mins at 360 degrees Fahrenheit.

3. Take a bowl whisk together the honey, soy sauce and remaining jerk dry rub.

   Whisk well.

4. When the Jerk Meatballs(Jamaican) are cooked, toss them in the sauce.

5. Serve them on sticks.

6. Easy sweet potato beef chili

Cook Time: 1 day 16 hrs, Prep Time: 10 hrs, Difficulty: Hard, Serving: 5

Ingredients

- 1/2 cup chopped red peppers
- 2-3 garlic cloves, minced
- 1 tsp olive oil
- 1/2 cup chopped green peppers
- 1/2 cup chopped onions
- 1 pound ground beef
- 2 15 oz cans chili beans
- 1/2 cup beef broth
- 1 medium sweet potato Cut into cubes
- 6 oz canned tomato paste
- 1 can of diced tomatoes and chilis

- Homemade Chili Seasoning

- 1 tsp cumin

- 1 tsp dried oregano

- salt and pepper to taste

- 1 tbsp chili powder

- 1 tsp red cayenne pepper

Instructions

1. Take a Dutch oven or big stockpot and heat it on medium-high heat. When hot, add the olive oil, green peppers, chopped onions and red peppers.

2. Saute until the veggies are soft, for a few mins.

3. Put the minced garlic in and stir.

4. Add in the minced beef. Break down the minced beef by Using a meat chopper.

5. With the chili seasoning, season the beef. Stir until you have cooked the minced beef, around 4 mins. Drain the extra fat.

6. Add the tomato paste, diced tomatoes and chilies, broth and sweet potatoes in cubes to the pan. Stir properly.

7. Cover the pan and leave the chili to cook for almost 40 mins on medium-low heat until the sweet potatoes are soft. Check after 10 mins.

8. Cool before serving.

7. The Ultimate Air-fryer Lamb Burgers

Cook Time: 18 mins, Prep Time: 3 mins, Difficulty: Easy, Serving: 4

Ingredients

- Burger Press

- Air-fryer

Lamb Burgers:

- 2 tsp Garlic Puree
- 1 tsp Harissa Paste
- 650 g Minced Lamb
- 1 tbsp Moroccan Spice
- Salt & Pepper

Greek Dip:

- ½ tsp Oregano
- 1 Small Lemon
- 1 tsp Moroccan Spice
- 3 tbsp Greek Yoghurt

Instructions

1. Put the lamb burger ingredients in a whisking bowl and whisk them well until all the lamb grind is properly seasoned.

2. Prepare the grind into lamb burger type shapes, Using a burger press.

3. Put the burgers in the air-fryer and cook for almost 18 mins at 360 degrees Fahrenheit.

4. While they are cooking, create the Dip sauce. Using a fork, whisk the ingredients together.

5. Serve it with your lamb burgers.

8. Air-fryer Burgers

Cook Time: 12 mins, Prep Time: 5 mins, Difficulty: Easy, Serving: 4

Ingredients

Kitchen Gadgets:

- Biscuit Cutters
- Air-fryer

Burger:

- 500 g Minced Pork
- ½ Small Onion
- 1 Tbsp Soft Cheese
- 1 Tsp Garlic Puree
- 2 Tsp Thyme
- 2 Tsp Oregano
- 500 g Minced Beef
- Salt and Pepper
- Metric – Imperial

Instructions

1. Dice and peel the onion and load it into a whisking bowl with the rest of the burger patty ingredients.
2. Whisk properly with your hands.
3. Add in the soft cheese and whisk a little more.
4. Cut into burger shapes by Using a biscuit cutter.
5. Place into the air-fryer basket and cook for almost 12 mins at 360 degrees Fahrenheit.
6. Add the burger bun lid
7. Serve immediately.

9. Perfect Air-fryer Steak

Cook Time: 12 mins, Prep Time: 20 mins, Difficulty: Medium, Serving: 2

Ingredients

- Salt
- Olive oil
- Freshly cracked black pepper
- 1 stick unsalted butter softened
- 2 tbsp fresh parsley
- 2 8 oz ribeye steak
- 1 tsp Worcestershire sauce
- 1 tsp Worcestershire sauce
- 2 tsp garlic minced
- Garlic butter
- 1/2 tsp salt

Instructions

1. Prepare Garlic Butter by whisking butter, Worcestershire sauce, parsley garlic, and salt until thoroughly mixed.

2. Put in parchment paper and roll the mixture into a log. Cool in the refrigerator

   until ready to use.

3. Remove steak from refrigerator and place at room temperature for almost 20 mins. Rub all steak sides with a little bit of olive oil and season with freshly cracked black pepper and salt.

4. Grease your Air-fryer basket by spraying a little bit of oil on the basket. Preheat the Air-fryer to 400 degrees Fahrenheit. Once preheated, put steaks in the air-fryer and cook for almost 12 mins, flipping midway through.

5. Remove from the air-fryer and allow to rest for almost 5 mins.

6. Top with garlic butter and serve.

10. Air-fryer Hot Dogs

Cook Time: 5 mins, Prep Time: 1 min, Difficulty: Easy, Serving: 4

Ingredients

- 4 hotdog buns

- 4 hotdogs

- Ketchup

- Mustard

Instructions

1. to prevent the hot dogs from inflating, ensure that a few small cuts (or prick the hot dogs) are made before cooking. Place the hot dogs in your air-fryer.

2. Cook on 390f degrees Fahrenheit for almost 6 mins.

3. Take the hot dogs out. Put the bread buns in the air-fryer now and air fry for almost 2 more mins for crunchy and toasted buns.

4. Serve and enjoy.

11. Air-fryer Meatballs

Cook Time: 20 mins, Prep Time: 5 mins, Difficulty: Easy, Serving: 4

Ingredients

- 3/4 tsp salt

- 1/2 cup dried bread crumbs

- 1/2 cup grated Parmesan cheese

- 1 lb ground beef

- 1/4 cup milk

- 1/4 tsp pepper

- 2 cloves garlic minced
- 1/2 tsp Italian seasoning

Instructions

1. Mix all the mentioned ingredients in a plate, then roll into 1 1/2 inch meatballs.
2. Put the meatballs into the air-fryer basket in a single layer, without them touching.
3. Air fry the meatballs at 375 degrees Fahrenheit for almost 15 mins.
4. Remove and serve.

12. Taco Meatballs | Air-fryer Keto Taco Meatballs

Cook Time: 15 mins, Prep Time: 10 mins, Difficulty: Easy, Serving: 4

Ingredients

- 1 tbsp (1 tbsp) Minced Garlic
- 1/4 cup (40 g) onions, chopped
- 1 pound (453.59 g) Lean Ground Beef
- 1/4 cup (4 g) Cilantro, chopped
- 2 tbsps (2 tbsps) Taco Seasoning
- 1/2 cup (118.29 g) Mexican Blend Shredded Cheese
- 1 Egg
- Kosher Salt
- Ground Black Pepper

For Dipping Sauce

- 1/2 cup (130 g) salsa
- 1-2 (1) Cholula hot sauce
- 1/4 cup (57.5 g) sour cream

Instructions

1. Put all the above ingredients in a stand mixer bowl. Using the paddle attachment, beat and whisk together until it forms a sticky paste, about 2-3 mins.

2. Form the mixture into 12 meatballs. Put meatballs in the air-fryer basket. Set the air-fryer to 400 degrees Fahrenheit for almost 10 mins.

3. Simultaneously, whisk together the sauce: In a small bowl, whisk together the salsa, sour cream and hot sauce.

4. Serve with the meatballs.

13. Air-fryer Asian Beef & Veggies

Cook Time: 8 mins, Prep Time: 10 mins, Difficulty: Easy, Serving: 4

Ingredients

*   1/2 medium yellow onion
*   1 medium red pepper
*   3 cloves garlic
*   2 tbsps cornstarch
*   1 lb sirloin steak
*   2 tbsp grated ginger
*   1/2 cup soy sauce
*   1/4 teaspoon red chili flakes
*   1/4 cup rice vinegar
*   1 tsp sesame oil
*   1/3 cup brown sugar
*   1 tsp Chinese 5 spice optional
*   1/4 cup water

Instructions

For Freezer Prep

1. Put all the above ingredients in a big-sized bag with a zip. Ensure all of the ingredients are mixed.

2. Label and freeze for up to 4 months.

To Cook

3. Overnight, thaw the bag in the refrigerator.

4. Remove the veggies and steak using tongs, and move to the Air-fryer.

5. Set the Air-fryer to 400 degrees Fahrenheit and the timer to almost 8 mins. Shake the basket midway through. It is not necessary.

6. Serve with rice, and garnish with scallions and sesame seeds.

14. Air-fryer Steak Tips

Cook Time: 20 mins, Prep Time: 10 mins, Difficulty: Medium, Serving: 4

Ingredients

- 1 tsp Worcestershire sauce

- 1/2 tsp garlic powder

- 2 Tbsps (30 ml) butter

- 1/2 lb. (227 g) potatoes

- 1 lb steaks

- Salt

- Minced parsley

- Black pepper

- Chili Flakes

- Melted butter

Instructions

1. Heat a pot containing water until boiling, put potatoes in it. Cook for almost 5 mins, or until tender or crispy. Drain and put aside

2. Combine the blanched potatoes and steak tips. Mix with the Worcestershire sauce, garlic powder, melted butter, salt and pepper.

3. Preheat the Air-fryer at 400 degrees Fahrenheit for almost 4 mins.

4. Spread the potatoes and steak in a single layer in the air-fryer basket. Air fry at 400 degrees Fahrenheit for almost 18 mins, flipping and shaking the potatoes and steak 2 times through a cooking process (time depends on your desired thickness, doneness of the steak, and size of the air-fryer).

5. Check the steak to see how well it is cooked. If you want the steak to be more done, add an extra 5 mins of cooking time.

6. If needed, garnish with parsley, optional drizzled the melted butter, and optional chili flakes. Season with additional salt and pepper according to taste.

7. Serve warm.

15. Air-fryer meatloaf

Cook Time: 50 mins, Prep Time: 10 mins, Difficulty: Hard, Serving: 3

Ingredients

- 1/2 pound minced beef

- 1/2 pound ground pork

- 1 cup almond flour

- 1/2 pound thick-cut bacon

- 1/2 yellow onion, diced

- 1 red bell pepper, diced

- 2 tbsp ketchup

- 1 tsp salt
- 1 tsp garlic powder
- 1 tbsp spicy brown mustard
- 1/2 tsp white pepper
- 1/2 tsp celery salt
- 1/4 tsp cayenne pepper
- 1 egg

For the sauce:

- 2–3 tbsps maple syrup
- 1/2 cup ketchup

Instructions

1. Preheat the air-fryer to 350 degrees Fahrenheit.

2. Take a big bowl and mix the meatloaf ingredients with a spoon or clean hands until completely mixed. Then whisk together the sauce ingredients in another bowl, set aside.

3. Top a loaf pan with slightly contrasting bacon strips. Place the meatloaf mixture on top of the bacon to fully cover the meatloaf, then tie the strips around the meat. Tip the pan over, then cut the meatloaf.

4. In an air-fryer, placed the meatloaf. Switch the heat of the oven up to 350 degrees Fahrenheit and timer up to 50 mins.

5. When the timer reaches the mark of 30 mins, click pause and brush around 3 tbsps of the sauce on top of the meatloaf using a basting brush. Lightly cover a slice of tin foil with the meatloaf.

6. Cook for almost 16 minutes, then cut the foil, pour the meatloaf once again in

   around 3 tbsps of sauce, then cook for the remaining 4 minutes without the foil.

7. When baked, before slicing and serving, let the meatloaf rest for 10 mins. Only a head up, it's certainly a little tough to pull the meatloaf out. You'll be able to gently press up and lift the wire rack from the basket until the wire rack has cooled. Or a few handy dandy spatulas you should still have. The toughest part of the day is going to be this.

16. Air-fryer beefy Swiss bundles

Cook Time: 10 mins, Prep Time: 20 mins, Difficulty: Easy, Serving: 4

Ingredients

- 1-1/2 cups sliced fresh mushrooms
- 1/2 cup chopped onion
- 1-1/2 tsps minced garlic
- 4 tsps Worcestershire sauce
- 1 pound ground beef
- 3/4 tsp dried rosemary, crushed
- 3/4 tsp paprika
- 1/2 tsp salt
- 1/4 tsp pepper
- 1 sheet frozen puff pastry, thawed
- 2/3 cup refrigerated mashed potatoes
- 1 cup shredded Swiss cheese
- 1 big egg
- 2 tbsps water
- Powered by Chicory

Instructions

1. Preheat the air-fryer to 375 degrees Fahrenheit. Take a big plate, cook mushrooms, beef and onion until vegetables are tender for almost 10

mins. Add garlic; cook 1 min longer. Drain and stir in seasonings and Worcestershire sauce. Remove from the heat; set aside.

2. Roll the puff pastry into a 15x13-inches piece on a lightly floured table. Split into 4 7-1/2x6-1/2-inches pieces. Over each piece, put around 2 tbsps of potatoes; scatter to within 1 inch from the margins. Cover with 3/4 cup of whisked beef each; top with 1/4 cup of cheese.

3. Toss the egg and water; rub some around the sides of the pastry. Place opposite pastry corners over each bundle; pinch the seams to seal. Brush the remaining whisked eggs. 1Place the pastries in batches in a single layer on the air-fryer basket tray; cook until golden brown for almost 12 minutes.

4. Option to freeze: Freeze unbaked pastries until firm on a parchment-lined baking sheet. Shift to a container that is airtight; return to the freezer. To use, cook frozen pastries until golden brown and heated, increasing time to almost 20 minutes, as instructed.

17. Air-fryer Beef Bulgogi

Cook Time: 12 mins, Prep Time: 10 mins, Difficulty: Easy, Serving: 6

Ingredients

- 3 Chopped Green Scallions
- 1 cup shredded carrots
- 3 tbsps Soy Sauce
- 1.5 pounds Sirloin Steak
- 2 tbsp Brown Sugar, or 2 tsps Splenda for low carb
- 2 tbsps Sesame Oil
- 2 tbsp Sesame Seeds
- 2 tsps Minced Garlic
- 1/2 tsp Ground Black Pepper

Instructions

1. Put sliced carrots, beef and green onions into a plastic zip-top bag. Add soy sauce, sesame oil, brown sugar, garlic, sesame seeds, and ground pepper. Squish the bag well to get the sauce and meat to incorporate well.

2. Leave the beef to marinate for almost 30 mins or up to a whole day by putting it in the refrigerator.

3. Put the veggies and meat into the air-fryer basket, leaving behind as much of the marinade as you can. Set the air-fryer to 400 degrees Fahrenheit for almost 12 mins, shaking midway through.

4. Serve with riced cauliflower, steamed rice or over a whisked salad.

18. Chipotle steak tacos

Cook Time: 8 mins, Prep Time: 10 mins, Difficulty: Easy, Serving: 4

Ingredients

For The Steak

- 2 cloves Garlic
- 1 canned chipotle chile
- 1 tbsp adobo sauce
- 1 tbsp Ancho Chile Powder
- 1 Chipotle Chile in Adobo Sauce
- 1.5 pounds flank steak
- 1 tsp Dried Oregano
- 1/2 cup Red Onion
- 1 tbsp Olive Oil
- 1.5 tsps Kosher Salt
- 1/2 tsp Ground Black Pepper
- 1 tsp Ground Cumin

- 2 tbsps Water

For Serving

- 1 cup Salsa
- 1/2 cup Cotija cheese
- 8 flour tortillas

Instructions

1. Put the strips of beef in a resealable plastic bag or a big bowl. In a food processor or blender, combine the onion, adobo sauce, garlic, chipotle chile, chile powder, cumin, oregano, salt, olive oil, pepper, and water. Blend until smooth.

2. To thoroughly coat and mix, spray the marinade over the meat and stir or seal the container and massage the bag. Marinate for almost 30 mins at room

   temperature or cover it and refrigerate for up to 24 hours.

3. Take the strips of beef out of the bag using tongs and lay them flat in the air-fryer basket, reducing as much overlap as doable. Set the air-fryer for 8 minutes to 400 degrees Fahrenheit, turning the strips of beef midway through the cooking period. It may occur   in two batches.

4. Place the steak on a pan with one single layer.

5. Set the oven to broil and cook the steak for almost 4 mins.

6. Flip and allow to cook for an additional 2 mins.

19. Za'atar lamb chops

Cook Time: 10 mins, Prep Time: 5 mins, Difficulty: Easy, Serving: 4

Ingredients

- 1 tsp extra-virgin olive oil
- 8 lamb loin chops
- 3 cloves garlic, crushed

- 1/2 fresh lemon
- 1 1/4 tsp kosher salt
- 1 tbsp za'atar
- Fresh ground pepper, to taste

Instructions

1. With oil and garlic, rub the lamb chops.
2. Squeeze the lemon over each side, then season with zatar, salt and black pepper.
3. Preheat the air-fryer to 400 degrees Fahrenheit. In batches in a single layer, cook for almost 5 mins on each side as the desired liking.
4. Remove and serve.

Chapter No.6: Pork Recipes

1. Mustard glazed pork fillet

Cook Time: 18 mins, Prep Time: 10 mins, Difficulty: Medium, Serving: 2

Ingredients

- ¼ tsp salt
- ¼ cup yellow mustard
- 1 tbsp peeled garlic
- 1 tsp Italian seasoning
- 1 1.5 lb pork fillet
- 3 tbsp brown sugar
- ⅛ tsp fresh cracked black pepper
- 1 tsp dried rosemary

Instructions

1. Dry and rinse the pork fillet. Cut slits into the top of the pork fillet. Put peeled garlic in the slits. Mix pork with pepper and salt.

2. Take a small bowl, whisk Italian seasoning, mustard, brown sugar, and rosemary in a bowl until entirely mixed. Place and rub the mustard mixture over the entire pork. Put it in the refrigerator for at least 2 hours to marinate.

3. Put pork fillet into greased air-fryer basket. Cook at 400 degrees Fahrenheit for almost 20 mins until an instant-read meat thermometer reads a temp of 145 degrees Fahrenheit.

4. Remove from the Air-fryer and allow to rest for 5 mins before slicing.

5. Serve and enjoy.

2. Breaded Air-fryer Breaded Pork Chops

Cook Time: 12 mins, Prep Time: 5 mins, Difficulty: Easy, Serving: 4

Ingredients

- Non-fat cooking spray, like Pam cooking spray
- 4 Bone-in center-cut pork chops

Liquid Dredge Station:

- 1 egg, beaten
- 1/4 cup water

Dry Dredge Station:

- 1 cup Panko breadcrumbs
- 1/2 cup flour
- 1/2 tsp black pepper
- 4 tsps paprika
- 2 tsps dried parsley

- 1/2 tsp powder of garlic
- 1/4 tsp cayenne pepper
- 1/4 tsp dry mustard
- 1/2 tsp salt

Instructions

1. Prepare the chops: Trim all the fat from the chops. Rinse with water to extract bone particles, if any.

2. Prepare the Stations to dredge: Take one, beat the egg with water. Take another baking pan or shallow dish, mix spices and Panko bread crumbs.

3. Set up another bowl with the flour.

4. Coating the Chops: If the flour step is used, gently coat the chop in flour first. Shake off the flour excess. This move allows the egg wash to stick to the pork chop. Skip to the next step if the flour is not used.

5. Place the chops in the mixture of egg wash and switch both sides to wet. Then, roll the chops in the crumb mixture to cover all ends.

6. In the Air-Fryer: Put chops in the Air-fryer pan. Drizzle gently with non-stick cooking spray. If needed, add a wire rack to make the second tier of pork chops. Place drawer into air-fryer and close.

7. Cook the Chops: Set the temp to 380 degrees Fahrenheit and the time for almost 12 mins. Turn the chops midway through the cooking time and gently spray with cooking spray. Close the drawer and continue the process of cooking. The chops are done when the internal temp reaches 145 degrees Fahrenheit and the center of the chops is no longer pink.

8. Give it a Rest: Leave the chops to rest for almost 3 mins then serve.

9. Serving Suggestions: For a 20-minute meal, serve with quick-cooking rice, steamed vegetables and a cucumber-tomato salad (fresh).

10. Storage: Leftovers may be kept in an air-tight jar in the refrigerator for up to 3 days.

3. Air-fryer Chinese Salt & Pepper Pork Chops

Cook Time: 15 mins, Prep Time: 5 mins, Difficulty: Easy, Serving: 1

Ingredients

- 1 Egg White
- 1/2 tsp Sea Salt
- Pork Chops
- 3/4 cup Potato Starch
- 1 Oil Mister
- Stir Fry
- 1/4 tsp Freshly Ground Black Pepper
- 2 Jalapeño Pepper stems
- 2 Scallions (Green Onions)
- 1/4 tsp Freshly Ground Black Pepper
- 2 tbsp Canola Oil
- Cast Iron Chicken Fryer
- 1 tsp Sea Salt

Instructions

1. Coat Air-fryer Basket with a thin coat of oil

2. Take a medium bowl, mix salt, egg white and pepper until foamy. Cut the chops of pork into pieces of cutlet, leaving a little dried on the bones and pat. Apply bits of pork chop to the egg white mixture. Marinate for 20 mins at least.

3. Move the chops of pork to a large bowl, then add Potato Starch to it. Dredge

the chops of pork entirely with the Potato Starch. Shake off the pork and place in a fully prepared air-fryer basket. Lightly spray oil on the pork.

4. Cook at 360 degrees Fahrenheit for almost 9 mins, shaking the basket often and spraying with oil between shakes. Cook an additional 6 mins at 400 degrees Fahrenheit, or until the pork is crispy and brown.

5. Stir Fry.

6. Cut Jalapeños thin and remove the seeds. Chop scallions. Put it in a small bowl and put it aside.

7. Skillet or Heat wok until screaming hot. Add oil, Scallions, Jalapeño peppers, salt and pepper and stir fry for almost a minute. To the wok or pan, apply air-fried pork strips and toss with the jalapeño and scallions. For another minute, stir fry the pork, making sure the hot oil and vegetables are coated.

4. Air-fryer pork schnitzel

Cook Time: 10 mins, Prep Time: 20 mins, Difficulty: Easy, Serving: 4

Ingredients

- 1 tsp seasoned salt
- 1/4 tsp pepper
- 1 large egg
- 2 tbsp milk
- 3/4 cup dry bread crumbs
- 1 tsp paprika
- 4 pork sirloin cutlets
- 1/4 cup all-purpose flour
- Cooking spray

Dill Sauce:

- 3/4 cup chicken broth

- 1/2 cup sour cream
- 1/4 tsp dill weed
- 1 tbsp all-purpose flour

Instructions

1. Preheat the air-fryer to 375 degrees Fahrenheit. Take a shallow bowl, mix seasoned salt, flour and pepper. Take another shallow bowl, mix milk and egg until blended. Take a third bowl, mix paprika and bread crumbs.

2. Pound pork cutlets to 1/4-in with a beef mallet. Of size. Dip the cutlets to cover all sides in the flour mixture; shake off the excess. Dip in the mixture of crumbs, then pat in the crumb mixture to help adhere to the coating.

3. Put the pork on a tray in a single layer in the air-fryer basket; sprinkle with cooking spray. Cook until golden brown for almost 5 mins. Turn; sprinkle with cooking spray. Cook until golden brown for almost 5 mins longer. Remove to a serving plate; keep it warm.

4. Simultaneously, in a small saucepan, mix broth and flour until smooth. Bring to a boil, stirring constantly; stir and cook for almost 2 mins or until thickened. Reduce the heat. Stir in sour and dill cream; heat through.

5. Serve with pork.

5. Air-fryer papas rellenas

Cook Time: 15 mins, Prep Time: 45 mins, Difficulty: Medium, Serving: 6

Ingredients

- 1/2 cup tomato sauce
- 1 small green pepper
- 1 small onion
- 1/2 cup raisins
- 2-1/2 pounds potatoes
- 1 pound lean ground beef

- 1-1/4 tsps salt

- 1-1/4 tsps pepper

- 1/2 tsp paprika

- 1 tsp powder of garlic

- 1/2 cup sliced green olives

- 2 large eggs, lightly beaten

- 1 cup seasoned bread crumbs

- Cooking spray

Instructions

1. Put potatoes in a big saucepan and coat with water. Make sure it's the boil. Reduce heat; cook and cover until tender for almost 20 mins.

2. Simultaneously, in a large pan, cook green pepper, onion and beef over medium-high heat until it is no longer pink; then drain. Stir in raisins, tomato

   sauce, olives, 1/4 tsp pepper, 1/4 tsp salt and paprika; heat entirely.

3. Drain potatoes; mash with remaining 1 tsp salt and pepper and powder of garlic. Make 2 tbsps potatoes into a small patty; put a tbsp of filling in the middle. Shape the potatoes around the filling, like a ball. Repeat the procedure.

4. Put bread crumbs and eggs in separate shallow bowls. Dip the potatoes in the egg mixture, then roll in the bread crumbs. Preheat the air-fryer to 400 degrees Fahrenheit. In batches, put on a greased tray in a single layer in the air-fryer basket; sprinkle with cooking spray. Cook until crispy or golden brown for almost 16 mins.

6. Air-fryer mini chimichangas

Cook Time: 10 mins, Prep Time: 1 hr, Difficulty: Medium, Serving: 14

Ingredients

- 3/4 cup water

- 1 cup sour cream
- 1 medium onion (chopped)
- 1 envelope taco
- 1 can chop green chiles
- 1 lb ground beef
- 14 egg roll wrappers
- 3 cups cheese(shredded)
- 1 large egg white
- Cooking spray
- Salsa

Instructions

1. Take a large pan, cook onion and beef over medium-high heat; drain. Stir in water taco and seasoning. Bring to a boil. Reduce heat; simmer, uncover it for almost 5 mins, stirring occasionally. Remove from the heat; cool slightly.

2. Preheat the air-fryer to 375 degrees Fahrenheit. Take a large bowl, combine sour cream, cheese and chiles. Stir in a mixture of beef. Put an egg roll wrapper on the work surface. Place 1/3 of a cup of filling in the middle. Fold one-third of the bottom of the wrapper over the filling; fold sideways.

3. Brush the surface with white eggs; roll up to cover. Repeat for the filling and leftover wrappers.

4. In batches, put chimichangas on a greased tray in a single layer in the air-fryer basket; spray with cooking spray. Cook until crispy or golden brown for almost 4 mins on both sides.

5. Serve warm with additional sour cream and salsa.

7. Air-fryer loaded pork burritos

Cook Time: 5 mins, Prep Time: 35 mins, Difficulty: Medium, Serving: 6

Ingredients

- 2 tsps salt
- 1-1/2 tsps pepper
- 1-1/2 pounds boneless pork loin
- 1 cup chopped seeded plum tomatoes
- 1 tbsp olive oil
- 1 small green pepper
- 3/4 cup thawed limeade concentrate
- 1 small onion
- 1/4 cup
- 1/3 cup peeled fresh cilantro
- 1 jalapeno pepper
- 1 tbsp lime juice
- 1 cup uncooked long-grain rice
- 1/4 tsp powder of garlic
- 3 cups Monterey Jack cheese(shredded)
- 6 flour tortillas
- 1 can (15 ounces) black beans
- Cooking spray

Instructions

1. Take a big shallow dish, whisk the limeade concentrate, 1 tsp salt, oil and 1/2 tsp pepper; add pork to it. Turn to coat; refrigerate and cover at least 20 mins.

2. For salsa, take a small bowl, combine the tomatoes, onion, green pepper, 1/4 cup cilantro, lime juice, jalapeno, powder of garlic and the rest of the pepper and salt. Set aside.

3. Simultaneously, cook rice according to the instructions written on the package. Stir in the rest of the cilantro; keep warm.

4. Drain the pork and discard the marinade. Preheat the air-fryer to 350 degrees Fahrenheit. Place pork in batches in a single layer in an air-fryer basket on a greased tray; sprinkle with cooking spray. Cook until the pork is no longer pink,

   turning midway through for almost 10 mins.

5. Sprinkle each tortilla with 1/3 cup cheese. Layer each with 1/4 cup of salsa, 1/2 cup of rice mixture, 1/4 cup of black beans and 1/4 cup of sour cream, top with 1/2 cup of pork. Fold the sides, and the filling ends.

6. Serve with the rest of the salsa.

8. Air-fryer fried pork chops southern style

Cook Time: 20 mins, Prep Time: 5 mins, Difficulty: Easy, Serving: 4

Ingredients

- 4 pork chops
- 3 tbsp buttermilk
- 1/4 cup all-purpose flour
- 1 Ziplock bag
- Pepper to taste
- Seasoning salt
- Cooking oil spray

Instructions

1. Pat until the chops of pork become dry.

2. Season the chops of pork with the seasoning pepper and salt.

3. Sprinkle the buttermilk over the chops of pork.

4. Put the chops of pork in a bag with the flour. Shake to coat entirely.

5. Marinate for almost 30 mins. It is optional. It helps the flour stick to the chops of pork.

6. Put the chops of pork in the air-fryer. Do not stack. Cook in batches if needed.

7. Drizzle the chops of pork with cooking oil.

8. Cook the chops of pork for almost 15 mins at 380 degrees Fahrenheit. Turn the chops of pork over to the side after almost 10 mins.

9. Air-fryer honey & mustard pork meatballs

Cook Time: 10 mins, Prep Time: 5 mins, Difficulty: Easy, Serving: 2

Ingredients

- 1 tsp Garlic Puree
- 1 tsp Mustard
- 2 tsp Honey
- Gluten-Free Oat Flour
- 500 g Peeled Pork
- 1 tsp Pork Seasoning
- Salt & Pepper
- 1 Small Red Onion

Instructions

1. thinly dice and peel the red onion.

2. Mix all the ingredients into a bowl properly until the pork mince is seasoned well.

3. Using a meatball press, make the meatballs. If needed, add some oat flour to mix them.

4. Put the pork meatballs into the air-fryer and cook for almost 10 mins at 360 degrees Fahrenheit.

5. Serve while still warm.

10. Air-fryer Pork Chops & Broccoli

Cook Time: 10 mins, Prep Time: 5 mins, Difficulty: Easy, Serving: 2

Ingredients

- 1/2 tsp paprika
- 2 tbsp avocado oil
- 1/2 tsp onion powder
- 2 5 ounce bone-in pork chops
- 1/2 tsp powder of garlic
- 1 tsp salt
- 2 cups broccoli florets
- 2 cloves garlic

Instructions

1. Preheat the air-fryer according to the instructions to 350 degrees Fahrenheit. Spray basket with non-stick spray.

2. Drizzle 1 tbsp of oil on each side of the chops of pork.

3. Season the chops of pork on each side with paprika, powder of garlic, onion powder and 1/2 tsp of salt.

4. Put pork chops in the air-fryer basket and cook for almost 5 mins.

5. When cooking pork chops, add the broccoli, rest of the 1/2 tsp of salt, garlic, and rest of the tbsp of oil to a bowl and toss to coat.

6. Open the air-fryer and gently turn the chops of pork over.

7. Add the broccoli and return it to the air-fryer basket.

8. Cook for almost 5 more mins, stirring the broccoli midway through.

9. Remove the food from the air-fryer carefully and serve.

11. Air-fryer English muffin pizzas

Cook Time: 5 mins, Prep Time: 5 mins, Difficulty: Easy, Serving: 4

Ingredients

- 4 English Muffins
- Toppings of choice
- Pizza Sauce of choice
- Shredded Mozzarella Cheese

Instructions

1. Set Air-fryer to 400 degrees Fahrenheit.
2. Once preheated, put halves of the English Muffins in the fryer for almost a minute
3. Remove from the air-fryer.
4. Add sauce, cheese and toppings.
5. Cook for an additional 5 mins after putting back into the Air-fryer.

12. Crispy pork belly

Cook Time: 30 mins, Prep Time: 10 mins, Difficulty: Medium, Serving: 4

Ingredients

- 3 cups Water
- 1 tsp Kosher Salt
- 1 tsp Ground Black Pepper
- 2 tbsps Soy Sauce
- 1 pound pork belly
- 2 Bay Leaves
- 6 cloves Garlic

Instructions

1. Slice the belly of the pork into 3 thick chunks, so it cooks more uniformly.

2. Put all ingredients into the inner liner of a pressure cooker or Instant Pot. Cook the pork belly at high pressure for almost 15 mins. Allow the pot to sit undisturbed for almost 10 mins and then release the rest of the pressure. Using a set of tongs, very gently remove the meat from the pressure cooker. Allow the meat to dry and drain for almost 10 mins.

3. Slice the three chunks of pork belly into 2 slices.

4. Put the pork belly slices in the air-fryer basket. Set the air-fryer to 400 degrees Fahrenheit for almost 15 mins or until the pork belly's fat is brown or has crisped up, and then serve.

5. Put the ingredients in a saucepan, cover and cook for about 60 minutes, if you do not have a pressure cooker before a knife can easily be inserted into the skin-side of the pork belly. For almost 10 mins, remove the meat and allow the meat to drain and dry.

6. Place the side of the pork belly skin on a baking sheet and set the oven to broil. Leave the meat to broil for almost 5 mins on the rack nearest to the broiler in the oven until the skin is crispy. Be sure to keep an eye on the oven so that the skin does not burn.

13. Sweet and Sour Pork

Cook Time: 15 mins, Prep Time: 25 mins, Difficulty: Easy, Serving: 2

Ingredients

- 1/4 cup sugar
- 1/4 cup packed dark brown sugar
- 1/4 cup ketchup
- 1 tbsp reduced-sodium soy sauce
- 1/2 cup unsweetened crushed pineapple
- 1/2 cup cider vinegar

- 1-1/2 tsps Dijon mustard
- 1/2 tsp powder of garlic
- 1 pork fillet (3/4 pound)
- 1/8 tsp salt
- 1/8 tsp pepper
- Sliced green onions, optional
- Cooking spray
- Powered by Chicory

Instructions

1. Take a small saucepan, mix the first 8 ingredients. Bring to a boil, then reduce heat. Simmer gently, uncover it until thickened, for almost 8 mins while stirring occasionally.

2. Preheat the air-fryer to 350 degrees Fahrenheit. Sprinkle pork with pepper and salt. Put pork on a greased tray in the air-fryer basket; spray with cooking spray. Cook until pork is lightly brown for almost 8 mins. Turn it over; pour 2 tbsps sauce over the pork. Cook until an instant thermometer put into pork reads 145 degrees Fahrenheit for almost 12 mins. Leave pork for almost 5 mins before slicing.

3. Serve with the rest of the sauce. If needed, top with green onions.

14. Air-fryer pork fillet

Cook Time: 20 mins, Prep Time: 5 mins, Difficulty: Medium, Serving: 4

Ingredients

- 1 tsp Powder of garlic
- 1 tsp Cumin
- 1 tsp Oregano
- 1 Pound Whole Pork Fillet
- 1 tsp Dried Thyme

- 2 cloves Garlic, peeled
- 1 Tbsp avocado oil
- 1 tsp Salt
- 1/2 tsp Pepper
- US Customary - Metric

Instructions

1. Take a small mixing bowl, mix all of the spices, pepper, salt and oil to create a rub.
2. Put the pork fillet onto a cutting board and coat entirely by rubbing.
3. Put in the air-fryer and cook at 400 degrees Fahrenheit for almost 20 mins or until the internal temp reaches 145 degrees Fahrenheit with an instant meat thermometer.

15. Air-fryer roasted pork loin

Cook Time: 50 mins, Prep Time: 10 mins, Difficulty: Easy, Serving: 3

Ingredients:

- 1 tbsp extra virgin olive oil
- 1 clove garlic
- 2 lb boneless pork loin
- 2 tsps sea salt
- 1 tsp freshly ground black pepper
- 1 tsp dried thyme
- 1/2 tsp dried sage

Instructions:

1. Take the roast of the pork out from the fridge 25 mins before cooking. Give it a fast rinse under cold water and then pat dry with a paper towel. Trim off a sliver of skin from the underside with a sharp knife.

If still on the pork, trim the tough skin, leaving about 1/4 inch of the fat cap. In a checkered pattern, score the fat gently.

2. Take a small bowl, mix the olive oil, thyme, salt, garlic, sage and pepper. Cover the loin entirely with the seasoning mixture and oil. Move the pork to a wire rack and set aside for almost 25 mins.

3. Preheat the air-fryer to 360 degrees Fahrenheit.

4. Put the roast in the basket of the air-fryer, fat side up. Set the timer for almost 60 mins. Cook for almost 45 mins and use a digital meat thermometer to monitor the internal temp. You're looking for 150° F. Continue to cook until the optimal temperature is reached.

5. Remove the roast to a new cutting board and tent with a foil. Before slicing, allow the meat to stay for at least 10 mins.

6. Cut the roast into 1/4 inch thick pieces against the grain. Put these on a platter and, if necessary, spoon any of the pan drippings over the top.

7. Serve with beverages and side dishes.

16. Crispy Breaded Air-fryer Pork Chops

Cook Time: 8 mins, Prep Time: 10 mins, Difficulty: Easy, Serving: 4

Ingredients

- 1/4 tsp black pepper
- 1/2 tsp kosher salt
- 1/2 cup all-purpose flour
- 1 pound boneless pork chops
- 1 tsp powder of garlic
- 1 tsp onion powder
- 2 large eggs
- Splash of water
- 1/3 cup seasoned Italian breadcrumbs

- 1/3 cup grated parmesan cheese
- Fresh chopped parsley

Instructions

1. Season the chops of pork with pepper and salt on each side.

2. Set up the breading station with 3 different shallow bowls:

3. Bowl 1: mix the flour, 1/2 tsp of the onion powder and 1/2 tsp of garlic.

4. Bowl 2: entirely mix the eggs, 1/2 tsp of the powder of garlic, a splash of water, and 1/2 tsp onion powder.

5. Bowl 3: mix parmesan cheese and breadcrumbs.

6. Put the chops of pork into the mixture of flour one by one and evenly coat.

   Shake off some extra flour and bring it into the egg mixture immediately, then coat evenly. Let the pork chop drip off any extra egg, bring it directly into the breadcrumb mixture and coat evenly, shake off any extra. Repeat for the chops of pork that remain.

7. Set the air-fryer to 400 degrees Fahrenheit for almost 5 mins.

8. Sprinkle the air-fryer basket with cooking spray; put 2 pork chops in the basket or as many as you can without touching. Sprinkle the tops of chops with cooking spray.

9. Air fry for almost 4 mins, turn them over, sprinkle the top with more cooking spray and air fry an additional 4 mins or until an internal temp reaches 145 degrees Fahrenheit.

10. Serve with more grated parmesan and a garnish of parsley, if needed.

17. Grilled Asian chili garlic pork chops

Cook Time: 15 mins, Prep Time: 10 mins, Difficulty: Easy, Serving: 5

Ingredients

- 5 medium cloves garlic

- 4 tbsps vegetable oil

- 4 pork chops

- 2 tbsps fish sauce

- 2 tbsps packed brown sugar

- 2 tbsps rice vinegar

- 3 tbsp ketchup

- 1-2 tbsps Sriracha sauce

- Salt

- Black pepper

Instructions

1. Make the marinade: take a big ziplock bag, mix vegetable oil, fish/soy sauce, ketchup, brown sugar, garlic, rice vinegar and hot sauce. Season with pepper and salt to taste. Rub the bag with your hands to mix all the ingredients. Place the chops of pork in a bag and rub the chops of pork with the marinade. For outstanding taste, close the bag and marinate the chops of pork for at least 30 minutes or overnight.

2. Preheat grill on medium-high heat. Clean the grill grates to ensure they are clean.

3. Put the chops of pork on the grill, make sure that you save the excess marinade for cleaning when you grill. Cook the chops of pork on either side for around 6 mins or until they are well grilled and fried. Brush the chops of pork with the additional marinade several times before grilling.

4. Serve tasty and hot.

18. Grilled garlic pork chops

Cook Time: 15 mins, Prep Time: 15 mins, Difficulty: Easy, Serving: 6

Ingredients

- 1 tbsp soy sauce

- 1 tbsp Worcestershire sauce

- 4 tbsp olive oil or vegetable oil

- 4 pork chops

- 3 tbsp ketchup

- 1/2 tsp onion powder

- 1 tsp Dijon mustard or yellow mustard

- 3-4 cloves garlic

- 1/2 tsp Kosher salt

- Black pepper

- 2 tbsps packed brown sugar

- Peeled parsley for garnish

Instructions

1. Make the marinade: take a large ziplock bag, combine 3 tbsps of olive oil, Worcestershire, soy sauce, ketchup, mustard, onion powder, brown sugar and garlic. Season with pepper and salt to taste. Rub the bag with your hands to mix all the ingredients.

2. Put pork chops in the bag and massage the marinade into the chops of pork. Seal the bag and marinate the chops of pork for at least 30 mins or overnight is best for great flavor.

3. Preheat grill on medium-high heat.

4. Clean the grill grates to ensure they are clean.

5. Put the chops of pork on the grill. Cook the chops of pork for about 6 mins per side or until nicely grilled and cooked through. While grilling, brush the chops of pork with the excess marinade several times.

6. Garnish with peeled parsley. It is optional.

7. Serve warm with baked potatoes, pasta or whatever you want.

19. Grilled pork shoulder steaks

Cook Time: 20 mins, Prep Time: 10 mins, Difficulty: Easy, Serving: 5

Ingredients

- 1/4 cup (60 ml) oil
- 4 pork shoulder steaks
- 4 large cloves garlic, peeled
- 3 tbsp (45 ml) soy sauce
- 1/2 tsp (2.5 ml) onion powder
- 1/2 tsp (2.5 ml) kosher salt
- 1/2 tsp (2.5 ml) fresh cracked black pepper
- 1 tbsp (15 ml) brown sugar

Instructions

1. Take a bowl, mix oil, garlic, onion powder, soy sauce, salt, brown sugar and black pepper. Add pork steaks in the mixture and coat them properly in the marinade.

2. Cover the bowl and marinate the pork for at least 30 mins or up to overnight.

3. Preheat grill on medium heat. Clean the grill grates to make sure they are clean.

4. Cook steaks for almost 10 mins per side or until nicely cooked through and charred (turning the pork steaks many times will help cook them quicker and more evenly).

5. Serve hot and delicious straight up, or for sandwiches, on rice.

Chapter No.7: Casseroles, Frittatas and Quickies

1. Air fried frittata

Cook Time: 16 mins, Prep Time: 15 mins, Difficulty: Easy, Serving: 3

Ingredients:

- Cheddar cheese
- Chopped spinach
- Mushrooms
- Eggs
- Fresh chopped herbs
- Green onion

- Salt

- Grape tomatoes

Instructions:

1. Preheat the air-fryer to 350 degrees Fahrenheit.

2. Line a shallow 7-inch baking pan with parchment paper, then spray oil on the pan and set it aside.

3. Take a bowl, mix the cream and eggs.

4. Add the remaining ingredients to the bowl, including the sea salt flakes, salt, and stir to mix.

5. Pour the mixture of breakfast frittata into the baking pan and put it inside the air-fryer basket.

6. Cook for almost 16 mins, or until eggs are cooked. To check if it is cooked, put a toothpick in the middle of the air-fryer frittata. The eggs are cooked if the toothpick comes out clean.

2. Air Fried Asparagus with Garlic and Parmesan

Cook Time: 8 mins, Prep Time: 2 mins, Difficulty: Easy, Serving: 4

Ingredients

- 1 tsp olive oil

- 1/8 tsp garlic salt

- 1 bundle asparagus

- Pepper to taste

- 1 tbsp parmesan cheese (powdered or grated)

Instructions

1. Clean asparagus and pat dry. Cut 1 inch off the bottom to take off the woody stems.

2. Lay asparagus in a single layer in the air-fryer and spritz with oil.

3. Sprinkle garlic salt evenly on top of asparagus. Season with pepper, and then add a little Parmesan cheese across the top.

4. Cook at 400 degrees Fahrenheit for 7-10 mins. Thinner asparagus may cook faster.

5. Once asparagus is removed from the air-fryer, add a little more Parmesan cheese to finish it off!

6. Enjoy immediately.

3. Air-fryer corn on the cob

Cook Time: 15 mins, Prep Time: 10 mins, Difficulty: Easy, Serving: 3

Ingredients:

- Butter
- Salt & pepper
- Cilantro
- Corn

Optional toppings:

- Basil & parmesan cheese
- Sriracha
- Bacon

Instructions:

Prep the Corn

1. Remove the husk and trim if required. Place the cobs flat in the air-fryer in a

    single layer.

2. Spray corn with cooking spray and cook at 400 degrees Fahrenheit for almost 15 mins (turn over midway) until they're slightly charred.

3. Add salt, butter and pepper to a bowl and microwave on high temp until butter is completely melted.

4. Put butter on corn and drizzle with cilantro.

5. Top with lots of cojita cheese, cilantro lime juice, chili powder and butter or mayonnaise for a Mexican street corn style.

4. Air-fryer Roasted Cauliflower

Cook Time: 12 mins, Prep Time: 17 mins, Difficulty: Easy, Serving: 3

Ingredients

- 1 Tbsp olive oil
- 1 tsp parsley
- 1 tsp thyme
- 4 cups chopped cauliflower
- 1 tsp minced garlic
- ¼ cup parmesan cheese
- 1 tsp salt
- Pepper and salt

Instructions

1. Take a large bowl, mix the cauliflower with minced garlic, olive oil, parsley, salt and thyme.

2. Shake to mix, and cauliflower is properly coated.

3. Put cauliflower in the air-fryer basket. Set to 400 degrees Fahrenheit for almost 20 mins.

4. Stir the cauliflower after 10 mins add parmesan cheese to it.

5. Serve immediately, season with pepper and salt to taste.

5. Air-fryer Green Beans

Cook Time: 10 mins, Prep Time: 2 mins, Difficulty: Easy, Serving: 4

Ingredients

- 1/2 tbsp oil
- 2 cups green beans

Instructions

1. Clean green beans and slice off ends if required. Toss beans with oil.
2. Put beans into the air-fryer. Cook at 390 Degrees Fahrenheit for almost 10 mins.
3. Remove and serve.

6. Air-fryer Garlic Roasted Green Beans

Cook Time: 8 mins, Prep Time: 2 mins, Difficulty: Easy, Serving: 4

Ingredients

- 1 tbsp olive oil
- 3/4-1 pound fresh green beans (trimmed)
- Salt and pepper to taste
- 1 tsp garlic powder

Instructions

1. Drizzle the olive oil over the trimmed beans. Drizzle the seasonings throughout. Toss to coat.
2. Put the green beans in the air-fryer basket.
3. Cook the green beans for almost 8 mins at 370 degrees Fahrenheit. Toss the basket midway through the total cook time.
4. Remove the green beans and serve.

7. Quick and Easy Air-fryer Roasted Asparagus

Cook Time: 10 mins, Prep Time: 5 mins, Difficulty: Easy, Serving: 5

Ingredients

- 1 bunch asparagus (fresh)
- Salt and pepper
- 1 tbsp olive oil
- 1 1/2 tsps seasoning
- Freshly lemon wedge

Instructions

1. Clean and cut off asparagus (hard ends).
2. Drizzle the asparagus with the seasonings and olive oil. Cooking oil spray can also be used.
3. Add these asparagus to the air-fryer basket.
4. Cook for almost 10 mins at 360 degrees Fahrenheit until brown or crisp. Sprinkle freshly squeezed lemon over the roasted asparagus.
5. Cooking over 10 mins in the air-fryer is not recommended. As every air-fryer brand works differently, monitor the asparagus carefully.
6. When the asparagus is cooked for almost 5 mins, start to notice it carefully.

8. Easy garlic knots

Cook Time: 20 mins, Prep Time: 10 mins, Difficulty: Easy, Serving: 4

Ingredients

- 1 cup whole wheat flour
- 3/4 tsp kosher salt

- 2 tsps baking powder
- Olive oil spray
- 1 cup fat-free Greek yogurt
- 2 tsps butter
- 3 cloves garlic, chopped
- 1 tbsp grated parmesan cheese
- 1 tbsp finely chopped fresh parsley

Instructions

1. Preheat the air-fryer 325 degrees Fahrenheit and set for almost 12 mins.
2. Cook in batches without overcrowding and bake for almost 12 mins, or until crisp or golden. No need to turn.

9. Air-fryer Crispy Balsamic Brussels Sprouts

Cook Time: 10 mins, Prep Time: 10 mins, Difficulty: Easy, Serving: 4

Ingredients

- 1/2 cup sliced red onions
- 1 1/2 -2 cups brussels sprouts (fresh and sliced in half)
- 1 tbsp balsamic vinegar
- 1 tbsp olive oil
- Cooking oil spray
- Salt and pepper

Instructions

1. Add sliced red onions and the brussels sprouts to a big bowl. Sprinkle olive oil (or sprinkle cooking oil spray) and balsamic vinegar throughout the mixture.
2. Sprinkle pepper and salt to taste. Stir to coat evenly.

3. Sprinkle cooking oil over the air-fryer basket.

4. Add the onions and brussels sprouts and. Do not overcrowd the basket. Cook in batches if needed according to the air-fryer model.

5. Cook for almost 5 mins at 350 degrees Fahrenheit.

6. Open the air-fryer and toss the veggies with kitchen tongs.

7. Cook for an additional 5 mins. Every air-fryer brand cooks differently. Almost after 8 mins, it will become slightly charred but still soft. Right at 10 mins, they will be crisp.

8. Cool before serving.

10. Garlic-herb fried patty pan squash

Cook Time: 15 mins, Prep Time: 10 mins, Difficulty: Easy, Serving: 3

Ingredients

- 2 garlic bulbs
- 1/4 tsp pepper
- 1/2 tsp salt
- 1/4 tsp oregano(dried)
- 1 tbsp olive oil
- 5 cups small pattypan squash (halved)
- 1 tbsp fresh parsley
- 1/4 tsp thyme (dried)

Instructions

1. Preheat the air-fryer at 375 degrees Fahrenheit.

2. Put the squash in a big bowl. Mix oregano, oil, thyme, garlic, salt and pepper, sprinkle over squash. Shake to coat. Put the squash on a greased tray in a single layer in the air-fryer basket. Continue to cook until soft for almost 15 mins, stirring frequently.

3. Drizzle with parsley and serve.

11. Air-fryer general tso's cauliflower

Cook Time: 20 mins, Prep Time: 5 mins, Difficulty: Easy, Serving: 2

Ingredients

- 1/2 cup cornstarch
- 1/2 cup all-purpose flour
- 1 tsp salt
- 3/4 cup club soda
- 1 tsp baking powder
- 1 medium head cauliflower

Sauce:

- 2 tsps sesame oil
- 3 tbsp sugar
- 3 tbsps soy sauce
- 3 tbsp vegetable broth
- 1/4 cup orange juice
- 2 tbsps rice vinegar
- 2 tsps cornstarch
- 2 tbsps canola oil
- 2 to 6 dried pasilla or other hot chiles
- 3 green onions, white part minced
- 3 garlic cloves, minced
- 1 teaspoon grated fresh ginger root
- 4 cups hot cooked rice
- 1/2 teaspoon grated orange zest

Instruction

1. Preheat the air-fryer to 400 degrees Fahrenheit. Combine flour, salt, cornstarch

   and baking powder. Stir in the club soda until combined (batter will be thin). Toss the florets in the batter; move over a baking sheet to a wire rack. Let it stand for almost 5 mins. Put cauliflower in batches on a greased tray in an air-fryer basket. Cook until tender and golden brown for almost 12 mins.

2. Simultaneously, mix the first 6 sauce ingredients; mix in the cornstarch until smooth.

3. Take a big saucepan, heat the canola oil over medium heat. Add chiles; cook and stir until it gets fragrant for almost 2 mins. Add the white part of onions, ginger, garlic and orange zest; cook until it gets fragrant for almost 1 min. Stir in the mixture of orange juice; return to the saucepan. Put to a boil; cook and stir for 2-4 mins until thickened.

4. Add cauliflower to sauce; shake to coat. Serve with cooked rice, sprinkle with tiny sliced green onions.

12. Air-fryer cumin carrots

Cook Time: 15 mins, Prep Time: 5 mins, Difficulty: Easy, Serving: 4

Ingredients

- 1-pound carrots
- 2 tsps coriander seeds
- 1 tbsp melted coconut oil or butter
- 2 garlic cloves
- 1/4 tsp salt
- 1/8 tsp pepper
- 2 tsps cumin seeds

- Minced fresh cilantro

Instructions

1. Preheat the air-fryer to 325 degrees Fahrenheit. Take a dry pan, cumin seeds and toast coriander over medium-high heat for almost 60 seconds or until crisp or aromatic, stirring occasionally. Cool the mixture slightly. Chop in a spice grinder until finely chopped.

2. Put carrots in a big bowl. Add melted coconut oil, pepper, salt, garlic and crushed spices; shake to coat. Put on a greased tray in the air-fryer basket.

3. Cook until lightly browned and crisp-tender for almost 15 mins, stirring occasionally.

4. If desired, sprinkle with cilantro and serve.

13. Air-fryer Blooming Onion

Cook Time: 25 mins, Prep Time: 15 mins, Difficulty: Easy, Serving: 4

Ingredients

For the Onion

- 3 large eggs
- 1 cup breadcrumbs
- 1 large yellow onion
- 2 tsp paprika
- 1 tsp garlic powder
- 1 tsp onion powder
- 3 tbsp extra-virgin olive oil
- 1 tsp kosher salt

For the Sauce

- 2/3 cup mayonnaise
- 2 tbsp ketchup

- 1/2 tsp paprika
- 1/2 tsp garlic powder
- 1/4 tsp dried oregano
- 1 tsp horseradish
- Kosher salt

Instructions

1. Cut off the onion stem and place the onion on the straight side. Cut from the root down(almost an inch) into different sections, being careful not to slice all the way through. Turnover and slowly pull-out sections of onion so that petals are separate.

2. Take a shallow bowl, mix 1 tbsp water and eggs. Take another shallow bowl, mix spices and breadcrumbs. Dip the onion into the egg mixture, then dredge in a mixture of breadcrumb, using a spoon to coat entirely. Drizzle onion with oil.

3. Put in the basket of air-fryer and cook at 375 degrees Fahrenheit until onion is soft all the way through for almost 25 mins. Drizzle with more oil as desired.

4. Simultaneously make the sauce: Take a medium bowl, mix ketchup, mayonnaise, paprika, garlic powder, horseradish, and dried oregano. Season it with salt.

5. Serve onion with sauce for dipping and enjoy.

14. The Ultimate Air-fryer Veggie Burgers

Cook Time: 25 mins, Prep Time: 5 mins, Difficulty: Easy, Serving: 2

Ingredients

- Tea Towel (Clean)
- 190 g Carrots
- 1 Tbsp Mixed Herbs
- 1 Cup Chickpeas

- 500 g Sweet Potato
- 2 cups Whole meal Breadcrumbs
- 800 g Cauliflower
- 1 Cup Grated Mozzarella Cheese
- 1 Tbsp Basil
- Salt and Pepper

Instructions

1. Chop and peel the vegetables. Put them in the inner pot bottom of the Instant Pot. Add 1 cup of hot water to an Instant Pot. Put the cap on the Instant Cooker, close the valve and cook manually for almost 10 mins.

2. Using a tea towel, rinse the vegetables and squeeze out the remaining moisture such that the vegetables are completely dry.

3. The chickpeas are added, and the vegetables are mashed completely.

4. Add the breadcrumbs and whisk well.

5. Seasonings are added and make into shapes like veggie burgers.

6. Dip in the grated cheese so that it is completely covered in cheese.

7. Put the veggie burgers in the air-fryer basket and cook for almost 10 mins at 360 degrees Fahrenheit. Repeat with a further 5 mins at 400 degrees Fahrenheit to get that brown and crusty veggie burger shape.

8. Serve hot in bread buns or serve with a salad.

15. Air-fryer Simple Grilled American Cheese Sandwich

Cook Time: 8 mins, Prep Time: 2 mins, Difficulty: Easy, Serving: 2

Ingredients

- 2-3 slices Cheddar Cheese
- 2 slices Sandwich Bread

- 2 tsps Butter or Mayonnaise

Instructions

1. Take bread slices, put cheese between them and butter the outside of each slice of bread.

2. Put in air-fryer and cook at 370 degrees Fahrenheit for almost 8 mins. Flip, midway through.

3. Take more bread slices, put cheese between them and butter the outside of each slice of bread.

4. Put a tall trivet in the pressure cooker and top it with a crisp basket.

5. Put the sandwich into the crisp lid basket and Put the crisp lid on top of the pressure cooker.

6. Cook at 400 degrees Fahrenheit for almost 8 mins, flipping over after almost 5 mins.

16. Weight Watchers Air-fryer Mozzarella Cheese Sticks

Cook Time: 4 mins, Prep Time: 5 mins, Difficulty: Easy, Serving: 3

Ingredients

- 1 cup Italian breadcrumbs
- 1 Egg
- 1/2 cup flour
- 1 package Sargento Light String Cheese
- 1 cup marinara sauce
- Salt and pepper to taste

Instructions

1. Take a bowl, add pepper and salt to breadcrumbs.

2. Take separate bowls, add breadcrumbs to 1 bowl, flour to another, and eggs in another.

3. Dip the cheese sticks in breadcrumbs, then flour and egg.

4. Freeze cheese sticks for about an hour; want them to firm up.

5. Set Air-fryer to 400 degrees Fahrenheit. Add the cheese sticks to the fryer.

6. Cook for 4 mins, then flip. Cook for another 4 mins (may need more or less time and keep looking at them).

17. Air-fryer Mac and Cheese

Cook Time: 20 mins, Prep Time: 25 mins, Difficulty: Medium, Serving: 3

Ingredients

- 1 cup water
- ½ cup heavy cream
- 1 ½ cup elbow macaroni
- 8 oz sharp cheddar cheese
- 1 tsp dry mustard
- ½ tsp black pepper
- 1/4 tsp garlic powder
- ½ tsp kosher salt

Instructions

1. Combine elbow macaroni, ¾ of the cheese, water, dry mustard, black pepper, heavy cream, kosher salt and garlic powder to hold all the ingredients in a 7-inch pan that is deep enough. Stir to mix.

2. Put in an Air-fryer basket and set Air-fryer on 360 degrees Fahrenheit. Set the timer for almost -20 mins and start the Air-fryer. Midway through cooking, open the Air-fryer basket and add the rest of the cheese and stir. Close the air-fryer and continue cooking.

3. Once the Air-fryer is done cooking, open the Air-fryer and mix the mac with cheese. Remove the pan from the basket and let it cool for almost 10 mins. The mac and cheese will become thick while it cools.

4. Serve and Enjoy.

18. Crispy avocado fries

Cook Time: 10 mins, Prep Time: 5 mins, Difficulty: Easy, Serving: 3

Ingredients

- 1 tsp garlic powder
- 1 cup Panko breadcrumbs
- 1 tsp paprika
- 1 cup purpose flour
- 2 large eggs
- 2 avocados
- Ranch

Instructions

1. Take a shallow bowl, mix garlic powder, panko and paprika together. Take another shallow bowl, put flour in it, and beat eggs in a third shallow bowl.

2. One at a time, roll avocado slices into Panko mixture, then egg, flour until entirely coated.

3. Put in air-fryer and fry at 400 degrees Fahrenheit for almost 10 mins.

4. Serve with ranch, if needed.

19. Bob harper's air-fried French fries

Cook Time: 35 mins, Prep Time: 15 mins, Difficulty: Easy, Serving: 4

Ingredients

- 1 tbsp olive oil
- 1 lb fingerling potatoes
- Salt and pepper

Instructions

1. Preheat an air-fryer to 390 degrees Fahrenheit.

2. Boil the potatoes for almost 10 mins. Drain, and cool. Slice Halve lengthwise,

   spray with olive oil, and season with salt and pepper.

3. Put potatoes in the air-fryer for almost 15 mins. Open the fryer, toss the potatoes around, and put them back in the air-fryer for another 12 mins.

20. Air-fryer pickles

Cook Time: 15 mins, Prep Time: 20 mins, Difficulty: Easy, Serving: 3

Ingredients

- 1/2 cup all-purpose flour
- 1/2 tsp salt
- 3 large eggs, lightly beaten
- 32 dill pickle slices
- 2 tbsp dill pickle juice
- 1/2 tsp cayenne pepper
- 1/2 tsp garlic powder
- 2 cups panko breadcrumbs
- 2 tbsp snipped fresh dill
- Cooking spray
- Ranch salad dressing, optional

Instructions

1. Preheat the air-fryer to 400 degrees Fahrenheit. Leave the pickles to stand on a paper towel until the liquid is almost absorbed for almost 15 mins.

2. Simultaneously, in a shallow bowl, mix flour and salt. In another shallow bowl, mix eggs, cayenne, pickle juice and garlic powder. Take a third shallow bowl and

   mix panko and dill in it.

3. Dip pickles in a mixture of flour to coat each side; shake off the extra. Dip in crumb mixture, then in egg mixture, patting to help the coating stick. In batches, Put pickles in one layer on a greased tray in the air-fryer basket. Cook until crispy and golden brown for almost 10 mins. Turn pickles, spray with cooking spray. Cook until crispy and golden brown for almost 10 mins longer.

4. Serve immediately. If needed, serve with a ranch dressing.

21. Tostones (twice air fried plantains)

Cook Time: 20 mins, Prep Time: 5 mins, Difficulty: Easy, Serving: 3

Ingredients

- Olive oil spray

- 1 cup water

- 1 large green plantain

- 1 tsp kosher salt

- 3/4 tsp garlic powder

Instructions

1. Cut a slice lengthwise of the plantain skin with a sharp knife; it will allow it easier to peel. Slice the plantain into small pieces, 8 total.

2. Take a small bowl mix the water with garlic powder and salt.

3. Preheat the air-fryer to 400 degrees Fahrenheit.

4. When ready, spray the plantain with olive oil and cook for almost 6 mins. You might have to do this in 2 batches.

5. Remove from the air-fryer and mash them with a tostonera while they are hot or measuring cup to flatten or the bottom of a jar.

6. Dip the mixture in the seasoned water and put it aside.

7. Preheat the air-fryer to 400 degrees Fahrenheit once again and cook in batches for almost 5 mins on both sides, spraying each side of the plantains with olive oil.

8. When done, give them another spray of oil and season with salt.

9. Serve and eat right away.

Chapter No.8: Fish And Seafood Recipes

1. Salmon and Broccoli Stir-Fry

Cook Time: 15 mins, Prep Time: 15 mins, Difficulty: Easy, Serving: 4

Ingredients

- Finely grated zest and juice of 1 medium orange
- 2 tsps reduced-sodium soy sauce, plus more for serving
- 1 large bunch of broccoli
- 1 pound salmon
- 2 cloves garlic
- Rice or noodles

Instructions

1. Add 1/2 inch water to a saute pan or large wok and transfer to a boil over high heat. Add the broccoli, covering loosely, so that steam can

escape, and cook until nearly fork-tender and bright green, about 4 mins. Transfer and Drain the broccoli to a plate. Clean the remaining broccoli debris out of the plate.

2. Take a small bowl, mix the juice, orange zest and soy sauce. Season the salmon with a pinch of black pepper and salt. Put the pan over medium-high heat. Add 1 tbsp high-heat cooking oil, canola, like rice bran or grapeseed. Put the salmon to a thoroughly coated surface, tilt the pan. Add the salmon to the hot oil carefully, reduce the heat to medium, and sprinkle with the garlic. Cook until browned on the bottom, undisturbed, and the sides of the salmon turn opaque about 3 mins. Put the orange and soy sauce in the mixture, then turn the salmon around. To reduce the heat to medium-low, add the broccoli. Cook for around 3 mins before the salmon is cooked through and the juice thickens a little. Serve with rice or pasta and extra soy sauce and spoon the sauce over the salmon and broccoli.

2. Perfect air-fryer salmon

Cook Time: 7 mins, Prep Time: 5 mins, Difficulty: Easy, Serving: 2

Ingredients

- Lemon wedges
- 2 tsps paprika
- 2 wild-caught salmon fillets
- Salt and coarse black pepper
- 2 tsps avocado oil or olive oil

Instructions

1. Remove any bones from the salmon if required and put fish on the counter for almost 1 hour. Rub every fillet with olive oil and drizzle with salt, paprika and pepper.

2. Put fillets in the air-fryer basket. Cook in the air-fryer at 380 degrees Fahrenheit for almost 7 mins for fillets (1-1/2-inch).

3. When the air-fryer goes off, open the basket and check fillets with a fork to make sure they are done to your needed doneness.

3. Easy Air-fryer Fish Sticks

Cook Time: 10 mins, Prep Time: 15 mins, Difficulty: Medium, Serving: 4

Ingredients

- 1/2 cup purpose flour
- 1/2 cup breadcrumbs
- 1/2 tsp salt
- 1/2 tsp paprika
- 1 pound skinless cod fillets
- 1/2 tsp lemon-pepper seasoning
- Cooking oil
- 1 egg beaten

Instructions

1. Slice the cod into any size you wish. Pat until it gets dry.
2. Spray the air-fryer basket with cooking oil with the help of a spray bottle.
3. Take a bowl big enough, add the breadcrumbs to dredge the sticks of fish with seasonings.
4. Set up a cooking station with the flour, beaten egg and seasoned breadcrumbs in 3 separate bowls big enough to put the sticks of fish.
5. Dip the fish in the breadcrumbs, then egg, and then the flour. Make sure there's a moist towel nearby. Breading is messy.
6. Put the fish sticks in the air-fryer basket. Spray with oil. Do not stack the fish. If necessary, cook in batches.
7. Cook for almost 5 mins at 400 degrees Fahrenheit.

8. Open the basket and flip the fish. Spray with cooking oil. Cook again for 7 mins or until crisp.

4. Easy Air-fryer 15 Minute Crab Cakes

Cook Time: 10 mins, Prep Time: 5 mins, Difficulty: Easy, Serving: 4

Ingredients

- 8 ounces of crab meat
- 1 tbs old bay seasoning
- 1/3 cup breadcrumbs
- ¼ cup red peppers
- ¼ cup green peppers
- 1 medium egg
- ¼ cup mayo
- ½ lemon juice of
- Cooking oil
- 1 tsp flour

Instructions

1. Spray the air-fryer basket with oil.
2. Mix every ingredient except flour.
3. The mixture is formed into 4 patties. Apply a dash of flour to every Pattie.
4. Put the cakes in the Air-fryer. Spray the cakes with oil.
5. Cook for almost 10 mins at 370 degrees Fahrenheit.
6. Cool before serving.

5. Air-fryer Salmon Patties

Cook Time: 16 mins, Prep Time: 15 mins, Difficulty: Easy, Serving: 8

Ingredients

- 2 ½ cups mashed potatoes
- ¼ cup milk
- 1 tsp chives generous
- 1 tsp dill
- ½ tsp white pepper
- ¼ tsp cayenne pepper
- 1 tbsp parsley generous
- ¼ tsp Creole seasoning
- 20 ounces canned Salmon wet, 16 ounces dry
- ½ cup flour
- 4 eggs beaten
- 1 cup breadcrumbs

Instructions

1. Mix every ingredient except the breading related ingredient.
2. Make the salmon mixture into small patties. Dip in flour, then breadcrumbs and then egg mixture.
3. Stovetop: Add olive oil to a preheated large frypan and Melt butter on the stove. Cook a few mins on each side until golden brown and a nice crust have formed.
4. Cook at 400-degrees Fahrenheit for 8 mins in the Air-fryer, and sprinkle with olive oil. Flip and spray with olive oil again, and cook for additional 8 mins.
5. Serve immediately or cool in an airtight container in a refrigerator for up to one week. It can be served with creamed peas.

6. Air-fryer Southern Fried Catfish Nuggets

Cook Time: 17 mins, Prep Time: 5 mins, Difficulty: Medium, Serving: 2

Ingredients

- 1/4 Cup Oil
- 1 Box Fish Fry Mix
- 2 lbs. Catfish Nuggets

Instructions

1. Rinse the fish and put it aside.
2. Put half the fish fry mix into a big bag.
3. Add few Catfish Nuggets into the bag, which contains the fry mix.
4. Shake properly to coat and Seal the bag.
5. Remove the nuggets using the tongs(one at a time), shake off the excess batter.
6. Put the catfish nuggets in the basket of the Air-fryer. Follow the directions of your Air-fryer for filling the basket. Leave a little room and do not overfill.
7. Pour the oil into a relatively small pan.
8. Dip the basting brush into the oil and Baste oil onto the top of every catfish nugget. No need to baste each side of the fish. We don't turn the fish over when cooking.
9. Turn the Air-fryer on to 380 degrees Fahrenheit and set the timer for almost 17 mins. Begin checking at about 12 mins. (All Air-fryers are different). Do not shake while cooking.
10. Remove from basket and drain when done on the paper toweling.
11. Add the other batch to the basket, repeat the procedure. Total cooking time varies depending on how many batches are done.

7. Parmesan crusted fish fillets

Cook Time: 10 mins, Prep Time: 10 mins, Difficulty: Easy, Serving: 4

Ingredients

- 1 lb Fish Fillets thawed
- 1/4 cup Coconut Flour
- 1/4 cup Parmesan Cheese
- 1/2 tsp. Lemon Pepper Seasoning
- Dijon Mustard Sauce
- 1/4 cup Sour Cream
- 1 Tbsp. Heavy Whipping Cream
- 1 Tbsp. Dijon Mustard
- Fried Fish Fillets
- 1/2 Tbsp. Chives dried

Instructions

1. Take a small container, add parmesan cheese, coconut flour and lemon pepper seasoning. Stir properly to mix.

2. Spray each side of the fish with a cooking spray. Add this to the parmesan mixture, and both sides are coated. Press parmesan mixture using fingers into fish, if necessary.

3. Add to air-fryer basket and cook at 400 degrees Fahrenheit for almost 10 mins or until the fish flakes easily. Stop the air-fryer halfway to flip the fish.

4. Take a small saucepan over medium heat, add sour cream, Dijon, heavy whipping cream and chives. Stir to mix and heat but do not boil.

5. Put mustard sauce overcooked fish.

6. Serve immediately.

8. Air-fryer pretzel-crusted catfish

Cook Time: 10 mins, Prep Time: 15 mins, Difficulty: Medium, Serving: 4

Ingredients

- 1/2 tsp salt
- 1/2 tsp pepper
- 2 large eggs
- 1/3 cup Dijon mustard
- 2 tbsp 2% milk
- 1/2 cup purpose flour
- 4 catfish fillets
- 4 cups honey mustard pretzels
- Cooking spray
- Lemon slices

Instructions

1. Preheat the air-fryer to 325 degrees Fahrenheit. Drizzle catfish with pepper and salt. Mix eggs, milk and mustard in a deep bowl. Put pretzels and flour in different bowls. Cover the fillets with the flour, then dip in a mixture of egg and cover with pretzels.

2. Put fillets on a greased tray in a single layer in the air-fryer basket (in batches); spritz with cooking spray. Cook for almost 12 mins until fish flakes easily with a fork.

3. Serve with lemon slices, If desired.

9. Air-fryer Crispy Fish Sandwich

Cook Time: 10 mins, Prep Time: 10 mins, Difficulty: Easy, Serving: 2

Ingredients

- 1/2 tsp garlic powder

- 1/4 tsp pepper
- 1/2 cup panko bread crumbs
- 1/4 tsp salt
- 1 egg
- 1 tbs fresh lemon juice
- Primal kitchen tartar sauce
- 1/2 tbs mayo
- 10 oz cod fillets sliced in half
- Cooking oil
- 2 buns
- 2 tbsp purpose flour

Instructions

1. Start by setting up a cooking station. Add the flour, salt, garlic powder, and pepper to a bowl big enough and dredge the fish in it.

2. Add the lemon juice, mayo and egg to a different bowl big enough and dredge the fish in it. Beat the egg and mix the remaining ingredients.

3. Take a separate bowl to add the panko breadcrumbs. Keep a wet towel nearby. The hands can get messy.

4. Ste by step, dredge the fish in the flour, egg mixture and breadcrumbs.

5. Put the fish in the basket after Spraying the air-fryer basket with cooking oil.

6. Spray the fish top with cooking oil.

7. Cook for almost 10 mins at 400 degrees Fahrenheit until golden and crisp. If you wish to flip the fish, do so at 5 mins and then continue to air fry until golden and crisp.

8. Whitefish is very tender and delicate. Be very careful while flipping the fish and while handling it when removing it from the air-fryer. Use a silicone spatula.

9. Preheat the oven to 425 degrees Fahrenheit.

10. Line a baking sheet with parchment paper. Put the fish on the parchment paper.

11. Bake for almost 12 mins or until golden and crisp.

10. Air-Fryer Salmon with Maple-Dijon Glaze

Cook Time: 15 mins, Prep Time: 10 mins, Difficulty: Medium, Serving: 4

Ingredients

- 3 tbsp maple syrup

- 1 tbs Dijon mustard

- 1 medium lemon (juiced)

- 1 garlic clove, minced

- 1 tbs olive oil

- 1/4 tsp salt

- 1/4 tsp pepper

- 3 tbsp butter

- 4 salmon fillets

Instructions

1. Preheat the air-fryer to 400 degrees Fahrenheit.

2. Simultaneously, melt butter in a small saucepan over medium heat. Add maple syrup, lemon juice, mustard and minced garlic. Simmer and reduce the heat until the mixture thickens slightly for almost 3 mins. Remove from heat and put aside.

3. Drizzle oil over the salmon fish and sprinkle with pepper and salt. Put fish in a single layer in the air-fryer basket. Cook until fish gets lightly browned and flake easily with a fork for almost 7 mins.

4. Drizzle with sauce, then serve.

11. Keto shrimp scampi

Cook Time: 10 mins, Prep Time: 5 mins, Difficulty: Easy, Serving: 4

Ingredients

- 1 tbs Lemon Juice

- 2 tsp Red Pepper Flakes

- 1 tbs chopped chives

- 1 tbs chopped fresh basil

- 1 tbs Minced Garlic

- 2 tbsp Chicken Stock

- 4 tbsp Butter

- 1 lb Raw Shrimp

Instructions

1. Turn the air-fryer to 330 degrees Fahrenheit. Put a metal pan in it and start heating while you gather your ingredients.

2. Put the garlic, butter and red pepper flakes into the hot pan.

3. Allow it to cook for 2 mins, stir only once, until the butter melt. This step is important. It infuses garlic into the butter, which makes it all so delicious.

4. Open the air-fryer, add butter, minced garlic, lemon juice, red pepper flakes, chives, chicken stock, basil and shrimp to the pan, stirring gently.

5. Allow shrimp to cook for 5 mins, stirring only once. At this point, the butter should be well-melted.

6. Mix very well, remove the pan using oven mitts, and let it rest for almost 1 minute on the table. Let the shrimp cook in less heat, rather than letting it overcook, which makes it rubbery.

7. Stir at the end of 1 minute. The shrimp is well-cooked now.

8. Sprinkle more fresh basil leaves, and it's ready.

12. Air-fryer fish and chips

Cook Time: 35 mins, Prep Time: 10 mins, Difficulty: Hard, Serving: 4

Ingredients

- 1 cup breadcrumbs

- 1 egg

- 1/4 cup flour

- 2 russet potatoes

- 1 tsp salt

- 2 tbsp oil

- 1 lb fish fillet (cod, catfish, tilapia)

Instructions

1. Cut potatoes like French fries or in wedges. Take a bowl, toss potatoes, salt and

   oil together.

2. Add potatoes to your air-fryer basket and cook at 400 degrees Fahrenheit for almost 20 mins, shake twice. Remove from the basket when done.

3. Simultaneously, ready the fish. Take a deep bowl and add flour; take a second bowl and add beaten egg and take the third bowl, add panko. Step by step, dredge the fish in fillet flour, then in egg and then in breadcrumbs, Working with one piece at a time.

4. Add fish to the air-fryer and set it to 330 degrees Fahrenheit for 15 mins. Check halfway through and flip when required.

5. Serve with any sauce.

13. Air-fryer Bang Bang Fried Shrimp

Cook Time: 20 mins, Prep Time: 10 mins, Difficulty: Medium, Serving: 4

Ingredients

- 1 Egg White 3 tbsp
- 1 Tsp Paprika
- Grill Mates Montreal Chicken
- Bang Bang Sauce
- 1/2 Cup Purpose Flour
- 1 Pound Raw Shrimp Peeled
- 3/4 cup of Panko Bread Crumbs
- Salt and pepper
- Cooking Oil
- 2 tbsp Sriracha
- 1/4 cup Sweet Chili Sauce
- 1/3 Cup Plain Greek Yogurt

Instructions

1. Preheat the Air-fryer to 400 degrees Fahrenheit.

2. The shrimp is seasoned with the seasonings.

3. Put the egg whites, panko bread crumbs and flour in 3 separate bowls.

4. Create a place for cooking. Dip the shrimp in steps, first in the egg whites, then the panko bread crumbs and flour in the end.

5. Spray the shrimp with cooking oil.

6. Add the shrimp to the Air-fryer basket. Cook for almost 4 mins. Open the air-fryer basket and flip the shrimp. Cook again for additional 4 mins or until brown or crisp.

7. Mix all of the ingredients in a bowl. Mix thoroughly to combine.

14. Low Carb Miso Salmon

Cook Time: 10 mins, Prep Time: 10 mins, Difficulty: Easy, Serving: 2

Ingredients

- 2 tbsp Soy Sauce
- 2 tbsp white miso
- 1 tsps Minced Garlic
- 1 tsp Minced Ginger
- 1/2 tsp Cracked Black Pepper
- Non-Stick Cooking Spray
- 2 5-oz Salmon Fillets
- 1 tsp Sesame Seeds
- 2 tsps Truvia
- 2 Chopped Green Scallions

Instructions

1. Take a small bowl mix brown sugar, hot water, soy sauce, garlic, miso, ginger and pepper. Mix to combine.

2. Put salmon fillets on a pan. Pour the sauce over the fillets, flip them over, and cover the next side of the salmon fish with the sauce.

3. Spray the air-fryer basket with nonstick oil spray. Put the salmon fish covered with sauce into the air-fryer basket. Set the air-fryer to 400 degrees Fahrenheit for almost 12 mins. Midway through, brush more miso sauce on the top.

4. Top fillets with scallions and sesame seeds.

15. Low carb shrimp scampi

Cook Time: 10 mins, Prep Time: 5 mins, Difficulty: Easy, Serving: 4

Ingredients

- 1 tbs Lemon Juice
- 1 tbs Minced Garlic
- 2 tsps Red Pepper Flakes
- 1 tbs chopped chives
- 1 tbs chopped fresh basil
- 2 tbsp Chicken Stock
- 4 tbsp Butter
- 1 lb Raw Shrimp

Instructions

1. Turn the air-fryer to 330 degrees Fahrenheit. Put a metal pan in it and start heating while you gather the ingredients.

2. Put the garlic, butter and red pepper flakes into the hot pan.

3. Allow it to cook for almost 2 mins, stir once until the butter is melted. This step is important. Garlic is infused into the butter, which will make it so good.

4. Open the air-fryer, add butter, minced garlic, lemon juice, red pepper flakes, basil, chives, chicken stock, shrimp to the pan, stirring gently.

5. Allow shrimp to cook for 5 mins, stir only once. At this moment, the butter is well-melted and in liquid form, dipping the shrimp in spice.

6. Combine very well, remove the pan using oven mitts, and let it rest for almost 1 minute on the table. Let the shrimp cook in the normal heat, do not overcook because it gets rubbery.

7. Stir at the end of a minute. At this point, the shrimp should be well-cooked.

8. Sprinkle more fresh basil leaves and serve.

16. Air-fryer Southern style catfish with green beans

Cook Time: 20 mins, Prep Time: 5 mins, Difficulty: Difficult, Serving: 2

Ingredients

- 1 tsp light brown sugar
- 1/2 tsp crushed red pepper
- 3/8 tsp kosher salt
- 2 Unit (6-oz.) catfish fillets
- 1/4 cup purpose flour
- 1 large egg, lightly beaten
- 12 ounces fresh green beans
- 1/3 cup panko
- 1/4 tsp black pepper
- 2 tbsp mayonnaise
- 3/4 tsp dill pickle relish
- 1/2 tsp apple cider vinegar
- 1/8 tsp granulated sugar Lemon wedges
- 1 1/2 tsps chopped fresh dill

Instructions

1. Put green beans in a bowl, and spray with cooking spray. Sprinkle with crushed red pepper, brown sugar and 1/8 tsp of the salt. Put in the air-fryer basket, and cook at 400 degrees Fahrenheit until tender and well browned about 12 mins. Move to a bowl; cover with aluminum foil.

2. Simultaneously, toss catfish in the flour to coat. Dip small pieces, only 1 at a time, in egg mixture to coat, then drizzle with panko, press with finger to coat evenly on every side.

3. Put the fish in the air-fryer basket, and spray with cooking spray. Cook at 400 degrees Fahrenheit until cooked through and browned, about 8 mins. Sprinkle the tops with pepper and the rest of the 1/4 tsp of salt.

4. While the fish is cooking, mix mayonnaise, relish, dill, vinegar, and sugar in a bowl. Serve green beans and fish with lemon wedges and tartar sauce.

17. Air-fryer coconut shrimp

Cook Time: 8 mins, Prep Time: 15 mins, Difficulty: Easy, Serving: 2

Ingredients

- 1/2 cup sweetened shredded coconut
- 3 tbsp panko bread crumbs
- 2 large egg whites
- 1/8 tsp salt
- 1/2 pound uncooked large shrimp
- Dash pepper
- Dash Louisiana-style hot sauce
- 3 tbsp purpose flour
- 1/3 cup apricot preserves
- 1/2 tsp cider vinegar
- Dash crushed red pepper flakes
- Powered by Chicory

Instructions

1. Preheat the air-fryer to 375 degrees Fahrenheit. Devein and peel shrimp, leave the tails on.

2. Take a deep bowl, toss the coconut with bread crumbs. Take another deep bowl, whisk egg whites, pepper, salt and hot sauce. Put flour in another bowl.

3. Coat lightly by Dipping shrimp in flour; shake off well. Dip this in coconut mixture, then in egg white mixture, pat it to help coating adhere.

4. Put shrimp in one layer on a greased tray in the air-fryer basket. Cook for almost 4 mins; turn the shrimp and continue cooking until coconut is lightly browned and shrimp turn pink, do this for another 4 mins.

5. Simultaneously, mix sauce ingredients in a saucepan; cook and stir over medium heat until they are melted.

6. Serve shrimp quickly with sauce.

18. Air fried salt & pepper shrimp

Cook Time: 10 mins, Prep Time: 10 mins, Difficulty: Easy, Serving: 4

Ingredients

- 2 tsps Sichuan peppercorns, ground

- 1 tsp Kosher Salt

- 1 pound Shrimp, 21-25 per pound

- 3 tbsp Rice Flour

- 2 tsps Whole Black Peppercorns

- 2 tbsp Oil

- 1 tsp Sugar

Instructions

1. Take a saucepan and heat it. Roast the Sichuan peppercorns and black peppercorns together for almost 2 mins before you can sense the peppercorn smell. Allow cooling them.

2. Apply salt and sugar and grind the spices together using a mortar and pestle to

   create a coarse powder.

3. In a big bowl, put the shrimp. Apply the seasoning, rice flour, and oil and combine well until well-coated with the shrimp.

4. In the air-fryer basket, put the shrimp, trying to keep them as smooth as possible, in a layer. Use a rack to put half of the shrimp in the basket and half of the shrimp on the rack.

5. For extra oil, spray well.

6. Set the 325 degrees Fahrenheit air-fryer and cook, flipping halfway through, for 8-10 mins.

19. Fried shrimp po' boy sandwich recipe

Cook Time: 10 mins, Prep Time: 20 mins, Difficulty: Medium, Serving: 4

Ingredients

- 1 tsp Creole Seasoning
- 1/2 cup Louisiana Fish Fry Coating
- Cooking oil spray
- 1 pound shrimp
- Canola or vegetable oil
- 4 French bread hoagie rolls
- 1/4 cup buttermilk
- 2 cups shredded iceberg lettuce
- 8 tomato slices
- Remoulade Sauce
- 1/2 cup mayo
- 1 tsp minced garlic
- 1/2 lemon juice of
- 1 tsp Worcestershire
- 1/2 tsp Creole Seasoning
- 1 tsp Dijon mustard
- 1 tsp hot sauce

- 1 green onion chopped

Instructions

1. Mix the ingredients in a bowl. Cool before serving while the shrimp cooks.

2. Marinate the shrimp in the buttermilk and Creole seasoning for almost 30 mins.

3. Add the fish fry to another bowl. Take out the shrimp from the bags and dip all into the fish fry. Add this to the air-fryer basket.

4. Heat a frying pan with oil to 350 degrees Fahrenheit. Test the heat Using a thermometer.

5. Fry the shrimp on each side for almost 4 mins until brown and crispy.

6. Take this out of the pan and drain the grease using paper towels.

7. Spray the air-fryer basket with cooking oil. Add the shrimp to the air-fryer basket.

8. Spray the shrimp with cooking oil.

9. Cook the shrimp for almost 5 mins at 400 degrees Fahrenheit. Open the basket and flip the shrimp. Cook for an additional 5 mins or until brown and crispy.

10. On the French toast, pour the remoulade sauce. Add the tomato and lettuce slices and then the shrimp.

Chapter No. 9: Dessert Recipes

1. Air-fryer fried Oreos

Cook Time: 4 mins, Prep Time: 10 mins, Difficulty: Easy, Serving: 4

Ingredients

- 1 crescent sheet roll
- 9 Oreo cookies

Instructions

1. Spread crescent on the table after popping it. Use a knife to line and cut 9 even squares of it.

2. Take 9 cookies and wrap them in those squares.

3. Turn on the Air-fryer and preheat to 360 degrees Fahrenheit. Put the wrapped cookies in a layer and cook for 4 min; halfway through, shake and flip them.

4. Sprinkle with cinnamon or powder sugar according to taste, and have fun.

2. Maple Pecan Bars with Sea Salt

Cook Time: 25 mins, Prep Time: 15 mins, Difficulty: Medium, Serving: 8

Ingredients

- 1/4 of tea Kosher Salt
- 1/3 of cup Butter, softened
- ¼ of cup Brown Sugar, firmly packed
- 1 cup of flour
- Non-Stick Cooking Spray
- ½ of cup Brown Sugar
- ¼ of cup Pure Maple Syrup
- 1/4 of cup Whole Milk
- 4 TBS Butter (1/2 stick), diced
- 1 ½ of cup Pecans, Finely Chopped
- ¼ of tsp Flaked Sea Salt, for Topping
- ¼ of tea Vanilla extract

Instructions

1. Take an 8x8-inch square baking pan and line it with foil. Leave a couple of inches of overhang. Spray nonstick baking spray over the foil.

2. Take a medium bowl, combine butter and sugar(brown). Make it fluffy and light by beating it in an electric mixer at medium-low speed. Add some salt and flour and combine it thoroughly by beating.

3. The mixture is then transferred to the prepared pan (it will be crumbly). Press the mixture into the pan's bottom (the bottom of a coffee mug is used to press it in

   the pan).

4. Put the pan into the air-fryer basket. The air-fryer is set to 350°F for almost 13 min. Start the filling when the crust has 5 min remaining to cook.

5. Take a medium saucepan, combine the brown sugar, butter, maple syrup, and milk. Take it to a simmer and stir. When it begins to simmer, cook it for a minute. Remove from the heat and stir it in finely chopped pecans and vanilla.

6. Pour the filling on the crust evenly, slowly spreading with a rubber spatula, so the liquid and pecans are distributed evenly.

7. Set the air-fryer for 12 min when the mixture is bubbling. (The center of the mixture should be jiggly–it will get thicken when it cools.)

8. Remove it from the air-fryer and sprinkle the salt. Put on a wire rack for cooling. When it reached room temperature, transfer it to the refrigerator. The foil overhang is used to remove from the pan and cut into bars.

9. Serve the dessert at room temp.

3. Air-fryer mini nutella doughnut holes

Cook Time: 5 mins, Prep Time: 30 mins, Difficulty: Medium, Serving: 16

Ingredients

- Oil for deep-fat frying
- 1 tbsp water
- 1 tube large refrigerated flaky biscuits
- 2/3 of cup Nutella
- 1 large egg
- Confectioners' sugar

Instructions

1. Preheat the air-fryer up to 300 degrees Fahrenheit. Mix the egg with water. Roll each biscuit into a 6-inches circle on a lightly floured surface, cut into 4 wedges. Brush slowly with an egg mixture, top every wedge

with 1 tsp of Nutella chocolate. Bring corners over the filling; pinch the edges firmly to seal it.

2. On an ungreased tray, arrange the batches of biscuits in a single layer in the air-fryer basket. Cook until it turns golden brown for about 10 min, only turning once. Serve warm after dusting with confectioners' sugar.

4. Easy Air-fryer Dessert Empanadas

Cook Time: 10 mins, Prep Time: 15 mins, Difficulty: Medium, Serving: 12

Ingredients

- 2 apples
- 2 tsp raw honey
- 1 tsp vanilla extract
- 12 empanada wrappers thawed
- 1 tsp cinnamon
- 2 tsp cornstarch
- 1 tsp water
- 1 egg beaten
- 1/8 tsp nutmeg
- Olive oil.

Instructions

1. Take a saucepan and place it on medium-high heat. Add cinnamon, apples, nutmeg, vanilla and honey. Stir the mixture and cook for 2 to 3 min until the apples become soft.

2. Mix the water and cornstarch in a small bowl. Add this to the pan and stir properly. Cook for just 30 sec.

3. The filling is left to cool for 5 min at least before the empanada wrappers are loaded onto the filling.

4. The empanada wrappers are laid on a surface. Dip the cooking brush in a glass of water. The empanada wrappers are glazed with the wet brush along the edges of the filling. The crust will get soften, and it is easier to roll then.

5. The apple mixture is added to each. Add 1 tbsp of the apple mix to each empanada. Don't overstuff. Flatten the mixture out with the help of a spoon.

6. Close the empanadas properly. A fork is used to seal them along edges, indents in the crust are created. Now press the fork down along the edge of each into the crust.

7. The air-fryer basket is then spritzed with cooking oil. Add this to the Air-fryer basket. Don't stack the empanadas. Cook in batches.

8. A cooking brush is used to brush the upper side of every empanada with the beaten egg (egg wash).

9. Put Air-fryer on 400 degrees Fahrenheit. Cook for 10 min when it gets crisped.

10. Cool it before serving.

5. Air-fryer bread pudding

Cook Time: 15 mins, Prep Time: 15 mins, Difficulty: Easy, Serving: 2

Ingredients

- 1/2 cup half-and-half cream
- 2/3 cup sugar
- 2 ounces semi-sweet chocolate, chopped
- 1 large egg, room temperature
- 1 tsp vanilla extract
- 1/2 cup 2% milk
- 1/4 tsp salt

- Optional toppings: Confectioners' sugar and whipped cream
- 4 slices of day-old bread, crusts removed and cut into cubes (about 3 cups)

Instructions

1. Take a small microwave-safe bowl and melt the chocolate in it, stir until it gets smooth. Stir in cream and set it aside.

2. Mix sugar, egg, milk, vanilla and salt in a large bowl. Stir in a mixture of chocolate. Add cubes of bread and toss it to coat. Wait 15 min.

3. Preheat the air-fryer to 325 degrees Fahrenheit. Spoon the mixture of bread into 2 greased ramekins. Place it on a tray inside the air-fryer basket. Cook for 15 mins until a knife comes out clean when inserted in the center.

4. According to the taste, top it with whipped cream and confectioners' sugar.

6. Air-fryer Sugar Doughnut Recipe

Cook Time: 5 mins, Prep Time: 3 mins, Difficulty: Easy, Serving: 4

Ingredients

- 1/2 Cup Sugar
- 1 Can Large Pillsbury Biscuits
- 5 Tsp Butter
- 1/2 Tbsp Cinnamon

Instructions

1. Preheat the air-fryer to 330 degrees Fahrenheit. To do this, simply turn the air-fryer onset temperature to 330 degrees Fahrenheit and let it run for about 5 min.

2. Take a medium bowl, mix the sugar and cinnamon. Set this aside.

3. Open the biscuit can and remove it by cutting the center out of every biscuit. (Use a small cookie cutter used as a doughnut cutter because it is small.)

4. Put in your air-fryer the larger and the outside portion of biscuits.

5. Run for 5 to 7 min at the same temperature (330 degrees Fahrenheit). You may need to vary this slightly, which depends on the model of the air-fryer. When you make the recipe, make sure it is properly cooked in the middle.

6. Melt the butter while the doughnuts are cooking.

7. Use a pastry brush; coat melted butter on the doughnuts. Use a spoon to coat the top after laying it in the bowl of cinnamon-sugar mixture.

8. Shake off excess sugar gently.

9. Serve doughnuts hot.

7. Air-fryer Caribbean wontons

Cook Time: 10 mins, Prep Time: 30 mins, Difficulty: Medium, Serving: 12

Ingredients

- 1/4 cup sweetened shredded coconut

- 1/4 cup mashed ripe banana

- 4 ounces cream cheese, softened

- 2 tsp chopped walnuts

- 1 cup marshmallow crème

- 2 tsp canned crushed pineapple

- 24 wonton wrappers

- Cooking spray

- 1/4 cup sugar

- 1 pound fresh strawberries, hulled

- 1 tsp cornstarch

- Confectioners' sugar and ground cinnamon
- Powered by Chicory

Instructions

1. Preheat the air-fryer to 350 degrees Fahrenheit. Take a small bowl, beat cream cheese in it until it gets smooth. Stir in coconut, walnuts, banana and pineapple. Fold the mixture in marshmallow cream.

2. A wonton wrapper with 1 point is positioned towards you. Keep the remaining covered with a paper towel that is damp until ready to use. Add 2 tsp of filling in the center of each wrapper. Moisten the edges with water, fold the opposite corners over the filling and press them to seal. Repeat this procedure with all wrappers and the filling.

3. Arrange wontons in a single layer on a greased tray and place them in the air-fryer basket (in batches); spritz each with cooking spray. Cook until crisp and golden brown for almost 12 min.

4. Place strawberries inside a food processor, close and process until pureed completely. Take a small saucepan, combine cornstarch and sugar in it. Stir this in strawberries. Place it in a boil, stir and cook until it gets thickened for almost 2 min. According to taste, strain the mixture, reserve the sauce and discard seeds. Sprinkle the wontons with cinnamon and confectioners' sugar.

5. Serve with the sauce.

8. Air-fryer peppermint lava cakes

Cook Time: 15 mins, Prep Time: 15 mins, Difficulty: Medium, Serving: 4

Ingredients

- 1 cup confectioners' sugar
- 2 large eggs, room temperature
- 1 tsp peppermint extract
- 1/2 cup butter

- 2 large egg yolks
- 2 tbsp finely crushed peppermint candies
- 2/3 cup semi-sweet chocolate chips
- 6 tbsps all-purpose flour

Instructions

1. Preheat the air-fryer to 375 degrees Fahrenheit. Take a microwave-safe bowl, melt the chocolate chips and butter it for almost 30 secs; stir until it gets smooth. Mix in eggs, egg yolks, confectioners' sugar, and extract until blended. Fold in flour.

2. Slowly grease it and flour ramekins over it; pour the batter into the ramekins. Don't overfill. Put ramekins on the tray in the air-fryer basket; cook this until a thermometer reads 160 degrees Fahrenheit and edges of cakes are set; it will take almost 12 min.

3. Remove from the basket; let it stand for 5 min. Use a knife around the border of ramekins to loosen the cake; place it onto the dessert plates. Drizzle it with crushed candies.

4. Serve immediately.

9. Air-fryer apple fritters

Cook Time: 8 mins, Prep Time: 10 mins, Difficulty: Easy, Serving: 15

Ingredients

- Cooking spray
- 1-1/2 cups all-purpose flour
- 1/4 cup sugar
- 2 tsp baking powder
- 1-1/2 tsp ground cinnamon
- 1/2 tsp salt
- 2/3 cup 2% milk

- 2 large eggs, room temperature
- 1 tbsp lemon juice
- 1-1/2 tsp vanilla extract, divided
- 2 medium Honeycrisp apples, peeled and chopped
- 1/4 cup butter
- 1 cup confectioners' sugar
- 1 tbsp 2% milk
- Buy Ingredients
- Powered by Chicory

Instructions

1. Line the air-fryer basket with parchment; spritz it with cooking spray. Preheat the air-fryer up to 410 degrees Fahrenheit.

2. Take a large bowl, combine sugar, flour, cinnamon, baking powder and salt. Add milk, lemon juice, eggs and 1 tsp of vanilla extract; stir until it gets moistened. Then fold in apples.

3. Drop the dough by 1/4 cupfuls and 2 inches apart and place in the air-fryer basket (in batches). Spritz with the cooking spray. Cook until it gets golden brown for almost 6 min. Continue to cook until golden brown for almost 2 min.

4. Take a small-sized saucepan and melt the butter in it over medium-high heat. Cook until butter starts to get brown and foamy for almost 5 min. Remove from heat; cool slowly. Add 1 tbsp milk, confectioners' sugar and remaining 1/2 tsp of vanilla extract to butter; mix until it gets smooth.

5. Drizzle this over fritters and then serve.

10. Air-fryer baked apples

Cook Time: 15 mins, Prep Time: 5 mins, Difficulty: Easy, Serving: 2

Ingredients

- ½ tsp of Cinnamon
- 1 tsp of butter, melted
- 2 Apples

Topping Ingredients

- 1 tbsp of Maple Syrup
- 1 tbsp butter (melted)
- ⅓ cup od Old Fashioned or Rolled Oats
- 1 tsp of Whole meal or Whole Wheat Flour (plain flour)
- ½ tsp Cinnamon

Instructions

1. Preheat the air-fryer up to 356 degrees Fahrenheit by either running your air-fryer for 5 min at that temperature or using the preheat setting.

2. Cut the apples and use a knife to remove the stem, core and seeds. Brush the butter over the cut sides of the apples evenly, then sprinkle ½ tsp of cinnamon over it.

3. In a small cup, mix the topping ingredients, then spoon them evenly on top of the apple halves.

4. Put the apple halves into the air-fryer basket carefully, then cook for almost 15 min or until it gets softened.

5. Serve warm with cream or ice cream according to taste.

11. Air-fryer carrot coffee cake

Cook Time: 35 mins, Prep Time: 15 mins, Difficulty: Medium, Serving: 6

Ingredients

- 1 large egg, lightly beaten
- 1/2 cup of buttermilk
- 2 tsp dark brown sugar
- 1/4 cup dried cranberries
- 1/3 cup sugar
- 1 tsp orange zest (grated)
- 2/3 cup purpose flour
- 1 tsp vanilla extract
- 1 tsp baking powder
- 1/4 tsp baking soda
- 1/3 cup white whole wheat flour
- 1/4 tsp salt
- 2 tsp pumpkin pie spice
- 1 cup shredded carrots
- 1/3 cup chopped walnuts

Instructions

1. Preheat the air-fryer to 350 degrees Fahrenheit. Flour and grease a round baking pan. Take a big bowl, buttermilk, mix egg, 1/3 cup of sugar, brown sugar, orange zest, oil and vanilla in it. Take another bowl, mix flours, 1 tsp of pumpkin pie spice, baking soda, baking powder and salt. Slowly beat into the mixture of egg. Fold in dried cranberries and carrots. Pour into the prepared pan.

2. Take a tiny bowl, combine the rest of the 2 tsp sugar, walnuts and the rest of the 1 tsp pumpkin spice. Drizzle evenly over the batter. Gently put the pan back in the basket of the air-fryer.

3. Cook for almost 40 min until a toothpick put in the middle comes out clean. If the top gets dark, cover tightly with foil. Cool this in a pan for almost 10 min before removing it from the pan.

4. Serve warm.

12. Fruit hand pies

Cook Time: 35 mins, Prep Time: 25 mins, Difficulty: Medium, Serving: 2

Ingredients

- 1/2 tsp (0.5 tsp) Kosher Salt

- 1.5 cups (187.5 g) Purpose Flour

- 1/4 cup (56.75 g) butter

- 1/4 cup (51.25 g) shortening

- 1/4-1/3 cup (62.5 g) cold water

- 1 tbsp (1 tbsp) Water

- 1 large (1 large) Eggs

- 1 tsp (1 tsp) coarse sugar

Instructions

1. Preheat the air-fryer to 320 degrees Fahrenheit.

2. Trace around a 6-inch circular baking pan onto a sheet of 8 1/2 x 11-inch paper. Cut the circle out (this would be the pie crusts pattern to be cut out); put aside.

3. Then mix the flour and salt in a medium bowl. Cut in the shortening and butter until the pieces are pea-sized, utilizing a pastry cutter. Sprinkle over half of the flour mixture with 1 tbsp of cold water. Toss with the help of a fork. To the side of the cup, transfer the moistened pastry. Repeat with the remaining flour until it is moist, using 1 tbsp of water at a time. In

a ball, collect the flour mixture and stir slowly for as long as it takes to fall together in a ball.

4. Slightly flatten the pastry on a lightly floured board, then roll it into a 13-inch circle from the middle to the end. Near one side, put the design on the pastry. Cut out a 6-inch circle of pastry using a thin, sharp knife. To make two rings and then repeat. Discard the bits of dough.

5. On half of the pastry circle, put half the required fruit filling, leaving a 1/4-inch border. With the help of spray, clean the bare edge. Fold over the filling with the empty half of the pastry. To close it, press along the side of the pastry using a fork. Poke the top of a fork in a few locations. Repeat for the filling and pastry left.

6. Beat the egg and the water together in a tiny cup. Brush and dust with the coarse sugar over the tops of the pies.

7. Put the pies and cook for 35 min in the air-fryer basket until the pies are golden brown.

8. Cool the pies for 20 min on a wire rack before eating or cool absolutely at room temperature and serve.

13. Air-Fryer French Toast Cups with Raspberries

Cook Time: 20 mins, Prep Time: 20 mins, Difficulty: Medium, Serving: 2

Ingredients

- 2 cups fresh raspberries
- 2 slices Italian bread
- 2 big eggs
- 1/2 cup whole milk
- 2 tsp cornstarch
- 2 ounces cream cheese
- 1 tbsp maple syrup

- 1 tbsp lemon juice

- 1/3 cup of water

- 1/2 cup of fresh raspberries

- 1/2 tsp lemon zest (grated)

- The ground cinnamon

- 1 tbsp maple syrup

- Powered by Chicory

Instructions

1. Carefully divide half of the cubes of bread between 2 greased 8-oz. custard cups. Sprinkle with cream cheese and raspberries. Top with the remaining bread. Take a small bowl, milk, mix eggs and syrup; pour it over the bread. Cover and cool for at least 1 hour in the refrigerator.

2. Preheat air-fryer up to 325 degrees Fahrenheit. Place the custard cups on the tray inside the air-fryer basket. Cook until it gets puffed and golden brown for almost 15 min.

3. At the same time, take a small saucepan, combine water and cornstarch until it gets smooth. Add 1-1/2 cups raspberries, syrup, lemon juice and lemon zest. Bring to boil; reduce the heat. Stir and cook until thickened for 2 min. Discard and strain seeds; cool moderately.

4. Softly stir the remaining half cup of berries into syrup. According to taste, sprinkle French toast cups including cinnamon

5. serve with syrup.

14. Air-fryer lemon slice sugar cookies

Cook Time: 10 mins, Prep Time: 15 mins, Difficulty: Easy, Serving: 12

Ingredients

- 1/4 tsp salt

- 1 package (3.4 ounces) instant lemon pudding mix

- 1/2 cup unsalted butter

- 1/2 cup sugar

- 2 tsp 2% milk

- 1 large egg

- 1-1/2 cups purpose flour

- 1 tsp baking powder

- 2/3 cup confectioners' sugar

- 2 to 4 tsp lemon juice

- Powered by Chicory

Instructions

1. Take a large bowl put pudding mix, cream, butter and sugar until fluffy and light for almost 7 min. Beat the mixture in milk and egg. Take another bowl, mix baking powder, flour and salt; slowly beat into the creamed mixture.

2. Divide the dough with a knife. Shape each into a 6-in.-long roll on a lightly floured surface. Wrap and cool for 3 hours in the refrigerator or until it gets firm.

3. Preheat the air-fryer to 325 degrees Fahrenheit. Cut and unwrap the dough crosswise into 1/2-inches pieces. Put slices in a single layer on a tray properly greased in the air-fryer basket (in batches). Keep cooking until the edges get light brown for 12 min. Cool in the basket for 2 min. Remove the wire racks to cool completely.

4. Mix the confectioner's sugar and sufficient lemon juice in a small bowl to achieve drizzling consistency. Drizzle the cookies over. Enable it to stand when fixed.

5. To Make Ahead: It is possible to produce dough 2 days in advance. Cover and put in a jar. Store it in the freezer.

6. Freeze option: Put wrapped logs and freeze them in a jar. Unwrap the frozen logs for use and split them into slices. Cook as instructed, with a 1-2 minute increase in time.

15. Brazilian grilled pineapple

Cook Time: 10 mins, Prep Time: 10 mins, Difficulty: Easy, Serving: 4

Ingredients

- 1/2 cup (110 g) Brown Sugar
- 2 tsp of Ground Cinnamon
- 3 tsp of melted butter
- 1 pineapple

Instructions

1. Take a small bowl, mix cinnamon and brown sugar.

2. Brush the spears of pineapple with already melted butter. Sprinkle cinnamon sugar over them, pressing lightly.

3. Put the pineapple spears into the air-fryer basket in one layer. Preheat the fryer to 400degrees Fahrenheit for almost 10 min for the first batch (8 min for the other batch as the air-fryer will be already running). Halfway through, brush with the remaining butter.

4. Pineapples look done when they are heated and the sugar over it bubbling.

16. Homemade cannoli

Cook Time: 12 mins, Prep Time: 10 mins, Difficulty: Medium, Serving: 10

Ingredients

- 1/2 cup mascarpone cheese
- 1/2 cup powdered sugar
- 3/4 cup heavy cream
- 1 tsp. pure vanilla extract

- 1 container ricotta
- 1/4 tsp. kosher salt
- 1/2 cup mini chocolate chips for garnish
- 2 cup purpose flour
- 1 tsp. orange zest
- 1/4 cup granulated sugar
- 1 tsp. kosher salt
- 1/2 tsp. cinnamon
- 4 tbsp. cold butter, cut into cubes
- 1 large egg
- 1 egg white for brushing
- 6 tbsp. white wine
- Vegetable oil for frying

Instructions

1. Put molds in the air-fryer basket (in batches) and cook at 350 degrees Fahrenheit for almost 12 min or until it gets golden.

2. When it is cool enough to handle or using a cloth or towel to hold, slowly remove twist shells from the molds.

3. Put the filling in a bag of pastry fitted, which is open. Place filling into shells, then dip the ends in small chocolate chips.

17. Easy Air-fryer Chocolate Chip Cookies

Cook Time: 8 mins, Prep Time: 15 mins, Difficulty: Easy, Serving: 5

Ingredients

- 1/4 tsp cinnamon
- 1/3 cup granulated sugar
- 1/3 cup packed light brown sugar
- 1/2 cup chopped walnuts
- 1 egg
- 8 tsp butter softened
- 1 tsp vanilla extract
- 1/2 tsp of baking soda
- 1 cup flour
- 1/4 cup rolled oats
- 1/8 tsp freshly squeezed lemon juice
- 1 1/2 cups semi-sweet chocolate chips
- Optional sea salt for sprinkling
- 1/2 tsp of salt

Instructions

1. Sugar, cream butter and brown sugar in a mixing bowl for around 2 min using a medium-speed stand or hand mixer.

2. Place the egg, vanilla and lemon juice together. Using the blender and blend for 30 seconds at low heat. Then, blend for a few min on medium or until light and fluffy, rubbing the bowl away.

3. Add the rice, oats, baking soda, salt and cinnamon and combine for around 45 seconds with a low-speed mixer. Only don't over mix.

4. Fold in the walnuts and chocolate chips.

5. Cover air-fryer basket with parchment paper for the air-fryer. Scoop the cookie dough (about 2 tsp) into balls and put them about 1 1/2 to 2 inches apart in the basket. Using damp hands to flatten the cookies at the tip. The batter is sticky indeed. When holding it, damp hands work well.

6. Fry for 6-8 min at 300 degrees Fahrenheit Celsius.

7. Remove the basket from the air-fryer and allow the cookies to cool for 5 min until they are extracted from the basket. They will crumble if you treat them too fast.

8. For an additional 10 min, move the cookies to a wire rack to cool.

9. If you wish, sprinkle sea salt with it.

18. Air-fryer caramelized bananas

Cook Time: 6 mins, Prep Time: 1 min, Difficulty: Easy, Serving: 12

Ingredients:

- 1/4 of a lemon, juiced

- 2 bananas

- Optional toppings: cinnamon, nuts, yogurt, coconut cream, granola

- 1 tbsp coconut sugar

Instructions:

1. Clean bananas by washing with the peel on, then cut them through the middle, lengthwise.

2. Squeeze the lemon juice on top of every banana.

3. Use cinnamon mix with the coconut sugar, then sprinkle it over the top of bananas until it is fully coated.

4. Place into air-fryer for almost 8 min at 400 degrees Fahrenheit

5. Take it out of the air-fryer, eat as is or according to taste top with any toppings.

19. Quick Air-fryer Cinnamon Rolls

Cook Time: 7 mins, Prep Time: 8 mins, Difficulty: Medium, Serving: 8

Ingredients

- ¾ stick Unsalted Butter

- 1 tbsp Ground Cinnamon

- 6 tsp Brown Sugar

- 1 Sheet Puff Pastry

- 1 tbsp Milk

- 2 tsp Fresh Lemon Juice

- ½ cup Powdered Sugar

Instructions

1. Take a small bowl, mix cinnamon, sugar and softened butter.

2. Preheat the air-fryer to 400 degrees Fahrenheit for almost 4 min.

3. Gently roll out the pastry and spread the cinnamon mixture across the whole sheet.

4. Roll it very gently and loosely. Cut the pastry into about 1-inch slices.

5. Put them into a preheated air-fryer and cook at 400 degrees Fahrenheit for 7 min or until the rolls are golden brown.

6. Take them out, let them cool before topping them with icing.

7. Enjoy while warm.

20. Air-fryer Homemade Strawberry Pop-Tarts

Cook Time: 10 mins, Prep Time: 15 mins, Difficulty: Medium, Serving: 4

Ingredients

- 1/3 cup strawberry preserves (low-sugar)
- Cooking oil
- 2 refrigerated pie crusts
- 1 tsp cornstarch
- 1 oz cream cheese
- 1 tbsp sweetener
- 1/2 cup plain vanilla Greek yogurt
- 1 tsp sugar sprinkles

Instructions

1. Put the pie crust on a straight surface.
2. Cut the 2 pie crusts into 6 rectangles by using a knife.
3. Put the cornstarch and preserves in a bowl and whisk it.
4. Add a tbs of the strawberry preserves to the crust. Put the preserves on the top of the crust.
5. Put the pop tarts in the Air-Fryer. Spray with the cooking oil.
6. Cook at 370 degrees Fahrenheit for almost 10 min. Check the Pop-Tarts after 8 min to make sure they are not too crisp.
7. Mix the cream cheese, sweetener and Greek yogurt in a bowl.
8. First, cool it, then remove.
9. If it is not cooled, it may break.

30 Days food plan

By reusing ingredients and leftovers in innovative ways during the month, this plan is designed to save you time and energy. Weekly meal-prep measures demonstrate just a little legwork at the beginning of the week ensure little work throughout the busy weekdays. Whenever possible, check the plan to see what else you might buy from the supermarket (like frozen riced cauliflower, cooked brown rice and spiralized zucchini noodles). You'll be inspired to stay with it until the end by making this strategy simple, fun and tasty.

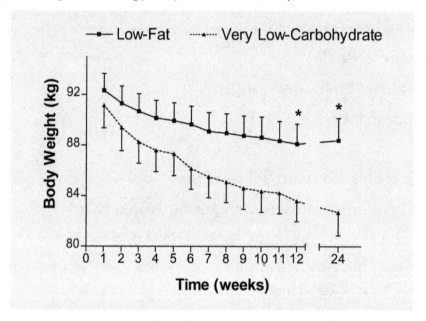

Week 1

Cook the Slow-Cooker Vegetable Soup on Day 1 overnight, so it's ready on Day 2 for lunch. Portion two 1 1/2-cup servings into leak-proof cans to use on Days 3 and 5 for lunch later in the week. In Week 3, freeze an extra two 1 1/2-cup portions to use for lunch. Freeze any leftover soup for up to 6 months in an air-tight jar.

In the morning of Day 2, make the Blueberry-Banana Overnight Oats so that they are ready to grab-and-go. Store in leak-proof jars of glass that will go from the refrigerator to the microwave.

Week 2

Create the Meal-Prep Sheet-Pan Chicken Thighs to include in the Freezer Pack recipes for Curried Chicken Apple Wraps and Slow-Cooker Pasta e Fagioli Soup.

Store to keep fresh in an air-tight meal prep jar.

To have dinner on days 12 And 13, make Pasta e Fagioli Soup Freezer Pack for dinner.

On Day 8, wrap the leftovers separately in plastic while making the biscuit pastries with Smoked Cheddar and Potato for breakfast and put them in an air-tight jar. Up to 3 days to cool in a refrigerator or up to 1 month to freeze. Remove the plastic for reheating, cover it in a paper towel and microwave for 30 to 60 seconds on high temp.

Week 3

On Days 21 and 22, you'll be making the Slow-Cooker Vegetable soup for lunch. On the evening of Day 19, remember to remove the soup from the freezer to defrost overnight in the fridge.

Prepare the Shrimp & Edamame Spicy Slaw Bowls and store them for lunch on days 16, 17, 18 and 19 in 4 air-tight meal prep jars. For the Spicy Cabbage Slaw, leave the cabbage mixture and dressing separate and wait to mix before ready to eat. Using pre-cooked frozen shrimp and wait until you are about to consume rather than all at once to defrost the shrimp, and wait to include the avocado, too. It will help keep the shrimp taste fresh and avoid the browning of the avocado.

Week 4

By using Smoked cheddar and potato, make pastry cheesecakes. You'll need them for breakfast during the week. Cover the leftovers individually in plastic and cool for up to 3 days or freeze for up to 1 month. Remove the plastic for reheating,

cover it in a paper towel and microwave for 30 to 60 seconds on high temp.

You'll get Blueberry-Pecan Pancakes on Day 22 for breakfast. You should reheat the pancakes in the microwave or toaster oven if you have leftovers frozen from Week 2.

Low-Carb Eating

A few factors depend on your food habits, like how safe you are, how much you work out, or how much weight you need to lose.

View this meal program as a general checklist, not something set in stone.

Eat meat, fruit, fish, eggs, vegetables, healthy oils, high-fat dairy, nuts, seeds, fats and maybe even non-gluten grains and some tubers.

Don't eat sugar, seed oils, HFCS, Trans fats, wheat, low-fat and diet products and highly cooked foods.

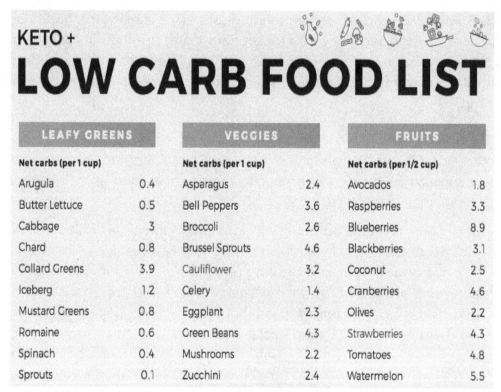

KETO +
LOW CARB FOOD LIST

LEAFY GREENS		VEGGIES		FRUITS	
Net carbs (per 1 cup)		Net carbs (per 1 cup)		Net carbs (per 1/2 cup)	
Arugula	0.4	Asparagus	2.4	Avocados	1.8
Butter Lettuce	0.5	Bell Peppers	3.6	Raspberries	3.3
Cabbage	3	Broccoli	2.6	Blueberries	8.9
Chard	0.8	Brussel Sprouts	4.6	Blackberries	3.1
Collard Greens	3.9	Cauliflower	3.2	Coconut	2.5
Iceberg	1.2	Celery	1.4	Cranberries	4.6
Mustard Greens	0.8	Eggplant	2.3	Olives	2.2
Romaine	0.6	Green Beans	4.3	Strawberries	4.3
Spinach	0.4	Mushrooms	2.2	Tomatoes	4.8
Sprouts	0.1	Zucchini	2.4	Watermelon	5.5

Foods to Avoid

These six food groups and nutrients can be avoided, in order of priority:

Sugar: Soft drinks, ice cream, agave, candy, fruit juices and many other foods that include sugar.

Refined grains: Wheat, barley, rice and rye, and cereal, bread and pasta.

Trans fats: Hydrogenated oils.

Low-fat and diet products: crackers, many dairy products, or cereals are fat-reduced but have sugar.

Highly cooked foods: If it looks factory-made, don't eat it.

Starchy vegetables: If you follow a low-carb diet, it's better to limit your diet's starchy vegetables.

Carbs Counting

Food Items	Carb Counts
Bread	15g Carbs
Cereal	15g Carbs
Crackers/Snack Foods	15g Carbs
Pasta/Grains	15g Carbs
Potatoes/Vegetables/Beans	15g Carbs
Fruits	15g Carbs
Soups	15g Carbs
Sweets	30g Carbs
Sweets	45g Carbs
Milk/Yogurt	15g Carbs
Sweets	15g Carbs
Vegetables	5g Carbs

Conclusion

When it comes to toppings and dressings, be careful. Be aware of fat-packed salad dressings, sauces, and sides like sour cream when selecting products. Mayonnaise- and oil-based sauces add some calories. Try keeping the mayo, and you can introduce yourself to ask for a bottle of ketchup or mustard, controlling how many you place on the sandwich.

Stick to zero-calorie drinks. Soda is a major source of calories that are hidden. Around 300 calories are included in the typical big drink, which will easily gulp up a large portion of your regular calorie intake. With up to 800 calories, shakes are worse. And don't be deceived by lemonade and fruit beverages that introduce calories and sugar in the form of nutrients without much. Instead, order water, diet soda, or unsweetened tea.

Be smart from both sides. Look for things on the menu that come with one or two side dishes. Fries, chips, rice, pasta, onion rings, coleslaw, macaroni and cheese, cookies, and mashed potatoes with gravy provide sides that will easily send calories soaring. Side salads with light sauce, baked potato (easy on the toppings), fresh fruit cups, cob corn, or apple slices are safer bets.

Pass the French fries on. Do you need those fries for real? A burger or sandwich can have plenty of filling on its own. Or if your meal without fries doesn't sound complete, pick the smallest size (which can be 400 calories less than a large serving).

Just ignore the bacon. Adding bacon to sandwiches and salads for added taste is often appealing, but bacon has relatively fewer nutrients and is rich in fat and calories. Instead, add spice without the fat by ordering additional pickles, peppers, tomatoes, or mustard.

Effect on the cardiovascular and digestive processes

Most fast food is filled with carbs with little to no fiber, like drinks and sides.

As these carbohydrates break down in your digestive system, the carbohydrates are released into the bloodstream. The blood sugar rises as a result.

Through producing insulin, the pancreas reacts to the increase of glucose. Insulin transports sugar to cells that need it for energy all over the body. Your blood sugar rises to usual when the body uses the sugar.

This blood sugar phase strongly controls your body, and as long as you're stable, your kidneys can manage these sugar spikes properly.

But consuming high levels of carbohydrates regularly will result in regular spikes in your blood sugar.

Over time, these spikes of insulin can cause the usual insulin response of your body to falter. It raises the chance of resistance to insulin, weight gain and diabetes.

Sugar and fat

There's extra sugar to several fast-food meals. This not only involves more calories but very little nutrition. The American Heart Association (AHA) tells that only 100 to 150 calories of added sugar a day be eaten. That's six to nine tsps or so.

Many fast-food beverages keep well over 12 ounces on their own. 8 tsps of sugar was contained in a 12-ounce can of soda. This is equivalent to 39 grams, 140 calories of sugar.

During food production, trans fat is produced fat. It's widely used in:

- Pastry
- Dough for pizza
- Fried cakes
- Crackers
- Cookies

No amount of trans fat is safe or healthy. It will raise your LDL (bad cholesterol), lower your HDL (good cholesterol), and increase your risk for diabetes and heart failure by eating foods that include it.

Restaurants can also intensify the calorie-counting issue. In one report, people dining at restaurants referred to as "healthy" also underestimated by 20 percent the number of calories in their meal.

Sodium

For some people, the mixture of sugar, fat and salt will make fast food tastier. Although diets rich in sodium can cause water retention. After consuming fast food, you may feel bloated, puffy or swollen.

For those with blood pressure problems, a diet rich in sodium is often harmful. Sodium will increase your blood pressure and put your heart and cardiovascular system under stress.

993 adults were surveyed and observed that their guesses were six times smaller than the real figure (1,292 milligrams). It suggests more than 1,000 mg of sodium estimates is off.

Please remember that the AHA advises that adults do not consume more than 2,300 milligrams per day of sodium.

Effect on the respiratory system

Impact on the breathing mechanism

Excess calories can cause weight gain from fast-food meals. It will cause obesity.

Obesity raises the chance, like asthma and shortness of breath, for respiratory issues.

The extra weight can cause heart and lung diseases, and even with no effort, signs can turn up. When you're driving, climbing stairs, or exercising, you can have trouble breathing.

Effect on the central nervous system

In the short term, fast food can satisfy hunger, but the long-term effects are less favorable.

People who consume fast food and packaged pastries are 51 percent more likely than people who don't eat such items or eat very little of them to experience depression.

Effect on the reproductive system

Junk food ingredients and fast food can affect fertility.

One analysis showed that there are phthalates in cooked food. Phthalates are molecules that can disrupt how the body's hormones function. Reproductive complications, like congenital disabilities, may arise from exposure to high levels of these chemicals.

Effect on the integumentary system (skin, hair, nails)

The foods you consume that change your skin's appearance, but maybe it's not

the foods you suspect.

According to one report, children and teens who consume fast food at least three days a week are even more prone to experience eczema. Eczema is a skin disease that causes areas of inflamed, itchy skin to become irritated.

Effect on the skeletal system (bones)

Carbs and sugar can increase acids in your mouth in fast food. These acids can cause tooth enamel to break down. Bacteria may grow back when tooth enamel disappears, and cavities may appear.

Obesity may also result in bone density and muscle mass problems. There is a higher chance of slipping and fracturing bones of people that are obese.

Effects of fast food on society

In the United States now, more than 2 in 3 people are deemed overweight or obese. About one-third of children aged 6 to 19 are either considered obese or overweight.

In America, the rise of fast food appears to correlate with the increase of obesity.

CPSIA information can be obtained
at www.ICGtesting.com
Printed in the USA
BVHW051221270421
605865BV00004B/531